The Film Audience:

An International Bibliography
of Research

With Annotations and an Essay

by
Bruce A. Austin

The Scarecrow Press, Inc.
Metuchen, N.J., and London
1983

Permission to reprint annotations originally appearing in the following has been granted by Heldref Publications:

Bruce A. Austin, "Film Audience Research, 1960-1980: An Annotated Bibliography," Journal of Popular Film and Television 8 (1981, no. 2): 53-60.

Bruce A. Austin, "Film Audience Research, 1960-1980: An Update," Journal of Popular Film and Television 8 (Winter 1981): 57-59.

The Journal is a publication of the Helen Dwight Reid Educational Foundation.

Library of Congress Cataloging in Publication Data

Austin, Bruce A., 1952-
   The film audience.

   Includes indexes.
   1. Moving-picture audiences--Bibliography.
I. Title.
Z5784.M9A87 1983   [PN1995.9.A8]   016.79143   83-3316
ISBN 0-8108-1622-9

Copyright © 1983 by Bruce A. Austin

Manufactured in the United States of America

CONTENTS

Acknowledgments	iv
How to Use the Bibliography	v
The Literature Search Process	vii
The Motion Picture Audience: A Neglected Aspect of Film Research	xvii
Bibliography	1
Subject Index	133
Title Index	139
Index of Nonprimary Authors	175
About the Editor	179

ACKNOWLEDGMENTS

Several individuals provided me with valuable assistance in the process of compiling this bibliography. I am greatly indebted to Sheila Simmons, Interlibrary Loan Librarian at Rochester Institute of Technology, who generously, diligently, and professionally gave her attention and care to the processing of literally hundreds and hundreds of my interlibrary loan requests. Without Ms. Simmons' uncomplaining, friendly, and cheerful help over more than half a year, it would not have been possible to complete this project. Sarah Reynolds, also at RIT, assisted with the processing of these requests.

Christopher H. Sterling introduced me to the method of systematic bibliographic research and was always receptive and encouraging in this project, as he has been with others I have done. Sterling, along with Douglas Gomery and Timothy Lyons, read the Sources Searched section and made useful suggestions for additional bibliographic tools to be consulted. Michael and Madonna Marsden helped by checking past Popular Culture Association conference programs for papers related to this book.

HOW TO USE THE BIBLIOGRAPHY

The present volume is an annotated bibliography of film audience research. The time span covered by this bibliography is indicated in the "Sources Searched" portion of the Search Process chapter. I have tried to find and present relevant writings from the earliest to the most recent, though very recent material will be missed because of publishing constraints.

As a rule, only empirical studies using the methods of social science and available in non-book form are presented. Speculative or advocacy pieces that are included here are clearly labeled as such in their annotations; these articles are included based on my subjective evaluation of their theoretical, historical, or heuristic value.

The subject investigated by the studies in this bibliography was the relationship of commercial cinema to its audience. Thus, research reports in which the focus of investigation was other than the film audience and theatrical motion pictures per se (e.g., the myriad studies on filmed aggression and anti-social behavior, educational applications of motion pictures, etc.) have, by and large, not been included.

Some entries are not annotated due to unavailability of the document despite attempts to retrieve it (through, for instance, interlibrary loan services) and the absence of an abstract of the item in the various standard abstracting services. Thus, while the appropriateness of such entries cannot be unequivocally verified, nor an annotation provided, the item was included here for the following reasons: 1/ the title of the article made its inclusion seem relevant and 2/ the article was listed in an abstracting service, bibliography, or index in which most of the other entries gathered from this same source proved relevant.

Each entry includes an entry number, the author name, the title of the article, and publication information (including volume, issue, year, and page numbers).

Since many of the entries address more than one topic or content area, I decided to arrange the bibliography alphabetically by the first author's last name (rather than attempting to group the entries by subtopic). In instances of unknown authorship, the entry was integrated by alphabetical inclusion according to the first key word in the title. Each entry has been assigned a citation number. To find material on any given topic the reader has been supplied with three additional tools: a subject index, a title index arranged alphabetically, and an index to the studies that have multiple authors.

Finally, it is my hope that this bibliography will serve at least two functions: 1/ to provide interested scholars with a handy reference tool that may be employed in their own research and 2/ to act as an impetus for vigorous scholarly inquiry on the subject of film audience research.

THE LITERATURE SEARCH PROCESS

The entries in the present volume are the result of what is believed to be an exhaustive search of the literature. In addition to the specific sources itemized below, the bibliographies, references, and footnotes included in this work's individual entries were also searched for relevant writings. As it turned out, this proved to be of immense value in locating additional entries that, for one reason or another, were not included in standard bibliographic research tools. Furthermore, unpublished works (e.g., conference papers) were solicited through four publications: Digest of the University Film Association 28 (March 1981):16, ICA [International Communication Association] Newsletter 9 (Spring 1981): 8, Popular Culture Association Newsletter 10 (July 1981):12, and Spectra [Speech Communication Association] (March 1981):4.

Sources Searched

Indices of book, periodical, thesis and dissertation, and governmental literature were systematically and thoroughly searched for writings related to and appropriate for this bibliography. The following is a list of the key words and/or headings used in the search: Attend; Attendance; Attending; Audience; Audience Research; Audience Analysis; Audience Measurement and Viewing; Audiences; Cinema; Cinematic; Communication Theory, Process and Effects; Film; Film Industry; Film Study; Filmed; Filmic; Films; Miscellaneous; Motion; Motion Picture; Motion Picture Film; Motion Pictures; Movie; Movies; Moving Picture; Moving Pictures; Radio, Television and Film; Research; Spectators.

The following is a list of sources searched using the key words and/or headings presented above.

Computer Literature Search

Wallace Memorial Library, Rochester Institute of Technology, Rochester, New York, 21 December 1981. The following data bases were searched:

   America: History and Life: beginning 1963.
   Comprehensive Dissertation Abstracts: beginning 1861.
   Educational Resources Information Center (ERIC): beginning 1966.
   Historical Abstracts: beginning 1973.
   Institute for Scientific Information (Social Scisearch): beginning 1972.
   National Technical Information Service (NTIS): beginning 1964.
   Psychological Abstracts: beginning 1967.
   Public Affairs Information Service (PAIS): beginning 1976.
   Sociological Abstracts: beginning 1963.

Bibliographies of Bibliographies

Besterman, Theodore. A World Bibliography of Bibliographies, 4th ed. Lausanne: Societas Bibliographica, 1965.
Bibliographic Index: A Cumulative Bibliography of Bibliographies. N.Y.: H.W. Wilson Co., 1960--April 1979.
Brockett, Oscar G., Samuel L. Becker, Donald C. Bryant. A Bibliographic Guide to Research in Speech and Dramatic Art. Chicago: Scott, Foresman and Co., 1963.
Bush, Deborah, et al. "A Bibliography of Selected Bibliographies in Radio, Television and Tele-Film, 1958-1968." Educational Broadcasting Review 3 (April 1969): 62-69.
Toomey, Alice F. (compiler). A World Bibliography of Bibliographies, 1964-1974. Totowa, New Jersey: Rowman and Littlefield, 1977.

Bibliographies

Armour, Robert A. Film: A Reference Guide. Westport, CT, 1980.
Austin, Bruce A. "A Bibliography of Film Audience Research Since 1960." ERIC ED 175 073.
_____. "Film Audience Research, 1960-1980: An Annotated Bibliography." Journal of Popular Film and Television 8 (1980, no. 2): 53-60.

ix   Literature Search Process

_____. "Film Audience Research, 1960-1980: An Update." Journal of Popular Film and Television 8 (Winter 1981): 57-59.
Baden, Anne L. (compiler). Moving Pictures in the United States and Foreign Countries: A Selected List of Recent Writings. Washington, D.C.: U.S. Library of Congress, Division of Bibliography, 1936.
_____. Moving Pictures in the United States and Foreign Countries: A Selected List of Recent Writings. Washington, D.C.: U.S. Library of Congress, Division of Bibliography, 1940.
Batty, Linda. Retrospective Index to Film Periodicals 1930-1971. N.Y.: Bowker, 1975.
Bergsma, F. "Bibliography." Gazette 25 (1980).
_____ and H. M. Schuijtvlot. "Bibliography." Gazette 26 (1980): 121-147.
Berry, Christine and Derick Unwin. "PLET Monitoring: A Selected Bibliography of Production and Audience Variables in Film and Television." Programmed Learning and Educational Technology 12 (January 1975): 54-70.
Blum, Eleanor. Basic Books in the Mass Media, 2nd ed. Urbana: University of Illinois Press, 1980.
Bouman, Jan C. Bibliography on Filmology as Related to the Social Sciences. Paris: United Nations Educational, Scientific and Cultural Organization, 1954.
Bukalski, Peter J. (compiler). Film Research: A Critical Bibliography with Annotations and Essay. Boston: G.K. Hall, 1972.
Canadian Radio-Television Commission. Bibliography: Some Writings on the Canadian Mass Media. Ottawa: Information Canada, 1974.
Canadiana: Canada's National Bibliography. 1950- September 1981.
Cannon, Carl L. Journalism: A Bibliography. N.Y.: The New York Public Library, 1924 (reprinted by Gale Research Co., Detroit, 1967).
Cinema: A Dissertation Catalog. Ann Arbor, MI: University Microfilms International, n.d.
Commission on Educational and Cultural Films. The Film in National Life. London: George Allen and Unwin Ltd., 1932, "Appendix J, Bibliography," pp. 195-200.
Comstock, George and Marilyn Fisher. Television and Human Behavior: A Guide to the Pertinent Scientific Literature. Santa Monica, CA: Rand (R-1746-CF), 1975.
Conant, Michael. Antitrust in the Motion Picture Industry. Berkeley: University of California Press, 1960, "Bibliography," pp. 221-226.

Danielson, Wayne A. and G.C. Wilhoit, Jr. A Computerized Bibliography of Mass Communication Research, 1944-1964. N.Y.: Magazine Publishers Association, 1967.

Denny, Reuel and Mary Lea Meyersohn. "A Preliminary Bibliography on Leisure." American Journal of Sociology 62 (May 1957): 602-615.

Ellis, Jack C., Charles Derry, and Sharon Kern. The Film Book Bibliography 1940-1975. Metuchen, N.J.: Scarecrow Press, 1979.

Fearing, Franklin and Genevieve Rogge. "A Selected and Annotated Bibliography in Communications Research." Quarterly of Film, Radio and Television 6 (Spring 1952): 283-315.

Fielding, Raymond (compiler). A Bibliography of Theses and Dissertations on the Subject of Film: 1916-1979. University Film Association, Monograph no. 3, Fall 1979.

──────. "Sixth Bibliographic Survey of Theses and Dissertations on the Subject of Film Filed at U.S. Universities 1916-1981." Journal of the University Film and Video Association 34 (Winter 1982): 41-54.

Gerlach, John C. and Lana Gerlach. The Critical Index: A Bibliography of Articles on Film in English, 1946-1973. N.Y.: Teachers College Press, 1974.

Gitter, A. George and Robert Grunin. Communication: A Guide to Information Sources. Detroit: Gale Research Co., 1980.

Gordon, Thomas F. and Mary Ellen Verna. Mass Media and Socialization: A Selected Bibliography. Philadelphia: Temple University, School of Communications and Theater, 1973.

──────. Mass Communication Effects and Processes: A Comprehensive Bibliography, 1950-1975. Beverly Hills: Sage Publications, 1978.

Gottesman, Ronald and Harry M. Geduld. Guidebook to Film. N.Y.: Holt, Rinehart and Winston, 1972.

Handel, Leo A. Hollywood Looks at Its Audience. Urbana: University of Illinois Press, 1950, "Publications on Film Audience Research and Related Fields," pp. 228-234.

Hansen, Donald A. and Herschel Parsons. Mass Communication: A Research Bibliography. Santa Barbara, CA: Glendessary Press, 1968.

Heusch, Luc de. The Cinema and Social Science. Paris: Unesco, 1962, "Bibliography," pp. 77-80.

International Committee for Social Science Information and Documentation. International Bibliography of the Social Sciences--Sociology. Paris: Unesco, vol. 5--9 (1955-

1959); Chicago: Aldine Publishing Co., vol. 10--13
(1960-1963); N.Y.: Tavistock Publications, vol. 14--
29 (1964-1979).
Jarvie, I.C. Movies and Society. N.Y.: Basic Books,
1970, "Bibliography," pp. 229-366.
Jowett, Garth. Film: The Democratic Art. Boston: Little,
Brown and Co., 1976, "Bibliography," pp. 487-505.
_____ and James M. Linton. Movies as Mass Communication. Beverly Hills: Sage Publications, 1980, "References," pp. 133-142.
Leonard, Harold (ed.) The Film Index: A Bibliography. Volume 1, The Film as Art. N.Y.: The Museum of Modern Art Film Library and the H.W. Wilson Company, 1941.
Liebert, Robert M. and Neala S. Schwartzberg. "Effects of Mass Media" in Mark R. Rosenzweig and Lyman W. Porter (eds.), Annual Review of Psychology, vol. 28. Palo Alto, CA: Annual Reviews, Inc., 1977, pp. 141-173.
Lipstein, Benjamin and William J. McGuire. Evaluating Advertising: A Bibliography of the Communications Process. N.Y.: Advertising Research Foundation, 1978.
A London Bibliography of the Social Sciences. London: London School of Economics and Political Science. First Supplement (June 1929--May 1931), Second Supplement (June 1931--May 1936), and Volume 1--38 (1934-1980).
Lumsdaine, Arthur A. and Mark A. May. "Mass Communication and Educational Media" in Paul R. Farnsworth (ed.), Annual Review of Psychology, vol. 16. Palo Alto, CA: Annual Reviews, Inc., 1965, pp. 475-534.
MacCann, Richard Dyer and Edward S. Perry. The New Film Index: A Bibliography of Magazine Articles in English, 1930-1970. N.Y.: E.P. Dutton, 1975.
Matlon, Ronald J. and Irene R. Matlon. Index to Journals in Communication Studies Through 1974. Falls Church, Virginia: Speech Communication Association, 1975.
Manchel, Frank. Film Study: A Resource Guide. Rutherford, N.J.: Fairleigh Dickinson University Press, 1973.
May, Lary. Screening Out the Past. N.Y.: Oxford University Press, 1980, "Notes," pp. 260-297.
McKerns, Joseph P., Carole L. McNall, and Elizabeth M. Johnson. "Mass Media Criticism: An Annotated Bibliography." Mass Comm Review 3 (Winter 1975/1976): 9-18.
Mowlana, Hamid. International Communication: A Selected Bibliography. Dubuque, Iowa: Kendall Hunt Pub. Co., 1971.

Nordicom (Nordic Documentation Center for Mass Communication Research). Bibliography of Nordic Mass Communication Literature. Aarhaus, Denmark: NDCMC, 1980.
Price, Warren C. The Literature of Journalism: An Annotated Bibliography. Minneapolis: University of Minnesota Press, 1959.
――――― and Calder M. Picket. An Annotated Journalism Bibliography 1958-1968. Minneapolis: University of Minnesota Press, 1970.
"Recherches sur le Cinéma: Enquête Bibliographique." Revue Internationale de Filmologie 3 (July-December 1952): 233-247.
Rehrauer, George. Cinema Booklist. Metuchen, N.J.: Scarecrow Press, 1972.
―――――. Cinema Booklist: Supplement One. Metuchen, N.J.: Scarecrow Press, 1974.
―――――. Cinema Booklist: Supplement Two. Metuchen, N.J.: Scarecrow Press, 1977.
Roberts, Donald F. and Christine Bachen. "Mass Communication Effects" in Mark R. Rosenzweig and Lyman W. Porter (eds.), Annual Review of Psychology, vol. 32. Palo Alto, CA: Annual Reviews, Inc., 1981, pp. 307-356.
Schramm, Wilbur. "Mass Communication" in Paul R. Farnsworth (ed.). Annual Review of Psychology, vol. 13. Palo Alto, CA: Annual Reviews, Inc., 1962, pp. 251-284.
Sheahan, Eileen. Moving Pictures: A Bibliography of Selected Reference Works for the Study of Film. New Haven: Yale University Library, 1973.
―――――. Moving Pictures: An Annotated Guide to Selected Film Literature with Suggestions for the Study of Film. N.Y.: A.S. Barnes, 1979.
Sproul, Edward, William F. Crawford, and Timothy J. Lyons. "Annotated Bibliography of the Journal 1947-1979." Journal of the University Film Association 31 (Fall 1979).
Stanley, Robert. The Celluloid Empire. N.Y.: Hastings House, 1978, "A Selective Bibliography," pp. 291-306.
Tannenbaum, Percy H. and Bradley S. Greenberg. "Mass Communication" in Paul R. Farnsworth, Mark R. Rosenzweig, and Judith T. Polefka (eds.), Annual Review of Psychology, vol. 19. Palo Alto, CA: Annual Reviews, Inc., 1968, pp. 351-386.
Tudor, Andrew. Image and Influence: Studies in the Sociology of Film. N.Y.: St. Martin's Press, 1974," Selected Bibliography," pp. 238-250.

Tunstall, Jeremy. <u>The Media are American.</u> N.Y.: Columbia University Press, 1977, "Bibliography," pp. 315-342.

─────── (ed.). <u>Media Sociology: A Reader.</u> Urbana: University of Illinois Press, 1970, "Selected Bibliography," pp. 545-558.

Unesco. <u>The Influence of the Cinema on Children and Adolescents: An Annotated International Bibliography.</u> Reports and Papers on Mass Communication No. 31, 1961.

Unesco. <u>World Communications: Press, Radio, Film, Television.</u> Paris: Unesco, 1951, "Bibliography," pp. 220-221.

Unesco. <u>World Communications: Press, Radio, Television, Film.</u> N.Y.: Unesco Publications Center, 1964, "Selective Bibliography," pp. 378-380.

United States. <u>Monthly Catalog of United States Government Publications</u> (1956-1981). Washington, D.C.: U.S. Government Printing Office.

─────── . Department of Commerce, Foreign Manpower Research Office, Bureau of the Census. <u>Bibliography of Social Science Periodicals and Monograph Series.</u> Washington, D.C.: U.S. Government Printing Office.
  <u>Bulgaria, 1944-1960,</u> 1961
  <u>Republic of China, 1949-1961,</u> 1961.
  <u>Mainland China, 1949-1960,</u> 1961
  <u>Rumania, 1947-1960,</u> 1961.
  <u>Albania, 1944-1961,</u> 1962.
  <u>Greece, 1950-1961,</u> 1962.
  <u>Hong Kong, 1950-1961,</u> 1962.
  <u>North Korea, 1945-1961,</u> 1962.
  <u>Republic of Korea, 1945-1961,</u> 1962.

─────── . Department of Commerce, Foreign Demographic Analysis Division, Bureau of the Census. <u>Bibliography of Social Science Periodicals and Monograph Series.</u> Washington, D.C.: U.S. Government Printing Office.
  <u>Denmark, 1945-1961,</u> 1963.
  <u>Finland, 1950-1962,</u> 1963.
  <u>Hungary, 1947-1962,</u> 1964.
  <u>Norway, 1945-1962,</u> 1964.
  <u>Poland, 1945-1962,</u> 1964.
  <u>Turkey, 1950-1962,</u> 1964.
  <u>Czechoslovakia, 1948-1963,</u> 1965.
  <u>Japan, 1950-1963,</u> 1965.
  <u>Soviet Zone of Germany, 1948-1963,</u> 1965.
  <u>Sweden, 1950-1963,</u> 1965.
  <u>U.S.S.R., 1950-1963,</u> 1965.
  <u>Yugoslavia, 1945-1963,</u> 1965.

Unwin, Derick. "Production and Audience Variables in Film
    and Television: A Second Selected Bibliography."
    Programmed Learning and Educational Technology 16
    (August 1979): 232-239.
Weiss, Walter. "Effects of Mass Media on Communication"
    in G. Lindzey and E. Aaronsen (eds.), Handbook of
    Social Psychology. Boston: Addison-Wesley, 1970,
    pp. 77-195.
──────. "Mass Communication" in Paul H. Mussen and
    Mark R. Rosenzweig (eds.), Annual Review of Psychology, vol. 22. Palo Alto, CA: Annual Reviews, Inc.,
    1971, pp. 309-336.
White, Carl M. Sources of Information in the Social Sciences. Totowa, N.J.: Bedminster Press, 1964.
Woronitzin, Sergei (compiler). Bibliography of Social Research in the Soviet Union (1960-1970). Munich: Verlag Dokumentation, 1973.
Wright, Basil. The Long View. N.Y.: Alfred A. Knopf,
    1974, "Selected Bibliography," pp. 697-709.

Abstracting Services (dates are inclusive)

Abstracts of Popular Culture, 1A (1976)--2C & D
Communication Abstracts, 1 (1978)--5 (no. 1, March 1982)
Communications Abstracts, 1 (1960)
Dissertation Abstracts International, January 1972--June 1982,
    "The Humanities and Social Sciences" and "The Sciences
    and Engineering."
    Comprehensive Dissertation Index 1861-1972, parts 1
    and 2 (Social Sciences and the Humanities), vol. 17
    (Social Sciences), vol. 18 and 19 (Psychology), vol. 25
    and 26 (Business and Economics), and vol. 31 (Communication and the Arts)
Historical Abstracts, 1 (1955)--33 (1982)
Journalism Abstracts, 1 (1963)--19 (1981)
Masters Abstracts, 1 (1962)--20 (no. 1, March 1982)
Psychological Abstracts, 1 (1927)--67 (no. 6, June 1982)
Social Science Abstracts, 1 (1929)--4 (1932)
Sociological Abstracts, 1 (November 1952)--30 (April 1982)

Indices (dates are inclusive)

American Humanities Index, 1 (1975)--8 (no. 1, Spring 1982)
British Humanities Index, 1962--January-March 1982
Business Periodicals Index, 1 (July 1959)--24 (no. 9, May
    1982)

Canadian Index to Periodicals and Documentary Films (after
    1976, Canadian Periodical Index), 1 (1948)--34 (no. 10,
    December 1981)
Film Literature Index, 1 (1973)--8 (no. 3, 1980)
Humanities Index, 1 (April 1974)--9 (June 1982)
Index to Psychoanalytic Writings, 1 (1954)--14 (1969)
Index to the Journal of the Society of Motion Picture (and
    Television) Engineers, July 1916--184 (1975)
International Index to Film Periodicals, 1972--1980
International Index to Periodicals (beginning with vol. 14 be-
    comes International Index: A Guide to Periodical Liter-
    ature in the Social Sciences and Humanities), vol. 1
    (1907-1915)--18 (April 1964-March 1965)
National Technical Information Service (Government Reports
    Annual Index)
    Bibliography of Scientific and Industrial Reports: 1
      (1946)--11 (1949)
    Bibliography of Technical Reports: 12 (1949)--21 (1954)
    U.S. Government Research Reports: 22 (1954)--39
      (1964)
    U.S. Government Research and Development Reports:
      40 (1965)--81 (December 1981)
New Periodicals Index, 1 (1977)--3 (January-December 1979)
Nordicom Review of Nordic Mass Communication Research,
    no. 2, 1981
Popular Periodicals Index, 3 (1973)--18 (July-December 1981)
Public Affairs Information Service, 1 (1915)--68 (July 1982)
Readers' Guide to Periodical Literature, 1 (1900-1904)--82
    (June 25, 1982)
Social Sciences and Humanities Index, 19 (1965)--27 (March
    1974)
Social Sciences Index, 1 (April 1974)--9 (June 1982)
Topicator, 2 (1966)--18 (January-February 1982)

THE MOTION PICTURE AUDIENCE:

A NEGLECTED ASPECT OF FILM RESEARCH*

As an object for scholarly inquiry, the motion picture medium historically has drawn considerable research attention from historians, aestheticians, and students of law and technology. Research studies from these various disciplinary perspectives are justified as being needed for the individual wishing to gain a fuller understanding of cinema. For instance, one might validly argue that it is, prima facie, "natural" to study the creators--the filmmakers--of motion pictures; and even the most cursory search of the literature reveals a plethora of such work. Moreover, the history and development of the motion picture medium has been well-documented, as have a variety of legal issues.[1] Somewhat surprising, however, is the paucity of valid and reliable research on the recipients--the consumers-- of motion pictures. Leaving the purposes and goals of social science aside for the moment, it seems intuitively reasonable to presume that the "manufacturers" of the "commodity" would for, if no other reason, economic motives, be keenly interested in such research to maximize profits. A second intuitively sensible assumption, again based upon financial motivation, would be that the world's largest and most prolific film producers--Hollywood--should be among the most attentive, encouraging, and supportive patrons--if not initiators--for film audience studies. Historically, and contrary to intuition, however, this was not the case. After a half a century of existence and popular acceptance, the powers in Hollywood were, for the most part, antagonistic toward and showed disdain for audience research. As Handel recounts: "In 1942 there was only a handful of persons who did not reject film research outright. Most condemned it without trial even through research was an established and useful part of other businesses."[2] Contemporaneously, Lazarsfeld, writing from the perspective of social science research, noted that "mere descriptive audience research has not developed so much with movies as with the other media."[3] Handel was to reiterate his and Lazarsfeld's point again in 1953: "Audience research is well entrenched in all media of mass communications except the film."[4] Today, the state of the art in film audience research has perhaps

---

*A longer version of this essay was presented at the Ohio University Film Conference, April 1982, Athens, Ohio.

been best summarized by Simonet: "Motion picture audience research has been growing as a science from humble beginnings to more grandiose beginnings. But it seems always to have been making beginnings."[5]

The purposes of this essay are twofold: first, to enumerate, document, and sort out the variety of reasons--although in many instances "excuses" might be a better term--historically offered about why film audience research has not been conducted; second, to suggest four specific research directions for future film audience research. Preceding these discussions a brief rationale detailing the importance of film audience research will be presented.

Guback has written that "the literature about film deals overwhelmingly with surface phenomena" and that "this situation hardly contributes to a comprehensive understanding of what film is all about." He makes a compelling case for an "institutional approach" to film research; such an approach "analyzes the economic and industrial structures and arrangements involved in cinema, and the means by which information and entertainment are processed and allocated as commodities." The material discussed in the present essay, as will be seen, dovetails with and complements Guback's argument, albeit from a somewhat different point of view. Whereas the institutional approach Guback outlines "explains the way a society organizes the production and distribution of its entertainment and information,"[6] here the discussion is centered on the consumption process of such entertainment and information by various audience aggregates. Thus, the consumption process--in the broadest sense of the phrase--can be seen as an important and necessary correlate to the organizational aspects of motion pictures. In fact, it can be asserted, these two approaches are clearly not mutually exclusive and are separated at the present only for purposes of analytical clarity; future research will--or least should--be directed at a synthesis of the institutional and consumptional literature.

I: Why Study the Film Audience?

Systematic study of the film audience properly, but not necessarily exclusively, falls within the purview of social scientists trained in such allied academic disciplines as communications, psychology, and sociology. While social scientists, enamored with the other major media of mass communications, have consistently and prolifically gone about the business of conducting audience studies resulting in encyclopedic volumes devoted to the audience for the medium of their interest, the research field on film audiences is largely unexplored. The mass communications student in search of audience analysis for any of the contemporary mass media but one--motion pictures--is faced (perhaps intimidated would be a better term in some instances) with formidable and seemingly neverending card catalogue drawers, journal articles, convention papers, books, and governmental publications. Film audience researchers, on the other hand, typically find themselves inundated with a veritable forest of verbiage, little of which seems to be theoretically and methodologically systematic, coherent, or valid.[7]

The title of this essay implies that the study of film audiences is in some way a useful activity and therefore in need of research attention. Perhaps, it might be argued, such research is neither useful nor meaningful and hence therein lies the explanation for the scarcity of such work. Thus, to introduce this discussion, attention must be paid to assertions of this nature.

Historically one would think that A.O. Tate's published regret at not having noted even the name of the first kinetoscope patron on April 6, 1894 ought to have served as an impetus for related research endeavors.[8] Such was not to be the case. Systematic analysis of the early film audience would, today, be useful insofar as it would provide baseline data upon which a multitude of future comparisons might have been made; this, as with other historically-based arguments, is abundantly clear given the lucidity of 20-20 hindsight. Succintly stated, we have a sharp picture of the industrial and technological development of the medium while, comparatively, the development and growth of the medium's audience is, at best, a fuzzy, soft-focus image enlightened mostly by armchair philosophy and (often apocryphal) reminiscence.

A second important reason for studying film audiences is the amount of money consumers spend on movies. The most currently available and complete data (1976) show that, while motion pictures account for only 4.12 percent of the total U.S. recreational expenditures, they are responsible for an astonishing 53.36 percent of the total U.S. spectator amusement expenditures[9]--this despite the availability of a variety of alternative leisure time spectator choices. The popularity of movies, then, as measured by recreational expenditures, warrants research attention.

Third, although movies account for more than half the recreational (spectator) dollar, U.S. cinema attendance has dramatically declined over the years. What factors explain this? A brief example illustrates the importance of and one possible answer to this question. In 1930 the U.S. had a population of slightly more than 123 million [10] and an average weekly film attendance of 90 million.[11] That was also the year in which the first reliable study of attitudes toward movies was reported.[12] Results of the early attitude research showed that patrons held favorable attitudes toward the medium.[13] In 1970 the total U.S. population had grown by 65 percent to 203 million[14] while the average weekly film attendance had dropped by 83 percent (since 1930) to 15 million.[15] Concurrent with the declining weekly admissions were less favorable attitudes toward motion pictures. One reason the average U.S. weekly movie attendance has plummeted by more than half in the space of 40 years may be the shift in movie-goers' attitudes toward the medium; unfortunately, there is no way to know for certain because the study of peoples' attitudes toward movies has been neglected.[16]

Fourth, and closely related to the point made above, in spite of the precipitous decline in attendance over the years, box office records continue to be broken annually by a few films, inflation notwithstanding. This observation suggests the hypothesis that while movie attendance generally has diminished, there continues to exist what Jarvie has labeled "the special occasion audience": normally infrequent film-goers who attend only selected productions. [17] The composition and motivations of this audience, which responded in such tremendous numbers at films such as Star Wars ($175 million) or The Empire Strikes Back ($120 million), [18] beg for scholarly scrutiny yet have been neglected. [19]

Thus, if carefully and systematically conducted, movie audience research offers the potential for important historical and behavioral explanations regarding large audiences and their interaction with a popular mass medium. Clearly, the brief rationale presented here for investigating the film audience should be viewed as heuristic rather than definitive: a multitude of other reasons, of equal or greater importance, might also be suggested. Perhaps a final comment to the question "Why study the film audience?" is: to provide an accurate accounting, grounded in theory, of film-goers' motives for attendance, the gratifications they derive from the movie experience, and the effect of movies on audiences.

II: Reasons for the Dearth of Data on Film Audiences

In his first annual report to the Motion Picture Association of America (MPAA) in 1946, President Eric Johnson stated that "The motion picture industry probably knows less about itself than any other major industry in the United States."[20] Given the industry's own lack of knowledge about itself, Garrison's statement that "very little information has been made public about the post-television movie audience" seems a foregone conclusion. [21] In 1944 Mae D. Huettig wrote that Hollywood has shown "A great reluctance to disclose factual information with respect to its operations" and she raised a number of questions concerning the industry as a business and the composition of its patrons. Huettig concludes that "There are few reliable statistics available (and none of these compiled by the industry itself) with regard to these questions."[22] While reasons and explanations for what appears to be Hollywood's phobic attitude toward external examination and research will probably remain at the level of speculation and conjecture, Lincoln may have inadvertently tapped a responsive chord when he wrote that "The movie industry is notorious for its lack of accurate statistics."[23] (It should be noted that for Huettig and Lincoln's discussion of "statistics" the term "research studies" may be justifiably substituted.) This portion of the essay addresses itself to offering answers to the following questions: Why has there been so little research on the movie audience? What reasons have been offered to explain this? How valid are these reasons?[24] These questions will be approached from two perspectives, the industry's and the independent scholar's. That is, why have both Hollywood and the social science community been reluctant to examine the movie audience?

The Industry and Audience Research

To assert absolutely that Hollywood has completely ignored researching its audience would be in error. Ramsaye recounts an anecdote involving Carl Laemmle who inauspiciously began his film career conducting "field studies" of the audience for Hale's Tours:

> For two days the little man from Oshkosh [Laemmle] stood down in State Street [in Chicago], moving just enough to keep from being conspicuous, while he counted the attendance that went in to see Hale's Tours pictures. When he got through he had an accurate notion of what kind of people went to see the pictures, what hours of the day they found the time to do it in, and how many of them there were per hour and per day. [25]

In a similar vein is Hampton's discussion of the development of the film exchange system which:

> established a route of communication from audience through exhibitor to distributor and producer, enabling the nickelodeon patrons to make their wishes known to the makers of pictures. If spectators enjoyed a film and applauded it, the nickelodeon owner scurried around and tried to get more like it, and if they grumbled as they left the show he passed on the complaints to the exchange, and the exchange told the manufacturer. [26]

The initial forays by industry-connected individuals into the field of audience research, however, were obviously little more than shots in the dark. Columbia Pictures' Harry Cohn's reputed use of his seat-of-the-pants methodology, [27] Mack Sennett's personalized "laughter scale," [28] and Albert Sindlinger's "bugging" of the restrooms of the theaters he operated with porters who would ask patrons questions about the picture currently playing, [29] all offered little in the way of external validity. Nevertheless, examples of studio bosses who considered themselves as representative of the audience for their pictures is, by now, the stuff of which legends are made[30] and, in a certain sense, understandable. In the early 1900s, the medium, industry, and audience for the medium were all new and thus the initial confusion and uncertainty among producers, which resulted in their extrapolating of their own responses to those of their audience, can be seen as a means by which (reasonable) fears of financial failure were offset. Such fears were compounded by what appeared to be an extraordinarily fickle audience. Hampton suggested that "the orgy of extravagance that obsessed the studios from 1922 until 1927, when talking pictures wrought a fresh revolution," in confluence with the public's "broadening of tastes, noticeable after Armistice Day," together created an audience film-preference climate so unpredictable for producers that "a blind guess seemed to be as effective in predicting results [of the public's attraction to various film genres] as the most careful and intelligent analysis."[31] It was this combination of rapid technological and social change that, according to Jacobs, caused the genesis of the " 'cycle' in motion pictures, the unit of which was the 'formula' picture" as a means to at least reduce uncertainty if not ensure "sure-fire" hits. [32] And, with this rise of the formula film, it is reported, came a modicum of interest, if not sophistication, in marketing analysis:

> Movies were analyzed for the following selling points: (1) "Names"--that is, stars; (2) "Production Value"--elaborate sets, big crowds, and other proofs of great expense; (3) "Story Value"--the huge price paid for the original and its great reputation as a novel or play; (4) "Picture Sense"--a conglomeration of all these items; (5) "Box Office Appeal" --plenty of all the standardized values which had proved successful in years past. [33]

Unfortunately, and perhaps due to Hollywood's doctrine of secrecy, film historians have not recounted the methodologies (never mind the results) used in these analyses with any precision. By and large, such historical accounts are anecdotal in nature and are usually presented to illustrate some point other than a film audience research perspective. Thus, we learn that Harry Rapf, when he was production manager at Selznick-Select and Warner Brothers,

> often authorized his chauffeur to invite amateur critics to express opinions on new films and the chauffeur's committee consisted of carpenters, electricians, the studio barber, the young interne in charge of the hospital, the gate-keeper, the gymnasium masseur, and their wives and children. Harry Rapf, regarding this audience as fairly representative of average theater patronage, frequently made changes to win its approval, with gratifying box-office results. [34]

In this passage we have been offered a glimmer of insight, but little of substance, about early attempts at pretesting of movies.

In summary, while it would be inaccurate to assert that Hollywood has entirely dismissed or disdained audience research, it may be stated that neither Hollywood nor film historians have been very helpful in detailing what was done or what was found in the way of film audience analysis. [35] One industry insider summarized "Commercial Practices in Audience Analysis" within the film colony this way:

> we have usually worked in the past on the thesis that if we stand in the dark and throw a rock and hear a crash, we've hit the greenhouse. This is not an altogether dependable method. It means that if you don't hear a crash, you may no longer be in the motion picture business. [36]

Specific reasons for the industry's own inattention to audience research have been detailed by several authors. One popular explanation, noted by several scholars, is that since the film industry does not sell advertising, "it does not need to account to anyone for the size of its audience."[37] Thus, unlike the broadcast or print media, measurement of the effects and effectiveness of the film medium as a tool for selling a product is superfluous. The validity of this reason, of course, may be differentially assessed depending upon the terms by which the purpose of cinema is conceptualized: e.g., as an art form designed to bring aesthetic enjoyment to viewers, as a business designed to bring maximal return on investments, as a medium designed as an outlet for the creative energies of artists. And, this aside, most film companies were accountable to various financial sources of funding as well as their own shareholders.

The early popularity of films is another frequently mentioned reason for the industry's lack of research:

> The young industry, which could readily finance research projects, found little motivation to do so because the new, expanding market was active enough to provide a highly satisfactory volume of business for the leading firms. Most motion picture executives were content to let product improvement and sales policies rest on their intuitive insight of what the public wanted, rather than on direct contact with the consumer.[38]

Thus, in essence, it is argued that a sense of complacency was encouraged and reinforced by virtue of a long-lasting period in which films were a seller's market: with people attending the movies in droves, the industry assumed a "who-cares-why-they-go" posture.[39] The weakness of such a line of reasoning, as history would later show, was its short-sightedness: the presumption of an ever-increasing, or at least stable, movie audience, coupled with either ignorance of, or refusal to acknowledge, the possibility of other competitive media (e.g., broadcasting), as well as intra-industry competition, among other things,[40] were to prove the flimsiness of this rationale.

Handel has asserted that "Hollywood, by and large, resisted the development of high-level audience research" and suggests that the most frequently heard reason for this was that "movie making is basically an artistic endeavor." He quickly dismisses this reasoning as so much fluff by stating: "We would gladly accept this statement if the same people did not tell us, after turning out a series of utterly commercial cliché pictures without batting a solitary eyelash, that movie making is just a business like any other."[41]

Lazarsfeld and Handel suggest that industry executives feared and distrusted researchers which, consequently, led to their avoidance of audience research. Lazarsfeld only states that "the executives in the movie industry are probably more individualistic and more distrustful of systematic research than those in any other communication industry."[42] Handel offers the explanation for this distrust: "Some movie makers misinterpret the function of audience research. They see in it not an instrument for their use, but a substitute for executive acumen."[43] Fear of usurpation by researchers among industry executives, however, was not necessarily unfounded. For instance, in the 1940s, the account executives of Gallup's Audience Research, Inc.

> tried to assume too large a status within the organizations they served. Instead of advising what decisions might be taken as a result of the audience studies, they often told the industry executives what to do. [44]

Nevertheless, short-sightedness, again, and an unprofessional approach to business are factors militating against wholehearted acceptance of the cogency of this argument for the lack of research.

Yet another reason for the industry's failure to pursue audience research has been offered by Handel:

> the industry still clings to some archaic methods of measuring audience reaction, such as uncontrolled sneak previews, preview cards, too much reliance on fan mail, and naturally, the mystic "feel" of the market which seems to reach its heights of potency in the air-conditioned private dining rooms of Bel Air and Miami Beach. [45]

This is less a reason and more an excuse: industry laziness and inertia cannot be held as a sound reason justifying the virtually total neglect of audience research.

Finally, Lazarsfeld has written that "the assumption has been that each film presented a new problem, and could not be considered a typical product"[46]--hence the paucity of research. This statement has several implications. First, it is assumed that research results gathered from the study of any single film and its audience cannot be generalized to the next feature that unspools; i.e., every picture has to be sold and researched independently. [47] Yet this belies the notion that

> in a business in which hunches often carry more weight than demographic research, the box office record of a particular kind of film in a specific theater usually determines the releasing pattern for most future films. [48]

Moreover, given the absence of research this assumption can be neither supported nor refuted. Second, the "uniqueness assumption" is related to the short "shelf life" of motion pictures; the average exhibition run of any given film in any given locale is from three to five weeks. If audience research is constrained to a picture-by-picture basis, then the utility of such research may not be justifiable given its cost. Again, however, these assumptions have not been tested. Third, the "uniqueness assumption" may be seen as a direct cause for the lack of general audience research:

> Determining who might comprise the audience is basically a back-burner project. Since it is not associated with a specific film, its lack of urgency causes it occasionally to get lost in the shuffle. [49]

Basically, then, this final argument for the industry's avoidance of audience research can be seen as tautological: film audience research cannot be conducted in a general sense (or the value of such research would be minimal) since the "product" is unique and the uniqueness of the product, together with its short shelf life, makes such research of limited value. In short, research has been traditionally neglected since its benefits have not been revealed--or, perhaps more accurately, given a chance to be revealed.

Social Science and Audience Research

In this section, the focus of analysis shifts to the independent scholar and the social science community: again the question is, why has film audience research been largely neglected?

Denis McQuail, in his introductory note to Franklin Fearing's article on the "Influence of the Movies on Attitudes and Behavior," which was originally published in 1947, states that "the fact that it still reads so freshly is also a measure of how little cumulative knowledge we have yet."[50] The fact that social scientists have long overlooked the motion picture medium as an object for audience research cannot be doubted. For example we can examine what has been collected on film audiences in book form. Sterling and Haight[51] present tabular data (drawn from other sources) describing "Characteristics of Motion Picture Audiences." Most film history books offer a brief discussion of the film audience--especially from the developmental point of view--although such presentations are, by and large, cursory and global in scope. Jowett's Film: The Democratic Art[52] provides the most current and comprehensive source for film audience research in book form. Yet even here, in this 461 page work, only 46 pages (as itemized in the index under "audiences")--or 10 percent--are devoted to the topic of audiences. Moreover, Jowett's discussion of one "Special Study" of the film audience contains an error of omission which leaves the reader with an incorrect reason for why people go to the movies.[53] Jowett aside, few books exist for the film audience researcher who wishes to uncover empirical evidence. In terms of books which focus exclusively on the film audience the most recent title is Handel's 1950 work, Hollywood Looks at Its Audience.[54]

The reluctance shown by mass communications and other scholars to investigate the motion picture audience may be traced to at least six factors. One frequently voiced reason offered for the scarcity of film audience research by independent scholars is the "notorious difficulty of access to facts about the film industry which is secretive and insular."[55] Lazarsfeld wrote that independent researchers do not and cannot gain access to box office returns data, which therefore "makes it understandable that mere descriptive audience research has not developed so much with movies as with the other media."[56] Thus, it is argued, although at present film audience research is known to take place--primarily by the marketing departments of the major film producer-distributors--these data remain proprietary, [57] and hence conceptual and theoretical advances are stymied by the lack of any clear-cut directions from an existing body of knowledge. On the other hand, this same reason ought to challenge the inquisitive scholar to begin vigorous investigations; for clearly such research would not, as the saying goes, be "reinventing the wheel," since this wheel is a well-kept secret. Furthermore, while box office data may be of importance for some film audience research projects, it is certainly not the sine qua non or germane for most audience research which uses the social science lens to focus on the phenomenon. Motivational research, to take one example, would do better to employ such constructs as frequency of attendance and the importance respondents assign movie-going as a leisure activity in their theoretical and research designs than box office or rental data. Lastly, complaints that the movie audience research field lacks--or is being deprived of--theoretical underpinnings and guidelines are flimsy excuses for lazy scholars; at some point in time every research area suffered this same situation.

The film industry's assumption, presented above, that "each film presented a new problem, and could not be considered a typical product" [58] may also have been a priori endorsed and adopted by the social science community, thereby causing researchers to neglect the field of film audience research in favor of other media audiences. If the "uniqueness assumption" is valid, scholars might be justified in arguing that the traditional predictive and explanatory functions of theory (including the process of theory-building) would be inoperative. However, as was noted earlier, the validity of this assumption has yet to be demonstrated. Moreover, the research interests and purposes of the film industry are not aligned with those of independent scholars: industry research may be broadly described as attempting to answer one question "How can any given picture best be marketed so as to achieve a profitable return on investment?"; social scientists, on the other hand, should approach the film audience with an interest that extends beyond the simple unidimensional one-film behavioral perspective; social science research can and should address itself to broader cognitive, affective, and behavioral issues, their interrelationships, and the search for explanations of these issues as applied in a theoretical sense.

A third reason offered by some writers for the noninvolvement of independent scholars in film audience research is the difficulty or inability to attract commercial, governmental, or foundation funding for such work. [59] The assertion that financial support might be hard to come by for film audience studies may have an element of truth. Compared to other mass media, the film medium's lobbying and self-regulatory organization (the Motion Picture Association of America) has rarely offered the opportunity for, sought out, or provided financial support for, independent research; conversely, both the National Association of Broadcasters and the American Newspaper Publishers Association--regardless of what might be their self-serving motives--have helped to foster and promote audience research for their media through grants to scholars. In 1946, "fact-minded" MPAA president Eric Johnson [60] established a Department of Research within the MPAA that might have led to the potential for involving independent scholars at some later time. Handel has stated that this Department had among its objectives "to eliminate the guesswork which had characterized industry statistics" and "to engage in research projects designed to furnish the industry with scientific data as a basis for the formation of policy."[61] The Department was short-lived, however, as the member companies of the MPAA did not approve a key research project advocated by Johnson [62] and "the research committee, after sponsoring some minor interindustry statistical studies, discontinued its activities."[63] However, even though there has been little financial support for film audience research, this still does not justify the inattention among independent scholars. While research can be costly, it is still possible even without external funding. Moreover, one would suspect that funding would be easier to attain--especially from research foundations and the industry--if one has a "track record" of such research.

Jarvie has written that two reasons the social dimensions of motion pictures have been paid such brief research attention are: 1/ "vulgar associations attached to the cinema, partly due because of its very newness and popularity, [and 2/] the feeling that what little there is to be said on the subject of the sociology of the cinema is trite and/or well-known."[64] The vulgarity argument may have held sufficient power in the early days of the movies to discourage research attention but this has doubtful, or at least limited, explanatory power. Myriad reports in the popular press [65] concerning the vulgarity, uncivilized, morally-threatening, and low-brow nature of the movies, as published in the early 1900s, can also be seen as acting as a catalyst to film audience research. Perhaps the best example in support of this is the Payne Fund studies. As Sklar has written, the initiator of the project, William A. Short, reform and procensorship-minded director of the National Committee for Study of Social Values in Motion Pictures, shaped the project "from the beginning by his special needs and goals: to get the goods on the movies, to nail them to the wall."[66] Today the cinema has reached and generally been accorded the status of at least a mid-level art form, thereby removing the stigma and obstacle for researchers. (Television has had the dubious distinction of usurping not only a large chunk of the cinema audience but also the pejorative aspects of the cinema's reputation.) The weakness of the "trite or well-known" argument lies in its assumption of a static industry, society, and audience.

A last explanation for the cold shoulder given to film audience research by social science is that the rapid and widespread diffusion and adoption of television, beginning in the early 1950s, "stole" whatever research interest might have been directed at the movies. Just as it has been shown that TV affected cinema attendance, [67] it is not coincidental that TV also affected social science research activity. That is, had the introduction of television come later, Handel's 1950 Hollywood Looks at Its Audience might now be viewed as the harbinger of an active research inquiry by independent scholars into the film audience field rather than the dying gasp of an unfashionable field presently of interest only to antiquarians. Television is, of course, a particularly attractive medium for audience research for many obvious and legitimate reasons. What is suggested here, though, is that TV's ubiquity and accessibility to both audience and researchers makes it a compellingly convenient medium (in contrast to motion pictures) to "do" research on. Simply put, film audience research isn't "where it's at," in part, because it is (or is perceived as being) less convenient, more difficult, and more time-consuming than television audience research. The pervasiveness of television, coupled with the public's attention to and appetite for the medium, is somewhat reminiscent of the pre-television motion picture audience; and perhaps recognizing the neglect it had shown the field of movie audience research, the social science community was quick to avoid making the same mistake with television. In any case, television audience research, while providing much needed information, may have also functioned--inadvertently maybe--to redirect the course of research away from the movie audience.

III: Four Areas for Further Research

Given the rather unstructured and unfocused state of the existing body of film audience literature, numerous diverse research endeavors could be enumerated for the future. This section will be selective, however, in its suggestions for such future film audience research studies: presented here are four areas in need of research attention. These particular areas for discussion were selected for primarily theoretical reasons.

Antecedent Conditions to Movie-Going

Several studies have inquired as to the salience individuals attribute to a number of film-specific variables which, in turn, may help to determine their particular movie-going experience.[68] Most studies of this nature have found that respondents evaluate subject matter as the most important factor in determining whether or not to see a movie and, conversely, behind-the-screen production personnel (e.g., producer, director, screenwriter) as the least important. In addition to this research on the importance of various variables in the film choice decision process, it has long been recognized that contemporary movie-goers are far more selective in their film attendance behavior than were their counterparts when the medium was at its height in popularity. The findings of several reports [69] support the concept of a discriminating audience: for most individuals, movie-going appears to be directionally specific activity; people go to a movie, not the movies. Thus, we have some insight as to the salience and predictive capacity of a host of variables as they relate to a specific film-going experience once an individual has decided to attend a movie (rather than engage in some other activity). This body of research presumes that the decision to alter existing activities--either immediately or sometime in the future--had already been reached by the individual. What this literature has not attempted to analyze is a central motivation theory question: What specific conditions determine how an individual initially becomes motivated to engage in movie-going as an activity? In other words, what is it about motion pictures--or a particular motion picture--that gives rise to an individual's change of behavior?

Movie audiences, their behavior, and their motives for that behavior, represent an interesting phenomenon from points of view of the leisure activity and consumption. Movies are a consumer product, unlike many other products, that do not offer "trialability." Also, the film consumer typically enters into a "consumption agreement/situation" with little precise knowledge of the commodity itself; while the form is perhaps familiar, the exact content remains enigmatic. Further, with movies, unlike other consumer products, few "repeat purchases" (i.e., attendance) of the same product (i.e., movie) are likely to occur. Additionally, movie selection and attendance is a costly commitment in terms of time, finances, and effort (i.e., one goes to a movie as opposed to sitting down to watch TV). Moreover, the "uniqueness assumption," discussed above, postulates that each movie is a product unlike other products within the same class and has unique characteristics. Thus, while a facial tissue is pretty much the same whether the brand name is Kleenex, Scott, or generic, the same cannot be said for motion pictures. If there are key differences between films, which may exert differential influences in terms of motivation and decision-making, as the uniqueness assumption would hypothesize, these differences would tend to limit one's ability to generalize the results of individual movie motivational research studies. Finally, the most common attendance unit is the couple (as opposed to either going alone or as part of a large group). This, therefore, might tend to affect the attendance decision and specific film to be attended processes; such processes might involve exponentially larger numbers of variables simply by one or more additional persons entering into the decision process. It may be that such involvement is in some cases direct (e.g., through verbal discussion) or indirect (e.g., one individual planning attendance in view of such considerations as appropriateness for dating activities and the needs, desires, and preferences of the other).

All of the points raised above presently exist at the level of speculation. While conjecture may be cognitively stimulating, research studies need to be designed to begin to address these issues for purposes of theory-building.

Contexts of the Movie Experience

Movie-going is not an isolated activity. Regardless of whether the individual elects to attend alone or in the company of others, the physical ambience of the theater, the form of exhibition, and a host of other factors may play important roles in determining not only attendance decisions but also the film experience itself. Just as one would not attempt to interpret, in any meaningful and valid sense, nonverbal communicative behavior without the benefit of context, so too film audience research needs to consider and address the role of varying contexts of the movie experience.

Intuitively it makes sense to assert that motives for attendance and gratifications derived (to name but two possible research directions) will vary depending upon different film contexts. But the present state of the art in audience research has, by and large, remained at the intuitive level. Whatever the benefits of intuitively appealing exegeses, they are no substitute for systematically conducted research. Armchair philosophy needs to be supported or refuted on the basis of empirical reality.

One context in need of audience research attention is the different forms of exhibition. What differences and similarities in composition, for instance, can be identified between the audience that attends first- and those who attend subsequent-run pictures? In 1955 Smythe, et al. [70] reported their study of the audience for first-run films; to date this study has not been replicated nor has there been a study conducted comparing first- to subsequent-run movie audiences. Similarly, research has, for the most part, failed to examine the audience for art films, cult films (e.g., The Rocky Horror Picture Show), and other specific film-types.[71] In fact, with the exception of governmentally sponsored research on pornography, [72] few investigations have sought to study and describe the audiences for specific types of films. A third film context on which little audience research has been reported is the type of exhibition hall: e.g., drive-ins, [73] single screen, and multiplexes.

Thus, the argument presented here is that a multitude of contextual dimensions are in need of research attention. It should be noted that such research need not--and ought not--be constrained to an asymmetric perspective (i.e., what does the context "do" to the audience?). Rather, a transactional research design may prove to be a richer and more meaningful point of view. Here we would ask such questions as: How does the audience go about constructing its own film context? How does the audience's construction interface with an existing (e.g., physical) context?

Public Preference for Movie-Types

The third research issue concerns the public's taste in movies. What kinds of films does the public enjoy? Why? How are film-type preferences developed? Why do tastes and preferences for various types of films change? What explains "cycles" of popularity?

Unlike the two research issues presented above, a good deal of research attention has been directed toward uncovering people's preferences for various story-types.[74] However, the methods used to discern taste preferences by researchers in this area tend to be unreliable and the coding categories non-comparable (thereby making trend analyses, for instance, impossible). One thing, at least, is abundantly clear: the public is very familiar with the many labels assigned to film-types (e.g., mystery, science fiction, musical, comedy) and has little trouble identifying their favorites and least favorites. The problem for researchers comes in interpreting the meaning that various individuals attach to these several labels and understanding the discriminations people make between the labels (e.g., what is the difference between films classified as thrillers, mysteries, horror, and suspense?).

The problem of sorting out film-type labels into meaningful, mutually exclusive, and exhaustive categories has been pointed out by other researchers. Smythe, et al., for instance, note that "there is ... a presumptive fuzziness (in the psychological and semantic sense of validity) in the meaning of names given program types by the respondents."[75] Their study used open-ended questions to determine film-type preferences. On the other hand, Lazarsfeld pointed out that if movie types were precoded (close-ended response options), experimental work and conceptual clarification were also needed:

> If we ask, "What type of movie do you like best?" the answers depend upon the way the movie types are classified and upon the respondents' understanding of the terms we are using. [76]

An understanding of the public's preference for different types of films is important insofar as it would help scholars in developing a theory of the motives for movie-going. Further, such information might also find application in the measurement of attitudes toward motion pictures (discussed below). Here it can be noted that content analysis, coupled with such tools as the semantic differential and multidimensional scaling, suggest a method which could be used to clarify how the audience conceptualizes film-types.

Attitude Toward Motion Pictures

As was briefly noted earlier, one plausible explanation for the dramatic decline in weekly film admissions is that a shift in moviegoers' attitude toward the medium has occurred. In general, one clear purpose and use of attitude measurement is that of predicting behavior. [77] Such predictions may be advanced through an understanding of the characteristics and values individuals expect to find, or associate with, when engaging in a particular activity (e.g., movie attendance). However, systematic study of people's attitudes toward movies has been scant; a much greater research emphasis has been placed on the flip-side of the attitude coin (i.e., studies which ask "What do movies do to patrons?"). [78]

The few attitude-toward-movies studies that have been reported, when placed in a historical context, show an unmistakable trend. Based on the extant literature, the public's attitude toward movies can be seen as shifting from a highly favorable one as reported by Williams in 1933, to a more tepid response as was documented by Patel's 1952 study and Panda and Kanungo's 1962 report, and finally, to Austin's (1981) finding of a somewhat unfavorable attitude. [79] The shift in attitudinal direction since the earliest research study to the most recent parallels the declining number of admissions over the years. While acknowledging the dangers of ex post facto explanations, the intuitive appeal and face validity of such an interpretation cannot be ignored. That is, this parallel shift may suggest that movie attendance has declined because of an increasingly unfavorable attitude toward films. [80] The causes for this change in attitude direction can only be speculated on, unfortunately, since research was not performed on this topic.

Several related attitude research directions may also be briefly identified here. First, and most urgently, construction of a reliable, valid, and contemporary movie attitude scale is needed. Such a scale should be developed and designed keeping in mind the multidimensional aspects of attitude. [81] A second area in need of investigation is that of discovering the process of formation and change of attitude toward movies. How many exposures to the medium are required before an individual forms a firm attitude? What variables might affect a shift in this attitude? How does the social context affect attitude formation and change? Furthermore, the well-documented observation that interpersonal contact affects individual's choice of movie, [82] as well as their evaluation of movies, [83] raises the question: What role does interpersonal influence play in affecting attitude toward films?

A third direction for future attitude research has to do with a drawback to all of the existing attitude toward movies research. All of these studies have used either high school or college students as respondents. The issue of external (especially population) validity, and the limitations to the results gathered with samples composed of such individuals--in addition to factors such as the demand characteristics of the setting in which the scales were administered--are obvious. While it can be argued that since the largest group of filmgoers fall within the high school-college age bracket, [84] therefore "for film research, the college student may be more representative than students used in other research," [85] this overlooks the importance of understanding the entire population's attitude toward the medium (especially non-movie-goers and infrequent movie-goers). Thus, attitude measurement performed on samples with a greater range of stratification and demographic attributes is needed.

IV: Conclusions

Presented in this essay was 1/ a rationale for the systematic study of the film audience, 2/ explanations why both the industry and social science community have neglected film audience research, as well as the validity of these explanations, and 3/ four theoretically important topics for future research in this field. In general it can be concluded that the reasons typically offered for the lack of film audience research are, at best, weak. Further, by viewing the four topics suggested here for further research as heuristic, one can see that much work needs to be done.

Methodologically, the domain of film audience research demands that a variety of approaches and tools be used. It should be emphasized that in going about the business of performing research and building theory in this area, the researcher must actively avoid the temptation to become married to either a particular tool or design since no one research method is without its drawbacks. As Webb, et al., state: " ... the issue is not choosing among individual methods. Rather it is the necessity for a multiple operationalism, a collection of methods combined to avoid sharing the same weaknesses." [86] Thus, the often presented choice between quantitative and qualitative approaches, for instance, can be seen for what it is: a spurious, artificial, constraint externally imposed. Just as number-crunching is not the answer, the same can be said for the qualitative perspective.

Perhaps the strongest methodological argument to be advanced here is that film audience researchers must get out of the classroom and the laboratory and into the field. The phenomenon of interest needs to be studied in the richness of its natural environment. This environment, as was suggested earlier, needs to be understood for its own sake as well as to assist researchers in the interpretation and explanation of data gathered outside of the natural context. All too often researchers have relied on the comfort and convenience of the sterile classroom or the mail or telephone survey. Such research settings, far removed from where the phenomenon under investigation occurs, limit the external validity of the research results; and, more important, usually offer only an incomplete (or, worse, distorted) image of the behavior or the motives for behavior.

Earlier it was noted that most people, when asked how important a number of variables were to their most recent movie attendance, report that the film's theme or plot was the most important variable. In and of itself this finding is probably not too surprising; it is also, however, illogical. People might be expected to refer to film content as the key determinant in their attendance decision ex post facto. However, one cannot possibly have first-hand knowledge of a film's plot prior to actually viewing the film itself. Thus, the influence of "plot" in drawing attention to and attendance at a given film is probably embedded in and dependent upon other variables (e.g., interpersonal interaction, reading of reviews, viewing and reading advertisements, seeing trailers, etc.). Field studies --interviews with patrons in line, before they see the picture they are queued up for--might, for instance, find a decrease in the frequency with which the film's plot is mentioned as an important variable in the attendance decision process. Moreover, personal interviews with patrons would provide the opportunity to follow-up and probe a response such as "theme/plot" to ascertain the underlying means by which patrons gained their perception of film content (unlike the printed survey). In short, the application of multiple methodologies, under a variety of conditions, all directed at understanding a given aspect of the movie audience, would tend to increase the meaningfulness of the data gathered.

The final paragraphs of this essay focus on theory vis-a-vis film audience research. At present, it is clear, we find ourselves not only with little audience research per se, but also devoid of theory. The cause(s) of this present state of affairs could be speculated on (it may be, for instance, a case of reciprocal causation), but the value to be derived from such speculation may not be so compelling as to warrant the effort. Moreover, regardless of the precise reason(s) for the atheoretical state of film audience research, the consequences are obvious. Without the guidance of theory, research falls prey to justifiable and well-deserved criticism aimed at its meaninglessness and unconnectedness. [87] The need for theoretical underpinnings is urgent.

Rather than taking, for instance, the shotgun empiricism approach to research, film audience investigators must begin by using existing theory as a means to develop film audience theory. An example will help to underscore and clarify this point. One might reasonably pose the question: What accounts for the vast, immediate, popularity of some films, such as Raiders of the Lost Ark, as compared to the less immediate popularity of a film such as Breaking Away? Another way of asking this same question would be: Why do some films "catch on" with the public so quickly, others more slowly, and others not at all? The scholar seeking an answer to this question might fruitfully draw research hypotheses and design considerations from the literature of at least two theories: diffusion of innovations and Expectancy X Value. The point is not simply to seek confirmation of any theory but rather to "check the fit" and then go about designing follow-up studies to "improve the fit" using, as appropriate, tenets of the same theory or hypotheses drawn from other existing or developing theories.

Finally, the argument and example offered above was not presented to suggest that film researchers become the beggars of social science: i.e., taking theoretical handouts from other disciplines. Instead, what is being proposed is that film audience research apply the available literature and evidence as a lens through which to focus on the properties of the film audience. This approach allows film scholars to determine what is truly unique to the field and what is shared with other disciplines. From this point the development of a theory of film audience can begin.

References

1. This is not to suggest that all--or any--such works are necessarily definitive nor that such research is no longer needed.
2. Leo Handel, "This Thing Called Audience Research," Hollywood Reporter, 1946 Anniversary Edition, unpaginated.
3. Paul F. Lazarsfeld, "Audience Research in the Movie Field," Annals of the American Academy of Political and Social Science 254 (November 1947): 162.
4. Leo A. Handel, "Hollywood Market Research," The Quarterly of Film, Radio and Television 7 (Spring 1953): 310.

5. Thomas Simonet, "Industry," Film Comment 14 (January-February 1978): 72.
6. Thomas H. Guback, "Are We Looking at the Right Things in Film?," paper presented at the Society for Cinema Studies Convention, Philadelphia, PA, March 1978. For a related discussion of this perspective see Graham Murdock and Peter Golding, "Capitalism, Communication and Class Relations," in James Curran, Michael Gurevitch, and Janet Woollacott (eds.), Mass Communication and Society (Beverly Hills: Sage, 1977), pp. 12-43.
7. One might wish to compare the simple frequency of movie audience studies with, for example, those of a much more recent medium, television. If, for instance, one wishes to assess the body of literature pertaining to television and motion pictures vis-a-vis their audiences, and could use only one book, the point regarding the depth and breadth of knowledge concerning film audience research is made abundantly clear. For TV audience research perhaps the most current and comprehensive book is George Comstock, et al., Television and Human Behavior (N.Y.: Columbia University Press, 1978) in which one would find 510 pages of text surveying more than 2500 research reports. In contrast, the most current film audience research book is Leo A. Handel's Hollywood Looks at Its Audience (Urbana: University of Illinois Press, 1950), containing 227 pages of text and fewer than 100 references. Some would maintain that this comparison between the contemporary TV research and the historical research on film audiences is spurious and argue that the appropriate comparison to Comstock would be the 1933 series of Payne Fund studies (which were conducted, it would be asserted, at a time when movie-going stood in the same relationship to society as TV does presently). While I am inclined to agree with this argument, three items prevent complete endorsement. First, it is important to note (as it will be later in the text) that the Payne Fund studies were initiated by William Short, a man with an ax to grind (see Garth Jowett, Film: The Democratic Art [Boston: Little, Brown and Co., 1976], p. 231, footnote 48). Second, the Payne Fund studies resulted in 12 volumes --certainly not an overwhelming number of researches. Third, methodological weaknesses abound in these works, especially the content analyses.
8. See Gordon Hendricks, "The History of the Kinetoscope," in Tino Balio (ed.), The American Film Industry (Madison: University of Wisconsin Press, 1976), pp. 38-39.
9. Richard Gertner (ed.), Motion Picture Almanac 1981 (N.Y.: Quigley Publishing Co., 1981), p. 30A.
10. Bureau of the Census, U.S. Department of Commerce, 1970 Census of Population, vol. 1 (Washington, D.C.: U.S. Government Printing Office, 1973), p. 42.
11. Christopher H. Sterling and Timothy R. Haight, The Mass Media (N.Y.: Praeger, 1978), p. 352.
12. L.L. Thurstone ("A Scale for Measuring Attitude Toward the Movies," Journal of Educational Research 22 [September

1930]: 89-94) reported his 40-item scale for measuring attitudes toward movies. The focus of his study was the development of an attitude assessment measure rather than its results; as a matter of fact, in this work the procedures employed for developing and utilizing this scale are presented but not the results of its implementation.

13. J. Harold Williams ("Attitudes of College Students Toward Motion Pictures," School and Society 38 [August 12, 1933]: 222-224) used Thurstone's scale and concluded that his sample, "on the whole, is more favorably than unfavorably disposed toward moving pictures; and that a large proportion of them exhibit extremely favorable attitudes" (p. 223).

14. Bureau of the Census, op. cit., p. 42.

15. Reported in Melvin L. DeFleur and Sandra Ball-Rokeach, Theories of Mass Communication, 4th ed. (N.Y.: Longman, 1982), p. 63.

16. For a discussion of this point, as well as presentation of the most current data, see Bruce A. Austin, "Attitudes Toward Motion Pictures Among College Students," ERIC ED 214 210.

17. I.C. Jarvie, Movies and Society (N.Y.: Basic Books, 1970), p. 113.

18. All box office figures reported represent domestic (U.S. and Canada) film rentals, not admissions. See "All-Time Film Rental Champs," Variety, May 13, 1981, pp. 49 ff.

19. One (limited in scope, methodology, and sample) study has been conducted on Star Wars' audience: James W. Arnold and Lennox Samuels, "Star Wars and its Audience," paper presented at the Popular Culture Association Conference, Cincinnati, Ohio, April 1978.

20. Quoted in Handel, Hollywood Looks at Its Audience, p. 93. Jowett (Film, op. cit., p. x) notes: "The continued reluctance of the motion picture industry to give its support to any form of research in the past now means that reliable industry statistics, and other relevant information, are generally not available. Thus the film historian is forced to fall back upon unsubstantiated material, or imprecise approximations."

21. Lee C. Garrison, "The Needs of Motion Picture Audiences," California Management Review 15 (Winter 1972): 148-149.

22. Mae D. Huettig, "The Motion Picture Industry Today," in Balio, op. cit., p. 229

23. Freeman Lincoln, "The Comeback of the Movies," in Balio, op. cit., p. 372, emphasis added.

24. It should be noted that Hollywood's seeming lack of interest in research is not limited to only audiences. Tino Balio has written that technical innovations (e.g., sound, color, and various widescreen processes) "were developed and perfected by either minor companies or individuals working outside of the mainstream of the industry." See "Retrenchment, Reappraisal, and Reorganization: 1948--," in Balio, op. cit., p. 321.

25. Terry Ramsaye, A Million and One Nights: A History of the Motion Picture Through 1925 (N.Y.: Simon and Schuster, 1926), p. 450

26. Benjamin B. Hampton, History of the American Film Industry from its Beginnings to 1931 (N. Y.: Dover Publications, 1970), p. 46.
27. See Bob Thomas, King Cohn: The Life and Times of Harry Cohn (N. Y.: G. P. Putnam's Sons, 1967), pp. 141-142.
28. Director Frank Capra recalled that Sennett ascertained the viability of his gag writers' schticks by his own reaction to them: "When he laughed, the audience was going to laugh. It was a real litmus test." See "Dialogue on Film: Frank Capra," American Film 4 (October 1978): 40.
29. Simonet, "Industry," op. cit., p. 72.
30. Hampton, for instance, reports that Adolph Zukor of Paramount was most prescient: he had "an amazing flair for sensing audience reactions long before the movie audiences themselves knew what they wanted." See Hampton, History of the American Film Industry, p. 154.
31. Ibid., pp. 338-339.
32. Lewis Jacobs, The Rise of the American Film: A Critical History (N. Y.: Teachers College Press, 1939), p. 296.
33. Ibid., pp. 295-296.
34. Hampton, History of the American Film Industry, pp. 311-312.
35. Ramsaye noted in his preface that: "The innumerable and complex racial, political, and geographical relations and reactions in which the screen has been importantly involved are yet to be explored. Largely the psychology of the motion picture is still awaiting an investigator." See Ramsaye, A Million and One Nights, p. vii.
36. C. A. Palmer, "Commercial Practices in Audience Analysis," Journal of the University Film Association 6 (Spring 1954): 9.
37. Lazarsfeld, "Audience Research," op. cit., p. 162. See also Jarvie, Movies and Society, pp. 5-6 and David Riesman and Evelyn Riesman, "Movies and Audiences," American Quarterly 4 (1952): 195-202.
38. Handel, Hollywood Looks at Its Audience, pp. 3-4. Robert W. Chambers ("Need for Statistical Research," Annals of the American Academy of Political and Social Science 254 [November 1947]: 169) offers a related explanation "To explain this factual deficiency ... the rapid growth of the industry has prevented it from taking a statistical inventory."
39. Jarvie, op. cit., p. 108.
40. For example anti-trust and monopoly rulings.
41. Handel, "Hollywood Market Research," p. 304. Richard Dyer MacCann ("Film Scholarship: Dead or Alive?" Journal of the University Film Association 28 [Winter 1976]: 5) notes: "the urge to construct scientific explanations for art naturally turns attention away from questions of quality." He goes on to ask: "Why don't the euphoric young semiologists who want to codify 'every square inch of the screen image' settle down and do a little honest audience research on what those codes really mean to various living viewers?"
42. Paul F. Lazarsfeld, "Foreword" in Handel, Hollywood Looks at Its Audience, p. xii.
43. Handel, "Hollywood Market Research," p. 304.

44. Ibid., pp. 308-309.
45. Ibid., p. 305.
46. Lazarsfeld, "Foreword," op. cit., p. xii. This argument has managed to linger on to the present. Most recently, Garth Jowett and James M. Linton have written (Movies as Mass Communication [Beverly Hills: Sage Publications, 1980], p. 27): "... each movie, while mass produced, is essentially a unique commodity" (emphasis in original).
47. As will be detailed later, this has an important implication for the independent scholar as well.
48. David Lees and Stan Berkowitz, The Movie Business (N.Y.: Vintage Books, 1981), p. 117.
49. Ibid., p. 144.
50. Denis McQuail (ed.), Sociology of Mass Communications (Baltimore: Penguin Books, 1972), p. 117. Fearing's article originally appeared in Annals of the American Academy of Political and Social Science 254 (November 1947): 70-79.
51. Sterling and Haight, op. cit., pp. 352-356.
52. Jowett, Film, op. cit.
53. Ibid. (pp. 386-387) discusses Marvin E. Olsen's study ("Motion Picture Attendance and Social Isolation," Sociological Quarterly 1 [April 1960]: 107-116) in which Olsen reported support for the hypothesis that one motive for movie attendance is that people use movies as a social substitute. What Jowett does not report is that five years after Olsen's study was published Olsen found and reported that a methodological error invalidated the major finding of the original study (see Marvin E. Olsen, "Correction of 'Motion Picture Attendance and Social Isolation,'" Sociological Quarterly 6 [Spring 1965]: 19).
54. Handel, Hollywood Looks at Its Audience. See also the 12 volumes reporting the Payne Fund studies which were published in 1933.
55. Jarvie, Movies and Society, p. 11. Jowett and Linton (Movies as Mass Communication, p. 28) have written: "... data from, and even the very existence and nature of, the industry's research on their product is treated as secretively as the data on various facets of the industry." Lees and Berkowitz (The Movie Business, p. ix) assert that "the film business, in which illusion is so important, likes to conceal its day-to-day realities." Sterling and Haight (op. cit., p. 354) state: "While many studies have been done on the motion picture audience, very little of such information has been released to the public. Hollywood appears to distrust statistics--and to show an interest in them only when times are bad."
56. Lazarsfeld, "Audience Research," op. cit., p. 162.
57. For a discussion of recent trends in research conducted by the film industry see Thomas Simonet, "Market Research: Beyond the Fanny of the Cohn," Film Comment 16 (January-February 1980): 66-69.
58. Lazarsfeld, "Foreword," op. cit., p. xii. MacCann ("Film Scholarship," op. cit., p. 5) has written: "the methods of science--at least if one thinks in terms of the familiar com-

bination of hypothesis and experiment--must usually be devoted to situations of great similarity. When a work or event can be replicated, something is proved. But of course a work of art, by definition, is unique."

59. See Lazarsfeld, "Foreword," op. cit., p. xii and Jeremy Tunstall, The Media are American (N.Y.: Columbia University Press, 1977), pp. 204-206.
60. Handel, "Hollywood Market Research," op. cit., p. 308.
61. Handel, Hollywood Looks at Its Audience, p. 5.
62. Johnson was pressing for research on American movie-goers and nonmovie-goers.
63. Handel, "Hollywood Market Research," op. cit., p. 308.
64. Jarvie, Movies and Society, p. 6. Jarvie also states (p. 11) that research is frustrated by the intermittent flow of films (both output by the producers and their exhibition) and the film's lack of pervasiveness as compared to other media.
65. See, for instance, Olivia Howard Dunbar, "The Lure of the Films," Harper's Weekly, January 18, 1913, pp. 20-22; Walter Prichard Eaton, "The Menace of the Movies," American Magazine, September 1913, pp. 55-60; Joseph R. Fulk, "The Effect on Education and Morals of the Moving-Picture Shows," Proceedings of the National Education Association Annual Meeting, 1912, pp. 456-461; William A. McKeever, "The Moving Picture: A Primary School for Criminals," Good Housekeeping, August 19, 1910, pp. 184-186; Harmon B. Stephens, "The Relationship of the Motion Picture to Changing Moral Standards," Annals of the American Academy of Political and Social Science (November 1929): 151-157.
66. Robert Sklar, Movie-Made America (N.Y.: Vintage Books, 1975), p. 134.
67. See Fredric Stuart, "The Effects of Television on the Motion Picture and Radio Industries," Ph.D. dissertation, Columbia University, 1960 (reprinted by Arno Press, 1976) and "Study Blames TV for Theatre Drop," Broadcasting, February 3, 1958, p. 58.
68. See Bruce A. Austin, "Film Attendance: Why College Students Chose to See Their Most Recent Film," Journal of Popular Film and Television 9 (Spring 1981): 43-49; Bruce A. Austin, "M.P.A.A. Film Rating Influence on Stated Likelihood of High School Student Film Attendance: A Test of Reactance Theory," unpublished Ph.D. dissertation, Temple University, 1981; Los Angeles Times, A Look at Southern California Movie-Going (Los Angeles: Los Angeles Times, 1972); Robert Silvey and Judy Kenyon, "Why You Go to the Pictures," Films and Filming 11 (June 1965): 4-5, 36.
69. See for example Los Angeles Times, op. cit. which found that nearly three-quarters (73 percent) of its respondents (teenagers and adults) reported they had decided to see a particular picture before deciding to go to the movies, rather than the other way around (i.e., deciding to go to the movies before deciding which film to see); William Fadiman (Hollywood Now [London: Thames and Hudson], 1973), among others, has noted that the concept of movie-going has shifted substantially from a habitual behavior to one bearing more special significance.

70. Dallas W. Smythe, John R. Gregory, Alvin Ostrin, Oliver R. Colvin, and William Moroney, "Portrait of a First-Run Audience," The Quarterly of Film, Radio and Television 9 (Summer 1955): 390-409.
71. A limited number of studies has been conducted on these topics. See for instance: Dallas W. Smythe, Parker B. Lusk, and Charles A. Lewis, "Portrait of an Art-Theater Audience," The Quarterly of Film, Radio and Television 8 (Fall 1953): 28-50; Bruce A. Austin, "Portrait of a Cult Film Audience: The Rocky Horror Picture Show," Journal of Communication 31 (Spring 1981): 43-54; Daniel J. Klenow and Jeffrey L. Crane, "Selected Characteristics of the X-Rated Movie Audience: Toward a National Profile of the Recidivist," Sociological Symposium 20 (Fall 1977): 73-83.
72. See the Commission on Obscenity and Pornography, Report of the Commission on Obscenity and Pornography (New York: Bantam Books, 1970), as well as the Technical Reports of this Commission published by the U.S. Government Printing Office.
73. See Steuart H. Britt, "What is the Nature of the Drive-In Theater Audience?," Media/scope 4 (June 1960): 100-102.
74. See for instance: Vernon E. Augustin, "Moving Picture Preferences," Journal of Delinquency 7 (1927): 206-209; Alice Miller Mitchell, "Movies Children Like," Survey 63 (November 15, 1929): 213-215; Harold E. Jones and Herbert S. Conrad, "Rural Preferences in Motion Pictures," Journal of Social Psychology 1 (1930): 419-423; W.D. Wall and E.M. Smith, "The Film Choices of Adolescents," British Journal of Educational Psychology 19 (June 1949): 121-136; W.J. Scott, Reading, Film and Radio Tastes of High School Boys and Girls (New Zealand Council for Educational Research, Educational Research Series No. 28 [New Zealand: Whitcombe and Tombs, Ltd., 1947]), Chapter III, pp. 112-145.
75. Smythe, et al., "Portrait of a First-Run Audience," op. cit., p. 398.
76. Lazarsfeld, "Audience Research," op. cit. p. 166.
77. See Charles R. Tittle and Richard J. Hill, "Attitude Measurement and Prediction of Behavior: An Evaluation of the Conditions and Measurement Techniques," Sociometry 30 (1967): 199-213. It should be noted that the attitude-causes-behavior position is not endorsed by all researchers. Daryl J. Bem ("Self-Perception Theory," in Leonard Berkowitz [ed.], Advances in Experimental Social Psychology, vol. 6 [N.Y.: Academic Press, 1972]) has discussed the hypothesis that behaviors cause attitudes while Herbert C. Kelman ("Attitudes are Alive and Well and Gainfully Employed in the Sphere of Action," American Psychologist 29 [May 1974]: 310-324) has examined the reciprocal causation hypothesis (i.e., attitudes cause behaviors and behaviors cause attitudes).
78. See for instance: J.E. Hulett, "Estimating the Net Effect of a Commercial Motion Picture Upon the Trend of Local Public Opinion," American Sociological Review 14 (April 1949): 263-275; Russell Middleton, "Ethnic Prejudice and Susceptibility to

Persuasion," American Sociological Review 25 (October 1960): 679-686; Douglas Cameron Moore, "A Study of the Influence of the Film, The Birth of a Nation, on Attitudes of Selected High School White Students Toward Negroes," unpublished Ph. D. dissertation, University of Illinois at Urbana-Champaign, 1971; Ruth Peterson and L. L. Thurstone, Motion Pictures and the Social Attitudes of Children (New York: Macmillan Co., 1933); Louis E. Raths and Frank N. Trager, "Public Opinion and 'Crossfire,'" Journal of Educational Sociology 21 (February 1948): 345-368; Irwin C. Rosen, "The Effect of the Motion Picture 'Gentleman's Agreement' on Attitudes Toward Jews," Journal of Psychology 26 (October 1948): 525-536.

79. J. Harold Williams, "Attitudes of College Students Toward Motion Pictures," op. cit.; A. S. Patel, "Attitudes of Adolescent Pupils Toward Cinema Films," Journal of Education and Psychology 9 (1952): 225-230; K. C. Panda and R. N. Kanungo, "A Study of Indian Students' Attitudes Towards the Motion Pictures," Journal of Social Psychology 57 (June 1962): 23-31; Bruce A. Austin, "Attitudes Toward Motion Pictures Among College Students," op. cit. For a review and summary of the attitude toward movies research see Bruce A. Austin, "People's Attitude Toward Motion Pictures," in Sari Thomas (ed.), Film/Culture: Explorations of Cinema in its Social Context (Metuchen, N. J.: Scarecrow Press, 1982).

80. For a discussion of three other possible explanations for this parallel shift see Austin, "Attitudes Toward Motion Pictures Among College Students," op. cit.

81. For further discussion on this point see Bruce A. Austin, "A Factor Analytic Study of Attitudes Toward Motion Pictures," Journal of Social Psychology 117 (August 1982): 211-217.

82. See for instance: Elihu Katz and Paul F. Lazarsfeld, Personal Influence (Glencoe, Ill.: The Free Press, 1955); Austin, "Film Attendance: Why College Students Chose to See Their Most Recent Film," op. cit.; Austin, "M. P. A. A. Film Rating Influence on Stated Likelihood of High School Student Film Attendance," op. cit.; Thomas O'Guinn, "The Audience's Choice: Movie Selection and Word of Mouth," paper presented at the International Communication Association Conference, Minneapolis, Minnesota, 1981.

83. Michael H. Burzynski and Dewey J. Bayer, "The Effect of Positive and Negative Prior Information on Motion Picture Appreciation," Journal of Social Psychology 101 (April 1977): 215-218.

84. Research presented in the early 1970s showed that 18-to-29-year-olds made up fully 48 percent of the movie-going public (National Association of Theatre Owners, Encyclopedia of Exhibition 1976 [N. Y.: National Association of Theatre Owners, 1976]). More recently, Richard Gertner (ed.), (Motion Picture Almanac 1980 [N. Y.: Quigley Publishing Co., 1980], p. 32A) reports that 58 percent of the total 1977 admissions were accounted for by 16-to-29-year-olds. Moreover, individuals with at least some college education comprised both the largest and most frequent movie-going aggregate.

85. William R. Elliott and William J. Schenk-Hamlin, "Film, Politics and the Press: The Influence of 'All the President's Men,'" Journalism Quarterly 56 (Autumn 1979), p. 553.
86. Eugene J. Webb, Donald T. Campbell, Richard D. Schwartz, and Lee Sechrest, Unobtrusive Measures (Chicago: Rand McNally, 1966), pp. 1-2.
87. For additional discussion of this point see Calvin Pryluck, "'There's Nothing So Practical as a Good Theory,'" AFI Education Newsletter 5 (September-October 1981): 1-2. However, for a discussion of the usefulness and necessity of basic descriptive and interpretational research, especially as applied to theory-building, see Leonard C. Hawes, "Alternative Theoretical Bases: Toward a Presuppositional Critique," Communication Quarterly 25 (Winter 1977): 63-68.

THE BIBLIOGRAPHY

1. Aaronson, Charles S. "Majority of Students Approve Film Ratings."
   Boxoffice, June 18, 1973, p. 7.
   Report of a survey analyzing attitudes toward the MPAA film rating system.

2. Abbott, Mary Allen. "A Study of the Motion Picture Preferences of the Horace Mann High Schools." Teachers College Record 28 (April 1927): 819-835.
   Frequency of attendance and film-type preferences among male and female pupils were measured by means of a questionnaire.

3. _____. "Motion-Picture Preferences of Adults and Children." School Review 41 (April 1933): 278-283.
   Differences in evaluation of 50 movies.

4. _____. "A Sampling of High-School Likes and Dislikes in Motion Pictures." Secondary Education 6 (March 1937): 74-76.

5. Abrams, Mark. "The British Cinema Audience." Hollywood Quarterly 3 (1947-1948): 155-158.
   Results of a survey involving 10,200 persons at least 16 years of age; data on frequency of attendance and reasons for attendance are presented and crosstabulated by age, sex, and socio-economic class of the respondents.

6. _____. "The British Cinema Audience, 1949." Quarterly of Film, Radio and Television 4 (Spring 1950): 251-255.
   Descriptive data on demographic characteristics of British moviegoers 16 years old and above; data are grouped by frequency of attendance.

7. Adams, William B. "A Definition of Motion-Picture Research." Quarterly of Film, Radio and Television 7 (1952-1953): 408-421.
   Brief definition and a discussion of motion picture research from four perspectives: theatrical, non-theatrical, social science, and historical.

8. Adler, Kenneth P. "Art Films and Eggheads." Studies in Public Communication 2 (Summer 1959): 7-15.
   Results of a study in which 128 interviews were conducted; data reported include art-film patron characteristics and their preferences for other cultural events; included is a copy of the interview schedule.

9. "The Adolescent and the Cinema." Education, November 19, 1948, pp. 889-892.

Review of research by various authors; reports on attendance habits, emotional effects of movies, enforcement of age attendance restrictions, and the content of film.

10. Adoni, Hanna. "The Functions of Mass Media in the Political Socialization of Adolescents." Communication Research 6 (January 1979): 84-106.
High school students' use of eight media, including cinema, as reported on questionnaires; relationships to political socialization and ties with primary socializing agents.

11. Afasizev, M. "Motiv Navstevnosti Filmu a Socialne Psychologicke Funkce Filmoveho Umen." Panorama 2 (Winter 1977): 59-63.
Motives for movie attendance among a sample from Estonia.

12. Aguirre, Ernesto Ego. "El Factor Cinematografico en la Delincuencia Infantil" (The Part of Motion Pictures in Juvenile Delinquency). Boletín de Criminologia 2 (1929): 245-254.
An advocacy piece suggesting that violence in movies may cause nervous disorders in children which may result in delinquency.

13. Aibauer, Rosa. "Zur Sittlichen Beurteilung von Filmen. Test mit 10-14 Jahrigen Mädchen über Teufelskerle" (The Moral Evaluation of Films. A Test with 10-14 Year Old Girls Concerning the Film Teufelskerle (Boys' Town)). Film, Jugend, Schule 45 (July 1954): 1-6.
A group of 32 10 to 14 year old girls evaluated the film on a number of dimensions including identification with the actors, best and least-liked sequences.

14. Albert, Robert S. "The Role of Mass Media and the Effect of Aggressive Film Content upon Children's Aggressive Responses and Identification Choices." Genetic Psychology Monographs 55 (May 1957): 221-285.
A mixed-sex group of 220 8 to 10 year olds responded to Rosenzweig's Picture-Frustration Scale before and after exposure to movies.

15. _____ and Peter Whitelam. "The Role of the Critic in Mass Communications: II. The Critic Speaks." Journal of Social Psychology 60 (1963): 153-156.
"Results of a survey of the opinions of literature, film, drama, radio-television, ballet, and fine-arts critics on some issues involved in their role definition and enactment."

16. Albertini, Laura and Maria Pia Caruso. "Percezione e Interpretazione di Immagini Cinematografiche nei Ragazzi" (Perception and Interpretation of Cinematographic Pictures by Children). Bianco e Nero 10 (May 1949): 9-27.
A study in which 576 8 to 14 year olds viewed Nanook of the North; the children's reactions to the film and their errors in observation and interpretation of the film were assessed through questioning.

17. _____. "Percezione e Interpretazione di Immagini Cinematografiche nei Ragazzi" (Perception and Interpretation of Cinematographic Pictures by Children). In Franziska Baumgarten, La Psychotechnique dans le Monde Moderne (Psychotechnology in the Modern

World) (Paris: Presses Universitaires de France, 1952, pp. 561-562).
Summary of the Bianco e Nero report.

18. Alfonsin, Julio A. "Un Factor Criminogeno Secundario (Cinematografo y Criminalidad)" (A Secondary Factor in the Genesis of Crime. Motion Pictures and Criminality). Revista de Psiquiatria y Criminologia 15 (June 1938): 275-288.
Review of literature which suggests that movies may be a secondary cause of delinquency among "idle" boys from unstable homes.

19. Allen, Marjorie. "Children and the Cinema." The Fortnightly, July 1946, pp. 1-6.
Discussion of British youth cinema clubs, their membership, and problems regarding age-appropriate films.

20. Altavilla, Enrico. "Film di Gangster e Riflessi Psicologici sui Fanciulli" (Gangster Films and Their Psychological Effects on Children). Bianco e Nero 10 (October 1949): 45-49.
A speculative discussion suggesting that such films cause moral disturbances moreso than encouraging imitation of criminal acts which are portrayed.

21. "American Films and Foreign Audiences." Film Comment 3 (Summer 1965): 50.
Results of several surveys conducted by the U.S. Information Agency; Japan and countries in Western Europe are included; frequency of attendance and attitudes toward U.S. films are reported.

22. Anast, Philip. "Personality Determinants of Mass Media Preferences." Journalism Quarterly 43 (Winter 1966): 729-732.
Using Jung's model of personality types high rankings for movies and TV correlated with sensation-orientation; on the thinking-feeling continuum, feeling correlated with frequent movie and TV consumption for males; males tended to be introverted while females tended to be extroverted in correlations with movie preference.

23. _____. "Differential Movie Appeals as Correlates of Attendance." Journalism Quarterly 44 (Spring 1967): 86-90.
Film content featuring eroticism, violence, mishaps, and luxury positively correlated with frequency of movie attendance; film content involving achievement and adventure was negatively correlated.

24. Ancona, Leonardo and Maria A. Croce. "Dinamica Psichica e Dinamismo Cinematografico" (Psychic Dynamics and Cinematographic Dynamism). Archivio di Psicologia, Neurologia e Psichiatria 28 (1967): 85-105.
Film-goers with depressed tendencies preferred slower moving plots; hypersensitive individuals preferred rapid-moving and action-packed content.

25. _____ and Maria A. Croce. "Dinamica Psichica e Dinamismo Cinematografico" (Psychic Dynamics and Cinematographic Dynamism). Contributi dell' Instituto di Psicologia 30 (1970): 1-19.
A reprint of the 1967 report.

26. _____ and M. Fontanesi. "Analisi delle Relazioni Dinamiche tra

Effetto Carartico ed Effetto Frustrante di uno Stimolo Cinematografico Emotivo" (Analysis of the Dynamic Relations Between Cathartic and Frustrating Effects from an Emotional Motion Picture). Contributi dell' Instituto di Psicologia 28 (1967): 30-48.
Pictures were shown to undergraduates and their reactions measured for increase of hostility and intensity of reaction.

27. Anderson, Irving H. and Walter F. Dearborn. "A Sound Motion-Picture Technique for Teaching Beginning Reading." School and Society 52 (October 19, 1940): 367-369.
Methods and procedures are presented while the application and its results are not.

28. Anzieu, Didier. "Filmologie et Sociologie" (Filmology and Sociology). Revue Internationale de Filmologie 1 (September-October 1947): 175-177.
Discussion of areas for research.

29. Arabadziev, M. "Posestaemost v Kinata." Kinoizkustvo 28 (May 1973): 33-38.
Discussion of sociological research on movie-going in Bulgaria.

30. Arcila-Rivera, Eduardo. "Opinions of the Columbian Movie Artist." Revista Latinoamericana de Psicologia 5 (1973): 355-362.
Survey of 990 persons in Bogota; film-type preferences were analyzed by sex of the respondents.

31. Arnold, James W. "Saturday Night Fever and its Audience." Paper presented at the Popular Culture Association conference, April 1979, Pittsburgh, PA.
Survey of 62 undergraduates; data on reactions to the film, repeat attendance, and comparisons to Star Wars are reported.

32. _____ and Lennox Samuels. "Star Wars and its Audience." Paper presented at the Popular Culture Association conference, April 1978, Cincinnati, OH.
Survey of 28 undergraduates; data on reactions to the film, repeat attendance, source of information about the film, scenes liked and disliked are reported.

33. Artus, Helmut M. "Critical Research on Movie Effects: On the Conduct of Inquiry in Communications." Publizistik 15 (1971): 48-63.
Reviews the literature and provides avenues for further research.

34. "Attitude of High School Students Toward Motion Pictures." Survey 51 (December 15, 1933): 338.
Reports on C. A. Perry's study of 37,505 high school pupils.

35. "Audience Reactions in Schools." Documentary NewsLetter, June-July 1947.
Preliminary report of 40 children's responses to a Road Safety film using four methods of measurement.

36. "The Audienscope Survey Technique." Film Bulletin 45 (November 1976): 4.
Briefly describes procedures for measuring film audience predispositions for motion pictures prior to release.

37. Augedal, Egil. "Patterns in Mass Media Use and Others Activities." Acta Sociologica 15 (1972): 145-156.

Not solely focused on film audiences but important to the film audience literature insofar as the data support a hypothesis for a "partial cumulative pattern" for different media activities.

38. Augustin, Vernon E. "Moving Picture Preferences." <u>Journal of Delinquency</u> 11 (1927): 206-209.
Film-type preferences, seasonal fluctuations in attendance, and day of week in which greatest attendance occurred; data were gathered over a seven-week period in Los Angeles.

39. Austin, Bruce A. "Psychological Reactance as a Causative Factor in Film Attendance." Paper presented at the Popular Culture Association conference, April 1979, Pittsburgh, PA.
Analysis of audience attraction to movies by rating symbol using film rental data.

40. _____. "Motion Picture Attendance and Factors Influencing Movie Selection Among High School Students." Paper presented at the University Film Association conference, August 1979, Ithaca, NY. Available in ERIC ED 177 630.
A pilot study measuring the importance of ten variables on film choice.

41. _____. "Rating the Movies." <u>Journal of Popular Film and Television</u> 7 (1980, no. 4): 384-399.
Somewhat abbreviated version of the author's Popular Culture Association conference paper.

42. _____. "The Influence of the MPAA's Film Rating System on Motion Picture Attendance: A Pilot Study." Paper presented at the Eastern Communication Association conference, April 1980, Ocean City, MD.
A longer version, with tables, of the author's <u>Journal of Psychology</u> article.

43. _____. "The Influence of the MPAA's Film-Rating System on Motion Picture Attendance: A Pilot Study." <u>Journal of Psychology</u> 106 (September 1980): 91-99.
Using reactance theory as its theoretical base, the experiment showed no significant difference for likelihood of attendance between films with the four rating symbols; self-report data indicated that participants in this study most frequently attended films rated either PG or R.

44. _____. "Film Attendance: Why College Students Chose to See Their Most Recent Film." <u>Journal of Popular Film and Television</u> 9 (Spring 1981): 43-49.
Results of a survey which investigated the importance of 28 variables (e.g., reviews, stars, advertising); more than one-quarter of the movie attendance variance was explained by the variables for the sample as a whole and 55 percent of the variance for frequent movie-goers.

45. _____. "Film Attendance: Why College Students Chose to See Their Most Recent Film." Paper presented at the Eastern Communication Association conference, April 1981, Pittsburgh, PA.
A longer version, with tables of the author's <u>Journal of Popular Film and Television</u> article.

46. _____. "Portrait of a Cult Film Audience: The Rocky Horror Picture Show." Journal of Communication 31 (Spring 1981): 43-54.
The findings of a field study which involved 562 patrons' responses to a 34-item questionnaire are presented; questionnaire items included demographic characteristics, reasons for attendance and repeat attendance, other media use habits; the sample was subdivided into three audience aggregates based on their previous attendance at Rocky Horror.

47. _____. "Portrait of a Cult Film Audience: The Rocky Horror Picture Show." Paper presented at the 4th International Conference on Culture and Communication, April 1981, Philadelphia, PA.
An extended treatment of the Journal of Communication article.

48. _____. "M.P.A.A. Film Rating Influence on Stated Likelihood of High School Student Film Attendance: A Test of Reactance Theory." Unpublished Ph.D. dissertation, Temple University, 1981.
Experimental, self-report, and unobtrusive measures were taken to ascertain the ratings influence on attendance; additional data on rating influence in the context of 28 other variables were gathered as well as attitudes toward age restrictions.

49. _____. "Movie Ratings and Their Effect on Movie Attendance." Paper presented at the Speech Communication Association conference, November 1981, Anaheim, CA. Available in ERIC ED 208 450.
An experiment involving undergraduates; self-report and unobtrusive measures were also taken.

50. _____. "The Salience of Selected Variables on Choice for Movie Attendance Among High School Students." Paper presented at the Western Speech Communication Association conference, February 1982, Denver, CO. Available in ERIC ED 210 754.
Results of a survey investigating the importance of 28 variables to film choice; nearly one-third of the movie attendance variance was explained for the sample as a whole and 89 percent of the variance for frequent movie-goers.

51. _____. "MPAA Film Ratings and Film Attendance: A Test of Reactance Theory." Paper presented at the Eastern Communication Association conference, May 1982, Hartford, CT. Available in ERIC 214 218.
A summary of the author's Ph.D. dissertation.

52. _____. "A Factor Analytic Study of Attitudes Toward Motion Pictures." Journal of Social Psychology 117 (August 1982): 211-217.
A pilot study involving undergraduates; factor analysis of Thurstone's movie attitude scale revealed nine dimensions.

53. _____. "Attitudes Toward Motion Pictures Among College Students." ERIC 214 210.
Replication of Bannerman and Lewis' study and reanalysis of their data; a somewhat unfavorable attitude toward movies was found.

54. _____. "G-PG-R-X: The Purpose, Promise, and Performance of the Movie Rating System." Journal of Arts Management and Law 12 (Summer 1982): 51-74. Also available in ERIC ED 212 029.
Review of the behavioral research as applied to policymaking and evaluation.

55. _____ and Thomas Simonet. "Ratings and Revenues." Paper presented at the University Film Association conference, August 1979, Ithaca, NY.
Examination of the relationship between film ratings and distributor rentals during 1977 and 1978.

56. _____, Mark J. Nicolich, and Thomas Simonet. "Movie Ratings and Revenues: Eleven Years of Success Ratios." Paper presented at the University Film Association conference, August 1980, Austin, TX. Available in ERIC ED 191 102.
Examination of the relationship between film ratings and box office success from 1969 to 1979.

57. _____. "M.P.A.A. Ratings and the Box Office: Some Tantalizing Statistics." Film Quarterly 35 (Winter 1981-82): 28-30.
A summary of the authors' University Film Association conference paper.

58. Avery, Robert K. "Adolescents' Use of the Mass Media." American Behavioral Scientist 23 (September-October 1979): 53-70.
A review of literature focusing mostly on television but also discussing print media and cinema.

59. Ayers, James Lawrence. "An Exploration on the Utility of Motion Picture Media in Personality Assessment." Unpublished Ph.D. dissertation, University of Minnesota, 1976.
Personality dimensions were danger seeking vs. avoidance and social closeness vs. distance; a self report scale and peer rating measure were developed for the study which involved 75 male undergraduates.

60. Bacal, Jeffrey Peter. "The Effect of Image Iconicity on Film Interpretation." Unpublished Ph.D. dissertation, University of Iowa, 1973.
Results of an experiment provide some support for iconicity theory.

61. Baggett, Patricia. "The Formation and Recall of Structurally Equivalent Stories in Movie and Text." Unpublished Ph.D. dissertation, University of Colorado, 1977.
Comparison between a text story and a dialogueless movie (from which the text story was constructed) showed similar recall for both media but quicker deterioration of recall for text.

62. _____. "Structurally Equivalent Stories in Movie and Text and the Effect of the Medium on Recall." Journal of Verbal Learning and Verbal Behavior 18 (June 1979): 333-346.
A summary of the author's dissertation.

63. Bailyn, Lotte. "Mass Media and Children: A Study of Exposure Habits and Cognitive Effects." Unpublished Ph.D. dissertation, Radcliffe College, 1956.
Examined television, comic books, comic strips, movies, radio, and books using a questionnaire; reports exposure habits, content preferences, and cognitive, affective and behavioral effects.

64. _____. "Mass Media and Children: A Study of Exposure Habits and

Cognitive Effects." Psychological Monographs 73 (no. 1, whole no. 471, 1959): 1-48.
A summary of the author's dissertation.

65. Banisson, M. "Consistenza Intraindividuale e Differenze di Gruppo nella Testimonianza sul Contenuto di Breve Sequenze Filmiche a Significato Ambiguo" (Self-Consistency and Group Differences in Reports on the Content of Short Ambiguous Film Sequences). Revista di Psicologia 59 (1965): 701-721.
Accuracy of recall of information presented in a film did not differ by sex of the respondents but did differ by occupation.

66. Bannerman, Julia and Jerry M. Lewis. "College Students' Attitudes Toward Movies." Journal of Popular Film 6 (1977, no. 2): 126-139.
Using a modified version of L. L. Thurstone's Movie Attitude Scale, this study found a slightly to moderately favorable attitude toward films on the part of the majority of respondents.

67. Baran, Stanley J. "How TV and Film Portrayals Affect Sexual Satisfaction in College Students." Journalism Quarterly 53 (Autumn 1976): 468-473.
Respondents who perceived media portrayals as real reported greater satisfaction in first and subsequent coital experiences.

68. Bassett, H. Thomas, James E. Cowden, and Michael F. Cohen. "The Audio-Visual Viewing Habits of Selected Subgroups of Delinquents." Journal of Genetic Psychology 112 (1968): 37-41.
A 35-item questionnaire was completed by 101 boys aged 12 to 19 who were confined to the Wisconsin School for Boys; examined the relationship between TV and movie viewing habits and selected personality factors, racial background, and the kinds of disciplinary practices they had experienced.

69. Bauer, Raymond A. and Alice H. Bauer. "America, Mass Society, and Mass Media." Journal of Social Issues 16 (1960): 3-66.
Review of literature concluding that there is little evidence to suggest that TV and other media have had a negative impact on public tastes or values.

70. Baxter, William S. "The Mass Communication Behavior of Young People in Grades 5, 7, 9, and 11 in the Des Moines Public Schools in 1958 as Compared with the Mass Communication Behavior of an Equivalent Group in Des Moines Before the Advent of Television." Unpublished Ph.D. dissertation, State University of Iowa, 1960.
Responses to a questionnaire by students (n = 2306) and parents (n = 1636); reports attention given to various media, including movies, as well as content and media preferences.

71. _____. "The Mass Media and Young People." Journal of Broadcasting 4 (Winter 1960-61): 49-58.
A summary of the author's dissertation.

72. Bayer, Raymond. "Le Cinéma et les Etudes Humaines" (The Cinema and the Social Sciences). Revue Internationale de Filmologie 1 (July-August 1947): 31-35.
Discussion of sociology as applied to the cinema.

73. Beattie, Earle. "In Canada's Centennial Year, U.S. Mass Media Influence Probed." Journalism Quarterly 44 (Winter 1967): 667-672.
    Focuses on television and print media with brief mention of films.

74. Beauchamp, Mary Ella. "Certain Influences of Movies on Adolescent Youth." Unpublished M.A. thesis, University of Michigan, 1936.

75. Behringer, Gertrude. "Welche Rolle spielt der Film tatsächlich im Leben unseres Jugend? 16,000 Wiener Jugendliche Geben Antwort" (What, in fact, is the Role of the Cinema in the Life of our Young People? 16,000 Viennese Young People Give Their Answers). Oesterreichischer Jugend-Informations-dienst 7 (June-July 1954): 4-6.
    Questionnaires inquired as to frequency of attendance, reasons for attendance, attendance unit, film-type preferences, and how films are selected for attendance.

76. Bell, George H. "Visual Physiology of the Cinema." British Medical Journal, November 27, 1943, pp. 669-671.
    Discussion of "the physiological problems of moving pictures."

77. Bell, Oliver. "Sociological Aspects of the Cinema." Nature 144 (September 16, 1939): 520.
    Argues the need for research.

78. _____. "Public Tastes and the Entertainment Film." Advancement of Science 1 (1940): 443.
    Brief note deploring the lack of effort to discover psychological effects of movies.

79. Belson, William A. "The Effects of Television on the Interests and Initiatives of Adult Viewers." Unpublished Ph.D. dissertation, University of London, 1957.
    Survey of television's effect on a range of public interest items including movie-going.

80. _____. "The Effect of Television on Cinema Going." Audio-Visual Communication Review 6 (1958): 131-139.
    Survey of 782 persons in London and use of the Stable Correlate method; concludes that television reduced cinema attendance by 33 percent.

81. Bennike, Sigurd. "Befolkningens Forbrug af Kommunikation" (Consumption of Communication in the Danish Population). Dansk Media Komite, Kobenhavn, 1976.
    Summary of studies which investigated the consumption of mass media by the average Dane during 24 hours; data are partitioned by sex, age, education, and urbanization.

82. Berger, Alan S., John H. Gagnon, and William Simon. "Urban Working-Class Adolescents and Sexually Explicit Media." Technical Reports of the U.S. Commission on Obscenity and Pornography, vol. 9, pp. 209-272. Washington, D.C.: U.S. Government Printing Office, 1970.
    Demographic characteristics of adolescents attending adult movies are presented; study also examines other sexually explicit media.

83. Berichte. "Die Wirkung des Films auf Jugendliche" (The Effect of the Cinema on Young People). Bildung und Erziehung 3 (1950).

84. Berkovits, Gy. "A Film es Kozonsege" (The Film and its Public). Filmkultura 3 (1976): 92-98.

85. Berkowitz, Meyer. "Moving Pictures Attended and Preferred by Children." Unpublished Ed. M. thesis, Temple University, 1940. Results of a questionnaire completed by 338 fifth and sixth graders; reports frequency of attendance, adult guidance in movie-going, preferences for movies as compared to other activities, reading interests as related to movies, movie stars preferred and disliked, and activities engaged in as a result of movies seen.

86. Berman, Harold H. "Audio-Visual Psychotherapeutics: Portable Moving Pictures with Sound as a Rehabilitation Measure." Psychiatric Quarterly 20 (1946, Supplement): 197-203.
Shut-in patients were shown sound films and it was found that the movies were helpful in habit training.

87. Bernstein, S. L. "The Berstein Children's Film Questionnaire." London: Granada Theaters, Ltd., 1947.

88. Besco, Galen. "Television and its Effects on Other Related Interests of High School Pupils." English Journal 41 (March 1952): 151-152. Report of a questionnaire given to 223 students; most pupils reported that TV had caused them to do less radio listening and to attend fewer movies.

89. Bettecken, W. "Gefährdung der Jugend durch den Film" (The Film, Danger for Youth). Jugendwohl 32 (1951): 330.

90. Beuick, Marshall D. "The Limited Social Effect of Radio Broadcasting." American Journal of Sociology 32 (1927): 615-622.
An advocacy piece asserting that broadcasting can "never compete injuriously with the theater, the concert, the church, or the motion picture."

91. Biabi, B. "L'Adolescent et le Cinéma" (The Adolescent and the Cinema). Cahiers Zairois de la Recherche et du Developpement 19 (1974): 137-165.

92. "Bid for Teens." Business Week, May 14, 1955, pp. 114, 116. Report concerning a Texas theater chain's strategy to bring teenagers back into the movie audience through admission price incentives.

93. Billstrom, Jakob. "Psykisk Hygien och Filmkontroll" (Mental Hygiene and Film Control). Svenska Lakartidningen 33 (1936): 950-955. Advocacy piece asserting that individuals "intoxicated" by motion pictures are typically unstable and unbalanced prior to their attendance at movies; the influence of movies on neurasthenics is generally negligible.

94. Birkenhead Vigilance Committee. "Survey of Children's Cinema." Great Britain, 1931.

95. Birtha, Rachel Roxanne. "Pluralistic Perspectives on the Black-Directed

Black-Oriented Feature Film: A Study of Content, Intent and Audience Response." Unpublished Ph. D. dissertation, University of Minnesota, 1977.
Blacks (followed by Native American Indians and whites) were most enthusiastic about a black-oriented film; selective perception and retention related to cultural factors in accounting for differential interpretations of the film.

96. Bisbee, Donald Ward. "The Relationship Between Motion Picture Attendance and Scholastic Achievement in the Seventh Grade." Unpublished M. S. thesis, Boston University, 1950.
Responses by 107 pupils to a questionnaire; slight indication that frequency of movie attendance was inversely related to scholastic achievement.

97. Bisky, L. "Ansatzpunkte" (Points of Departure). Film und Fernsehen 5 (April 1977): 49-51.
Advocates the necessity of audience research on young people in particular.

98. Blaustein, Leopold. "Przyczynki do Psychologji widza Kinowego" (Contributions to the Psychology of the Cinema Spectator). Kwartalnik Psychologiczny 4 (1933): 192-236.
Description of the various experiences of film viewers who watch productions using modern film techniques.

99. Bleich, Dina M. "Films and Attitudes." High Points 30 (October 1948): 18-31.
Description of a school film program over a three year period.

100. Bloch, V. "L'Etude Objective du Comportement des Spectateurs" (The Objective Study of Spectators' Behavior). Revue Internationale de Filmologie 3 (1952): 221-222.
Discussion of methods for conducting audience research and problems encountered with these methodologies.

101. Bloom, Samuel William. "A Social Psychological Study of Motion Picture Audience Behavior: A Case Study of the Negro Image in Mass Communication." Unpublished Ph. D. dissertation, University of Wisconsin, 1956.
Reactions to the film Lost Boundaries were measured by a questionnaire given to the respondents immediately after their viewing of the film; results showed that social climate and subjective orientation (attitude) were significant determinants of response.

102. Blumer, Herbert. "Moulding of Mass Behavior Through the Motion Picture." Publications of the American Sociological Society 29 (1936): 115-127.
A critical analysis and definition of mass behavior; concludes that the general influence of the movies is "a reaffirmation of basic human values but an undermining of the mores."

103. Blyth, E. "Egyptian Picture-Goers." Near East and India 30 (September 2, 1926): 254.

104. Bode, Barbara. "An Experiment in Propaganda." Journal of Adult Education 13 (1941): 365-370.
Results of an experiment in which 75 adult females participated;

findings showed that the films used in the study affected the subjects' attitude toward increased liberalism, even among subjects who saw a film that was conservative in theme.

105. Bolle de Bal, Francoise. "Possibilités Actuelles de la Recherche en Belgique sur le Cinéma et son Publique" (Present Possibilities for Belgian Research Concerning the Cinema and its Public). Etudes et Recherches-Techniques de Diffusion Collectif 5 (1961).

106. Boring, Edwin G. "Capacity to Report Upon Moving Pictures as Conditioned by Sex and Age." Journal of the American Institute of Criminal Law and Criminology 6 (March 1916): 820-834.
An experiment involving 44 subjects including undergraduates, children, and adults with the purpose of testing the reliability of children as witnesses in judicial proceedings.

107. Bose, A. B. "Mass Communication: The Cinema in India." Indian Journal of Social Research 4 (1963): 80-88.
Survey of 400 adult males; film was most popular among the younger and more educated; reasons for non-attendance and factors influencing film choice are presented as well as attitudinal data and perceptions of film's effect on society.

108. Bosio, Luigi. "Inchiesta sul Cinematografo" (Inquiry on the Cinema). Stampa, Cinema, Radio per Ragazzi, n.d., pp. 84-92.
Results of a study conducted in Turin during April and May 1952; reports attendance habits and preferences of 1,500 children.

109. Bossard, Robert. "Film und Familie" (The Film and the Family). Pro Juventute 28 (January 1957): 3-11.
A discussion of the effects of cinema on children, advantages and dangers of movie-going for children, and means to maximize benefits of the cinema.

110. Bouman, Jan C. "The Social Psychology of Film." Unpublished M.A. thesis, Stockholm University, 1952.

111. Bouman, J.C., G. Heuyer, and S. Lebovici. "Le Processus de l'Identification et l'Importance de la Suggestibilité dans la Situation Cinematographique" (The Process of Identification and the Importance of Suggestibility in the Cinema). Revue Internationale de Filmologie 4 (April-June 1953): 111-141.
A pilot study using an experiment as the methodology; identification was influenced by suggestive explanations given to the subject prior to the screening of the film.

112. Bower, Henrietta. "Children and the Cinema: The Report of the Inter-Departmental Committee." The Tablet, May 13, 1950, pp. 377-378.
Data on frequency of attendance, children's increased movie attendance over the past 20 years, and their preference for movies as compared to other activities are presented.

113. ———. "Children and the Cinema: The Effect in Juvenile Delinquency." The Tablet, May 20, 1950, pp. 398-399.
The author presents her dissenting comments to the Inter-Departmental Committee's conclusion that movies were not judged as being responsible for "the delinquency or moral laxity of children under 16."

114. Boyanowsky, Ehor O. "Film Preferences Under Conditions of Threat: Whetting the Appetite for Violence, Information, or Excitement?" Communication Research 4 (April 1972): 133-144.
Subjects in the experimental groups showed greater preference for film clips containing male against male aggression and sexually explicit content.

115. _____, Darren Newston, and Elaine Walster. "The Effect of Murder on Movie Preference." Proceedings of the Annual Convention of the American Psychological Association 7 (1972): 235-236.
Two days after an actual murder, attendance at In Cold Blood increased 89 percent from the previous week.

116. _____, Darren Newston, and Elaine Walster. "Film Preferences Following a Murder." Communication Research 1 (January 1974): 32-43.
Attendance at a movie with murder as its theme rose 89 percent two days after an actual murder; attendance at a control film did not increase significantly.

117. Bozzuto, James C. "Cinematic Neurosis Following 'The Exorcist': Report of Four Cases." Journal of Nervous and Mental Disease 161 (July 1975): 43-48.
Traumatic neurosis was found to be precipitated by viewing The Exorcist in previously unidentified psychiatric patients; symptoms of the four individuals studied and treatment administered are discussed.

118. Brady, Beverly Duvall. "Nursery School Teacher and Parent Group Perceptions in Film Choices." Unpublished M. A. thesis, San Francisco State College, 1969.
Results of a survey examining choices of films and their relationship to socio-economic status.

119. Breitenstein, Ole and Eva Wikander. Kila pa Bio. Kop en Livsstil (Go to the Cinema. Buy a Life Style). Stockholm: LiberForlag, 1979.
A study of young people's movie-going habits in Sweden.

120. Bremond, Claude. "Le Public Français et le Film Japonais" (The French Public and the Japanese Film). Communications 6 (1965): 103-142.
Report of 140 non-directed interviews; discusses attitudes toward Japanese films such as slowness, violence, cruelty, liberalism vs. authoritarianism, tradition vs. modernity, authenticity vs. phoniness; no statistical data reported.

121. Brill, A. A. "The Value of the Motion Picture in Education with Special Reference to the Exceptional Child." Proceedings 6th Conference Child Research Clinic of the Woods School, 1940, pp. 15-22.
The value of movies in providing vicarious experience and catharsis is discussed.

122. Brislin, Thomas John. "Selective Retention by Attitude in Film." Unpublished M. A. thesis, Ohio State University, 1970.
Pretest-posttest involving 56 undergraduates; support was found for the type of images recalled by a viewer and the viewer's attitude (liberal to conservative) and between the viewer's perception of the film's theme and the viewer's attitude.

123. "Brit. Film Council Data Shows Deadly Effect on Cinema B. O. of Unrestricted Movies on TV." Variety, May 11, 1977, p. 358.
   Report from the Film Industry Council documenting the relationship between televiewing and decreased movie attendance.

124. "Brit. Filmgoing in 11% Decline." Variety, March 17, 1976, p. 44.
   Brief report from the Department of Trade.

125. "Brit. Study Undermines Belief that TV Movies Cut Exhib B. O." Variety, November 23, 1977, pp. 31, 32.
   Results of two studies, one by the BBC, both suggesting that films shown on TV do not diminish theater attendance; other data reported include demographics on film-goers, reasons for and against attending movies.

126. "The British Cinema at the Gallup." Documentary NewsLetter, June-July 1947, p. 99.
   Discussion of Audience Research Inc.'s methodology, as compared to the Bernstein Film Questionnaire.

127. "British Film; Statistics of Production, Exhibition, Total Cinemas, Attendance and Rates." Economist 147 (January 1937): 50-56.

128. "British Youth Dislikes Love in the Movies." Literary Digest 3 (1931): 22-25.
   Inquiry concerning film content likes and dislikes of British movie-going children.

129. Britt, Steuart H. "What Is the Nature of the Drive-In Theater Audience?" Media/scope 4 (June 1960): 100-102, 104.
   Results of a mail survey; demographic characteristics are presented.

130. Brock, R. Barrington. "The Effect of Motion Pictures on Body Temperature." Science 102 (September 7, 1945): 259.
   Response to N. Kleitman's report in which it is suggested that confounding variables not accounted for in the original study may have produced the results.

131. Brodbeck, Arthur J. "An Exception to the Law of 'Adult Discount': The Need to Take Film Content into Account." Psychological Reports 8 (1961): 59-61.
   Subjects rated a film (Wages of Fear) for degree of reality and strength of involvement; ratings increased with the age of the subjects; author concludes that problems of viewers and characters in a film must be measured and matched in order to accurately understand the influence of films on personality.

132. Brooker, Floyd E. "Le Cinéma dans l'Enseignement Americain" (The Cinema in American Education). Revue Internationale du Cinema 1 (1949).
   The author suggests that films offer a language and method to access historical events and to demonstrate various developmental processes through time lapse photography.

133. Brown, Walter A. "Anger Arousal by a Motion Picture: A Methodological Note." American Journal of Psychiatry 134 (August 1977): 930-931.

The study demonstrated that anger significantly increased (over a control group) among subjects who saw a film in which unjust accusation of a crime and mistreatment by police was displayed.

134. Browning, H. E. and A. A. Sorrell. "Cinemas and Cinema-Going in Great Britain." Journal of the Royal Statistical Society 117 (Series A, General, 1954, Part II): 133-165.
Reports data on admissions by age, sex, and geographic region from 1934 through 1952; non-audience data also reported.

135. Bruce, D. J. "Rememoration du Material Filmique: Etude Experimentale" (The Recall of Filmic Material: An Experimental Study). Revue Internationale de Filmologie 4 (January-March 1953): 21-38.
Investigation of the memory process as applied to film; 36 subjects viewed a short film; results suggest that abstraction plays an important role in memory and that viewers "fill-in" gaps of information left out of films to construct plausible sequences.

136. Brudny, Wolfgang. "Der Sensationskulturfilm-Eine Warnung?" (The Dangers of Sensational Films). Film-Bild-Ton 5 (December 1955): 18-19, 39-40.
Nonsystematic observation of trauma in children leads the author to suggest that films in which people are attacked by animals are more harmful to children than films in which humans alone engage in violence.

137. Bruel, Oluf. "Film als Psycho-Traumatisches Kindheitserlebnis Psychotherapie" (The Cinema as a Psycho-Traumatic Childhood Experience; Psychotherapy). Acta Psychiatrica et Neurologica 8 (1933): 447-454.
Case history of a 15 year old girl who developed a fear complex, the origin of which, it is claimed, could be traced back to a scene in The Hunchback of Notre Dame.

138. _____. "Film som Psyko-Traumatisk Barndomsoplevelse" (The Film as Psychotraumatic Experience in Childhood). Ugeskrift for Laeger 97 (1935): 305-309.
Case study of a phobia and its relation to movies.

139. _____. "A Moving Picture as a Psychopathogenic Factor: A Paper on Primary Psychotraumatic Neurosis." Character and Personality 7 (1938): 68-76.
A case study upon which it is concluded that "the apparently harmless visits of children to the cinema are potent with the danger of serious psychogenetic after-effects."

140. _____. "Psychic Trauma Through the Cinema - An Illustrative Case." International Journal of Sexology 7 (November 1953): 61-63.
Case study of a 15 year old girl.

141. Brule, M. "Pour une Sociologie du Cinéma" (For a Sociology of the Cinema). Sociologie et Societes 8 (April 1976): 3-143.

142. Bruner, Jerome S. and George Fowler. "The Strategy of Terror: Audience Response to Blitzkrieg im Westen." Journal of Abnormal and Social Psychology 36 (October 1941): 561-574.
260 responses to a questionnaire distributed following the screening

of this German propaganda film; four types of responses to the film were identified based on the data gathered: belligerent, defeatist, alarmist, and indifferent; most respondents fell into the first and last categories.

143. Bryan, James H. and Tanis Schwartz. "Effects of Film Material Upon Children's Behavior." Psychological Bulletin 75 (1971): 50-59.
Reviews literature on symbolic modeling (from TV and film) including influences on aggression, phobic and altruistic responses, social judgments, and communications.

144. Bryant, Jennings and Dolf Zillmann. "The Effects on Aggression of Viewing Sadomasochism and Bestiality After Longitudinal Exposure to Standard Erotica." Paper presented at the International Communication Association conference, May 1981, Minneapolis, MN. Physiological and self-report measures of undergraduates to erotic films.

145. Buccalo, William Raymond. "Mise-en-Scène Versus Montage: Viewer Response to Two Styles of Visual Communication." Unpublished Ph.D. dissertation, Ohio State University, 1977.
Style "did make a difference to the individual viewer"; stylistic variables of camera distance, shot length, and camera viewpoint affected viewers' perception of distance, realism and involvement; focused interview instrument was used in data collection.

146. Burge, Stewart A. "A Survey of the Relative Influence of Color and Black and White on Audience Recall and Emotional Response to a Documentary Motion Picture." Unpublished M.A. thesis, West Virginia University, 1970.
As compared to black and white, color did not significantly affect subjects' factual recall ability or emotional response to the documentary film; a slight but nonsignificant preference for the color version was found.

147. Burton, Wilbur. "Chinese Reactions to the Cinema." Asia 34 (October 1934): 594-600.
Mostly focused on such industry-related topics as distribution, number of theaters and seating capacity, financial returns, and censorship; brief mention of favorite actors and actresses and the kinds of films that are popular.

148. Burzynski, Michael H. and Dewey J. Bayer. "Effect of Positive and Negative Prior Information on Motion Picture Appreciation." Journal of Social Psychology 101 (April 1977): 215-218.
This field study found that audience appreciation for a movie can be altered by prior information cues; subjects rated a motion picture after viewing and after having overheard positive, negative, or no comments from confederates posing as patrons.

149. Butler, Robert A. "The Responsiveness of Rhesus Monkeys to Motion Pictures." Journal of Genetic Psychology 98 (1961): 239-245.
Two experiments involving eight monkeys and their visual attention to film subjects.

150. Butler, William Fay. "Some Effects of Motion Pictures Upon Junior High School Children." Unpublished M.A. thesis, Michigan State University, 1936.

151. Caillois, Roland. "Le Cinéma, le Meurtre et la Tragédie" (The Cinema, Murder and Tragedy). Revue Internationale de Filmologie 3 (1949): 87-91.

152. Callenbach, Ernest. "U.S. Film Journalism--A Survey." Hollywood Quarterly 5 (Summer 1951): 350-362.
Survey of film critics inquiring as to their background training, familiarity with film literature, and perception of their role.

153. Cameron, I. "Hard Night Out." Spectator, July 10, 1964, pp. 45-46.

154. "Campus Denizens Go-for-Pix, Disks, Radio, But Not TV." Variety, February 13, 1980, pp. 4, 210.
Reports some results of a survey of campus-dwelling college students; males reported higher frequency of movie attendance than females.

155. Canestrari, Renzo. "Rassegna Cinematografica" (Cinema Chronicle). Rivista di Psicologia Normale e Patologica 5 (1949): 130-131.
Discussion of The Quiet One and A Tree Grows in Brooklyn; non-empirical.

156. Canestrari, Renzo. "La Psicologia Differenziale ed il Cinema" (Differential Psychology and the Cinema). Infanzia Anormale 24 (1953): 284-293.
Review of literature concerning the various influences of movies on the personality of the mentally retarded adolescent.

157. Cantor, Joanne. "Developmental Studies of Children's Fright from Mass Media." Paper presented at the International Communication Association conference, May 1982, Boston, MA.
Uses Piaget's theory of cognitive development; reviews results of studies already completed and also in progress.

158. Cantor, Joanne and Sandra Reilly. "Adolescents' Fright Reactions to Television and Films." Journal of Communication 32 (Winter 1982): 87-99.
Results of a questionnaire completed by sixth and tenth graders and interviews with their mothers inquiring as to the frequency of fear response to TV shows and movies.

159. Capecchi, V. "Analisi delle Preferenze di Films, Scrittori e Riviste con il Metodo delle Componenti Principali" (Analysis of Preferences of Films, Writers and Reviews by the Method of Principal Components). Ikon 14 (1964): 25-80.

160. Caplan, Richard E. "Investigation of the Dimensions of an Instrument for Measuring Audience Reaction to Motion Pictures." Unpublished Ph.D. dissertation, Wayne State University, 1975.
Concluded that a valid and reliable instrument using bi-polar adjective scales could be constructed and that using this instrument five factors of audience response were identified: artistic merit, enjoyment, realism, activity, and purity.

161. Carancini, G. "Le Film pour Enfants en Italie" (The Film for Children in Italy). Revue Internationale du Cinema 4 (1949).

162. Carlson, Harry C. "Movies and the Teenager." Journal of the Screen Producers Guild, March 1963, pp. 23-26, 30.

Results of a survey completed by 3,012 high school pupils; reports pictures attended, pictures the respondents would like to see again, what was liked and disliked about movie content, and how they selected the films they saw.

163. Carpenter, C. R. "A Challenge for Research." Educational Screen 27 (March 1948): 119-121.
Discussion of previous research and future directions for research on the effectiveness of teaching films.

164. Carson, Frances. "Motion Pictures and Our Youth." Quarterly Journal of Speech 28 (April 1942): 186-189.
A review of some of the Payne Fund research, especially attitude and moral conduct studies.

165. Carter, Roy E., Jr. and Orlando Sepulveda. "Some Patterns of Mass Media Use in Santiago de Chile." Journalism Quarterly 41 (Spring 1964): 216-224.
Interviews with 452 Santiagans were conducted; media availability was determined; 60 percent said they went to the movies at least occasionally (2-3 times monthly); North American films were most popular.

166. Cartwright, Rosalind Dymond, Niles Bernick, and Gene Borowitz. "Effect of an Erotic Movie on the Sleep and Dreams of Young Men." Archives of General Psychiatry 20 (March 1969): 262-271.
Results of an experiment involving ten male graduate students; no effect on sleep experience but some significant effects on dreams and dream content.

167. Carver, Mary Vida. "The Critical Evaluation of Films by Repertory Grid: Value Patterns of Working and Middle Class Youths Compared with Those of Professional Critics." Unpublished Ph. D. dissertation, University of London, 1967.
Taste differences were explained by the interaction of perceptual skills and critical evaluation; critics used finer discrimination in making their evaluations than did the youths.

168. Casanet y Gea, Miguel. "Peligros e Inconvenientes de Cinematografo para los Niños" (Dangers and Disadvantages of Motion Pictures for Children). Medicina 8 (November 1927): 1-4 (Supplement).
A doctor reports numerous instances where children were physically and morally injured by attending movies; calls for careful regulation of movies by a formal regulatory board; suggests that movies for children be shown in the "open air" and that the medium be more widely used for educational purposes.

169. Caspers, Wesley. "An Experimental Evaluation of Certain Motion Picture Films in Selected Educational Psychology Classes in Kansas College." Unpublished Ph. D. dissertation, University of Minnesota, 1956.
Professional teacher attitudes improved significantly for the 216 experimental subjects; achievement in coursework was also measured.

170. Centro Italiano Femminile. Inchiesta sulla Cinematografia per Ragazzi (An Inquiry into Cinema for Children). Rome, 1952.
Results of questionnaires sent to adults (artists, scientists, educators) inquiring as to their perception and experience regarding the

cinema's influence on children and their opinions regarding legislative remedies to the dysfunctional aspects of children and the cinema.

171. Chambers, Robert W. "Need for Statistical Research." Annals of the American Academy of Political and Social Science 254 (November 1947): 169-172.
Explanations for the deficiency of audience research and suggestions for research.

172. Champlin, Charles. "Who's Watching?" Journal of the Producers Guild of America 15 (March 1973): 17-18.
Discussion of the audience composition based on data gathered in MPAA-commissioned polls.

173. Chandler, Edward H. "The Moving Picture Show." Religious Education, October 1911, pp. 344-349.
An advocacy piece suggesting movies usually are "informing and wholesomely entertaining" but warns of the dysfunctional social consequences that often coincide with--yet are not caused by--the exhibition of movies.

174. Chang, Won H. "A Typology Study of Movie Critics." Journalism Quarterly 52 (Winter 1975): 721-725.
Through factor analysis 38 New York City critics' (reviews) were sorted into three types: elites, auteurists, and entertainers.

175. Chapman, Cynthia, Kent Dolan, Kevin Sullivan, and Neil Thompson. "The Relationship of Marketing Strategies Used by Walt Disney Productions to the Evolving Family Audience." Unpublished M.B.A. thesis, University of California, Los Angeles, 1977.

176. Charters, W.W. "A Technique for Studying a Social Problem." Journal of Educational Sociology 6 (December 1932): 196-203.
A brief review of the National Committee for Study of Social Values in Motion Pictures' program.

177. Chassagne, G. "Le Cinéma et les Jeunes" (Cinema and Young People). Lyon: Office Familial de Documentation Artistique, 1945, 12 pp.

178. Chazal, J. "Cinema et Délinquence Juvenile" (The Cinema and Juvenile Delinquency). Educateurs, March-April 1950, pp. 55-63.

179. "Check on Picture Attendance." Educational Screen 8 (February 1929): 42.
Brief report discussing the Portland Motion Picture Censor Board's findings regarding school pupils' frequency of attendance and the types of pictures being exhibited.

180. "Chi Va al Cinema e Perche?" (Who Goes to the Cinema and Why?). Bianco e Nero 19 (February 1958).
Entire issue is devoted to a survey of youngsters reactions to the movies.

181. Childs, Gayle B. "The Frequency of Attendance at Motion Pictures by School Children in Nebraska, the Nature of Shows Attended." Unpublished M.A. thesis, University of Nebraska, 1936.

182. Cimatti, Leone. "I Ragazzi al Cinema" (Children at the Cinema). Aggiornamenti Sociali 3 (March 1952): 99-106.
Analysis of LeMoal and Faugere's data with regard to legislation concerning the cinema.

183. "Cinema Ad Assn. Analysis of Film Fans in Britain." Variety, October 14, 1981, p. 27.
Results of a survey on British film-going habits; attendance patterns by age-group presented as well as film-type preferences.

184. Cirlin, Bernard D. and Jack N. Peterman. "Pre-Testing a Motion Picture: A Case History." Journal of Social Issues 3 (Summer 1947): 39-41.
Discussion of the procedures employed and results gathered from the use of the Cirlin Reactograph.

185. Citron, Leonard. "Research into the U. K. Cinema Advertising Audience." Commentary, Summer 1962, pp. 13-16.
Survey of audiences commissioned by the Screen Advertising Association; discussion of some of the techniques used.

186. Clark, C. C. "The Talking Movie and Students' Interest." Science Education 17 (December 1933): 312-320.
Results of an experiment involving nearly 600 college students; films were shown to be an effective medium for arousing interests and in strengthening interests previously acquired.

187. Clarkson, H. K. "A Survey of the Leisure Time of West Lothian School Children." Educational Institute of Scotland, 1938.
Survey of some 6,600 9 to 15 year olds which reports only 6 percent of its sample never attending the cinema.

188. Clinard, Marshall B. "Secondary Community Influences and Juvenile Delinquency." Annals of the American Academy of Political and Social Science 261 (January 1949): 42-54.
With regard to movies, radio, and comic books the author concludes that "on the whole their direct influence on the juvenile is either almost nil or serves only to aggravate already existent attitudes and personality traits."

189. Cloninger, Sally Joan. "The Sexually Dimorphic Image: An Empirical Analysis of the Influences of Gender Differences on Photographic Content." Unpublished Ph.D. dissertation, Ohio State University, 1974.
Use of a 13-set content analysis, a 7-item Ego Strength Differential Scale, and a Q-study to determine differences caused by sex in images made by males and females.

190. Clostermann, Gerhard. "Musische Erziehung nach Filmeindrucken. Schulerzeichnungen bezeugen Bildungsmöglichkeiten der Filmerziehung" (Artistic Education through Films. Children's Drawings Reveal the Cultural Possibilities of the Educational Cinema). Film, Jugend, Schule 6 (September 1953): 1-6.
Analysis of drawings made by 200 children after viewing a Lassie film.

191. _____. " 'Nanuk der Eskimo': Oberstufenkinder Urteilen uber Einen Film" ("Nanook of the North": Evaluation of a Film by

Secondary School Pupils). Film, Jugend, Schule 11 (January 1955): 1-4.
Questionnaire results from 128 children's auditory and visual perception, affective responses, and impressions produced by the film.

192. _____ and K. Preuss. "Abhandlungen zur Jugend-Filmpsychologie" (Discussions on Juvenile Film Psychology). Stadtisches Forschungsinstitut fur Psychologie des Arbeit und Bildung in Gelsenkirchen. Munster, Westfallen, Aschendorffsche Verlagsbuchhandlung, 1952 (Publication 3).
A two-part study of the relationship between films and juvenile delinquency and children's reactions to a film (Nanook of the North); case histories and questionnaires were used.

193. Cluydts, Raymond and Piet Visser. "Mood and Sleep: II. Effects of Aversive Pre-Sleep Stimulation." Waking and Sleeping 4 (July-September 1980): 199-203.
EEGs were recorded and the Profile of Mood States was administered to ten undergraduates who were shown a movie of a surgical operation; an experimental study.

194. Coffin, Thomas E. "Television's Effect on Leisure-Time Activities." Journal of Applied Psychology 32 (October 1948): 550-558.
Paired TV and non-TV families were questioned as to frequency of movie attendance, amount of reading, and their participation in other leisure activities during a sample week; at all socio-economic levels it was found that the rate of movie attendance was lower among TV families than non-TV families.

195. Cole, Kenneth. "Certain Aspects of the Motion Picture Problem: A Study in the Inventory of Interests." Unpublished Ph.D. dissertation, Harvard University, 1931.

196. Collier, John. "Cheap Amusements." Charities and Commons, April 11, 1908, pp. 73-76.
Discussion of the People's Institute, its origin and function.

197. The Community and the Motion Picture. Report of the National Conference on Motion Pictures held at the Hotel Montclair, New York City, September 24-27, 1929. New York: Motion Picture Producers and Distributors of America, Inc., 1929 (reprinted by Jerome S. Ozer, 1971).
Mostly devoted to industry issues such as exhibition and distribution; brief notes on audience aspects.

198. "Computer-Testing to Pick Up Lost Elements of Film Audience." Variety, March 26, 1975, pp. 7, 33.
Discussion of Sun Classic Pictures' audience research procedures.

199. Conrad, Herbert S. and Harold Ellis Jones. "Psychological Studies of Motion Pictures III. Fidelity of Report as a Measure of Adult Intelligence." University of California Publications in Psychology 3 (November 22, 1929): 245-276.
Tests of intelligence and comprehension and memory (of a movie) were given to some 1,500 10 to 60 year olds.

200. _____. "Psychological Studies of Motion Pictures IV. The Technique of Mental-Test Surveys Among Adults." University of Cali-

fornia Publications in Psychology 3 (November 22, 1929): 277-284.
Summary of suggestions presented in III and consideration of avenues for future research.

201. Consiglio, Alberto. "The Social Function of the Cinema." International Review of Educational Cinematography 5 (November 1933): 706-711.
Historical treatment of the context of the arts in society; discussion of censorship of cinema.

202. Cooper, Charles David. "The Reactions of Sixth Grade Children to Commercial Motion Pictures as a Medium for Character Education." Unpublished Ph. D. dissertation, Cornell University, 1938.
Results of a questionnaire to which 807 children responded; data presented include frequency of attendance, film-type preferences, reactions to events depicted, and children's learning from films.

203. _____. "The Reactions of Sixth Grade Children to Commercial Motion Pictures as a Medium for Character Education." Journal of Experimental Education 7 (June 1939): 268-273.
A summary of the author's dissertation.

204. Cooper, Eunice and Helen Dinerman. "Analysis of the Film 'Don't Be a Sucker': A Study in Communication." Public Opinion Quarterly 15 (Summer 1951): 243-264.
Use of the Program-Analyzer, intensive interviews with 24 persons, group interviews, and a written questionnaire to determine the effectiveness of the film in changing attitudes; findings suggest that the film was successful in changing attitudes among specific groups but that several of the filmic messages had a boomerang effect.

205. Corradini, Umberto. "Il Ragazzo al Cinema" (The Child at the Cinema). Lumen, February 1955, pp. 46-50.
A call for research to determine the influence of movies on children.

206. Corradini, Umberto. "Contributo allo Studio dei Rapporti tra Cinema e Gioventù" (Contributions to the Study of the Relations Between the Cinema and Young People). Lumen, May 1955, pp. 83-88; August 1955, pp. 114-116; January 1956, pp. 149-160.
A review of literature.

207. Council of Motion Picture Organizations. "Exploding a Myth: Motion Pictures Are Not Responsible for Juvenile Delinquency." New York, September 1950.
A 23 page booklet containing selected quotations from 54 authorities including psychiatrists, psychologists, educators, and criminal sociologists; this is a printed version of a nearly identical publication by the MPAA, "Juvenile Delinquency and Dramatized Entertainment."

208. Cowger, Richard Wright. "Retention of Film Content Under Conditions of Self-Selection and Individual Viewing." Unpublished Ed. D. dissertation, University of Oregon, 1968.
When film choices were offered, interested students retained more from their viewing than those less interested.

209. Cox, Carole Alice Shirreffs. "Film Preference Patterns of Fourth and Fifth Grade Children." Unpublished Ph. D. dissertation, University of Minnesota, 1975.

Interest patterns of 218 pupils were measured; data analyzed by sex, race, and SES.

210. Cox, William Michael. "American Limited Audience Cinema as an Art Form." Unpublished Ph. D. dissertation, Ohio University, 1970. General characteristics of the audience and artists are described.

211. Crawford, Paul John. "Movie Habits and Attitudes of the Underprivileged Boys of the All Nations Area in Los Angeles." Unpublished M. A. thesis, University of Southern California, 1934.

212. Creedon, Carol. "The Film as a Research Tool." Hollywood Quarterly 2 (1946-1947): 107-111.
Summary of Wiese and Cole's study on Tomorrow the World as it affects children's attitudes; suggests the usefulness of using other commercial films in social science research.

213. Cressey, Paul Frederick. "The Influence of Moving Pictures on Students in India." American Journal of Sociology 41 (November 1935): 341-350.
A questionnaire study of 233 undergraduates finds their chief interests in movies to be recreational and educational; foreign films gave them a better understanding of Europe and the U. S. but had only a superficial influence on their general attitudes and behavior.

214. Cressey, Paul G. "The Social Role of Motion Pictures in an Interstitial Area." Journal of Educational Sociology 6 (December 1932): 238-243.
Description of the procedures followed for the study; results are not presented (see the author's 1934 report for results).

215. _____. "The Social Role of the Motion Picture in an Interstitial Area." Publications American Sociological Society 28 (1934): 90-94.
A largely qualitative study of the effects of 19 films on 12 to 18 year old boys.

216. _____. "The Motion Picture as Informal Education." Journal of Educational Sociology 7 (1934): 504-515.
A review of literature, including some of the Payne Fund studies, in which the author suggests that the effect of movies on children are not uniform and that the full significance of films must be examined in reference to the specific social background of the individual.

217. _____. "The Motion Picture Experience as Modified by Social Background and Personality." American Sociological Review 3 (August 1938): 516-525.
A review of literature with suggestions for research; it is suggested that movies are reflexive in their influence on general conduct.

218. _____. "The Social Role of the Motion Picture in an Interstitial Area." Unpublished Ph. D. dissertation, New York University, 1943.

219. "Crime and the Cinema in the United States." International Review of Educational Cinematography 1 (September 1929): 303-314.
A review of literature concluding that "there is not ... nor can there be, any correlation between crime and film frequentation."

220. Croce, Maria A. "Condizionamenti Sociali Attraverso Tecniche Cinematografiche: Determinazione dell' Effetto 'Power' di Proiezioni Filmiche" (Social Conditioning Through Movies: The Determination of the "Power" Effect in Movie Projection). Contributi dell' Instituto di Psicologia 28 (1967): 173-177.
Various audience needs can be manipulated through motion pictures; this study demonstrated the need for power through presentation of particular films.

221. Cummins, E. Hulen. "An Investigation of the Influence of Motion-Pictures on a Group of High School Boys and Girls." Unpublished M.A. thesis, Oklahoma Agricultural and Mechanical College, 1937.

222. Cunningham, Robert P. "A Sociological Approach to Esthetics: An Analysis of Attitudes Toward the Motion Picture." Unpublished Ph.D. dissertation, State University of Iowa, 1954.
Use of a questionnaire to correlate social-psychological factors, the presence or absence of critical-esthetic abilities, with attitudes toward movies.

223. Currie, Barton W. "The Nickel Madness." Harper's Weekly, August 24, 1907, pp. 1246-1247.
Description of the nickelodeon theater and its audience.

224. Custen, George Frederick. "Film Talk: Viewers Responses to a Film as a Socially Situated Event." Unpublished Ph.D. dissertation, University of Pennsylvania, 1980.
Forty-three respondents saw Citizens Band and, in 12 groups, discussed the film; discussions were content analyzed and interpreted using Worth and Gross' model of interpretive behavior.

225. Dacruz, Efren Borrajo. "Esquema General de los Efectos Sociologicos del Cine" (General Outline of the Sociological Effects of the Motion Picture). Revista Internacional de Sociologia 17 (April-June 1959): 225-230.
Nonempirical discussion.

226. Dadek, Walter. "Der Gegenwärtige Stand der Filmsoziologie" (The Present Condition of the Sociology of the Cinema). Kölner Zeitschrift für Soziologie und Sozial Psychologie 12 (1960): 516-533.
A review of literature that also suggests new directions for research.

227. "Dailies Fuel Exhib Fear of Fans Lost to Stay-at-Homes; Menace of Cheap Cassettes." Variety, November 18, 1981, pp. 5, 32.
Results of survey of 1,500 U.S. and Canadian adults show that increasing numbers are staying home to watch movies on television.

228. Dale, Edgar. "Books Which Children Like to See Pictured." Educational Research Bulletin 10 (November 1931): 423-429.
Large scale study of fourth graders' preferences for novels they would like to see made as movies.

229. _____. "Methods for Analyzing the Content of Motion Pictures." Journal of Educational Sociology 6 (December 1932): 244-250.
Description of the study and procedures followed; results are not presented.

Bibliography

230. _____. "Diagnosis in Leisure-Time Activities." Yearbook: National Society for the Study of Education 34 (1935): 477-486.
Presents research methods for diagnosing areas of leisure time interests with a special focus on motion pictures; suggests that only a small percentage of parents and teachers provide guidance to high school students regarding their selection of movies.

231. _____. "Child Welfare and the Cinema." English Journal 26 (1937): 698-705.
A speech to the Child Welfare Committee of the League of Nations in Geneva; reports on Stoddard, Thurstone, and others' findings from the Payne Fund studies.

232. _____. "Need for Study of the Newsreel." Public Opinion Quarterly 3 (July 1937): 122-125.
Suggests that the content of newsreels effects public opinion and offers a methodology for content analyzing newsreels.

233. _____. "Analyzing the Movie Market." Educational Research Bulletin 16 (November 10, 1937): 212-216.
Results of a study of 71 female high school students' evaluations of 100 movies.

234. _____. "Motion Picture Industry and Public Relations." Public Opinion Quarterly 5 (April 1939): 251-262.
A discussion concerning Hollywood's attempts to influence public opinion and the degree of success these efforts have had.

235. Davies, Richard Ed. "Affective Response to the Film, Parable, as a Function of Theological Belief." Unpublished Ph.D. dissertation, Indiana University, 1975.
Subjects were 141 adult members from 16 United Methodist Churches; results of the pretest-posttest questionnaire showed that the film did have an emotional impact.

236. Davis, Keith E. and George N. Braucht. "Reactions to Viewing Films of Erotically Realistic Heterosexual Behavior." Technical Reports of the U.S. Commission on Obscenity and Pornography, vol. 8, pp. 68-98. Washington, D.C.: U.S. Government Printing Office, 1970.
Adults responding to a questionnaire.

237. Davis, Michael M., Jr. The Exploitation of Pleasure: A Study of Commercial Recreations in New York City. New York: Department of Child Hygiene of the Russell Sage Foundation, 1911.
Discussion of numerous leisure-time pursuits; pp. 33-35 discuss movies including children's frequency of attendance.

238. Davis, Ronald Dale. "Retention Related to Arousal in Film and Television." Unpublished Ph.D. dissertation, Auburn University, 1979.
The use of arousal techniques did not significantly increase long-term retention of information among students.

239. Davtyan, Susanna Ambartsumovna. "O Vliyani i Predvaritel' noy Informatsii na Vybor Fil'ma" (The Effect of Preliminary Information on Choice of Movie). Sotsiologicheskie Issledovaniya 4 (January-March 1977): 105-106.
Results of a survey which attempted to determine the kind of pre-

liminary prior information held by viewers before attending three films; interpersonal information accounted for 60 to 63 percent of prior information and reviews were a major factor for 23 percent of the respondents.

240. Dawson, Anthony H. "Motion Picture Economics." Hollywood Quarterly 3 (1947-1948): 217-240.
Contains data on consumer expenditures in movie theaters as a proportion of various other personal consumption expenditures.

241. Debesse, Maurice. "L'Enfant au Cinéma" (The Child at the Cinema). Revue Internationale de Filmologie 7 (April-June 1956): 99-109.
Summary of a lecture; discussion of literature on the film theater as a leisure time milieu for children and using the theater as a context for analyzing the influence of films on children.

242. Debongnie, Jean. "Cinéma, Grande École du Soir des Peuples" (The Cinema, Great Evening School of the People). Nouvelle Revue Pedagogique 3 (1947): 159-161.
A presentation of statistics demonstrating the importance of cinema in European life as applied to social psychology.

243. Decaigny, T. "Influence du Cinéma sur l'Enfant et l'Adolescent" (Influence of the Cinema on Children and Adolescents). Cahiers Jeunesse, Education Populaire, Bibliothèques Publiques 1 (February 1957).
Review of research since 1929; points out an overlooked area of research: the effect of movies on the perception of social reality.

244. DeCurtins, L. "Film und Jugendkriminalitaet" (Motion Pictures and Juvenile Delinquency). Kriminalistik 21 (1967): 349-355.

245. DeFeo, George. "Le Monde Scolaire et le Film d'Enseignement" (The School World and the Educational Film). International Review of Educational Cinematography 4 (June-July-August 1932): 504-518, 608-617, 696-702.
20,000 Italian school children were asked about film use in the classroom; most felt that movies could aid the teacher and preferred movies to slides; most indicated that movies could not be substituted for the teacher.

246. _____. "Quand et Comment les Jeunes Fréquentent le Cinéma" (When and How Children go to the Cinema). International Review of Educational Cinematography 4 (October-November 1932): 865-874, 944-955.
Study of Italian children; attendance and age were positively related, males attended more often than females, as age increased so did attendance at films of a higher quality.

247. _____. "Public Attendance at the Cinema." International Review of Educational Cinematography 4 (October-November 1932): 769-776, 845-855.
Results of a questionnaire completed by more than 18,000 elementary, middle, and technical students; frequency of attendance, days and hours of attendance, and attendance unit are presented; data are analyzed by sex, age, parents' occupation, and type of home environment (urban or rural).

248. _____. "Students and the Didactic Film." International Review of Educational Cinematography 5 (1933): 429-442, 519-528, 607-613.
Results of a questionnaire completed by 15,000 pupils; data are analyzed by sex, age, parents' occupation, and home environment (urban or rural).

249. _____. "Young Peoples' Impressions of War Films." International Review of Educational Cinematography 5 (1933, nos. 1-5): 33-44, 121-130, 204-209, 273-281, 357-367.
A large-scale questionnaire; data are analyzed by sex, age, parents' occupation, and type of home environment (urban or rural).

250. Degand, C. "Les Medias Audiovisuels Face à Leur Publique" (Audio-visual Media Meet Their Public). Filmechange 12 (Autumn 1980): 79-85.
Discussion of the extant research literature on Western European television and film audiences.

251. DeMaday, Andre. "An Enquiry Respecting the Cinematograph Made in the Schools of Geneva, Lausanne and Neuchâtel." International Review of Educational Cinematography 1 (November and December 1929): 531-552, 638-667.
Results of a large scale questionnaire distributed in 1914 to 8 to 15 year old school pupils; data reported include attendance unit, enjoyment of cinema, film-type preferences, factors attracting attendance.

252. Dembo, Richard. "Gratifications Found in Media by British Teenage Boys." Journalism Quarterly 50 (Autumn 1973): 517-526.
Twenty-six categories of uses and gratifications (e.g., relaxation, excitement, conversation) of the film experience were found in this study which is not exclusively focused on film; no significant differences in the uses and gratifications by aggressive and non-aggressive subjects were found.

253. Denis, Michel. "Orientations and Preferences Towards Motion Pictures." International Review of Applied Psychology 23 (October 1974): 89-109.
Describes the orientations and preferences of a small sample of French adults toward films.

254. Denk, P. "Der Einfluss des Kinos auf die Kinder (Zusammenfassung)" (The Influence of Movies on Children: Summary). Compte Rendu, 8th Conference Internationale Psychotechnique, Prague, 1935, pp. 741-742.

255. Department of Social Welfare and Community Development in Accra and Kumasi. Children and the Cinema: A Report of an Inquiry into Cinema-going Among Juveniles Undertaken by the Department of Social Welfare and Community Development in Accra and Kumasi, 1954, 14 pages (stencilled).
Results of a study conducted in response to concerns regarding the influence of movies on juvenile delinquency (in Ghana); also reports reactions of youngsters and their preferences for films.

256. DeProspo, Nicholas D. "Developing Scientific Attitudes by Responding Actively to Motion Pictures: A Study to Determine if Responding Actively to Selected Motion Pictures by Identifying the Problem-

Solving Skills They Portray Reinforces or Develops a Scientific Attitude in College Freshmen." Unpublished Ph. D. dissertation, New York University, 1957.
Experimental subjects showed a significant gain in attitude over the control group.

257. Deprun, Jean. "Le Cinéma et l'Identification" (Cinema and Identification). Revue Internationale de Filmologie 1 (July-August 1947): 36-38.
A nonempirical discussion.

258. _____. "Cinéma et Transfert" (Cinema and Transference). Revue Internationale de Filmologie 1 (September-October 1947): 205-207.
Argues that two conditions are necessary for transference to occur: concepts must be symbolically represented and must be projected "outside" the observer without danger of return; cinema satisfies both conditions.

259. Descamps, J. "Pourquoi les Jeunes Vont-ils au Cinéma?" (Why do Adolescents go to the Cinema?). La Nouvelle Revue Pédagogique 6 (March 1951): 326-342.
A 1950 study of more than 2,000 Belgian students over 16 years of age.

260. Deshaies, Gabriel. "Les Fonctions Psychologiques du Cinéma" (The Psychological Functions of the Cinema). Annales Medico-Psychologiques 1 (May 1951): 553-573.
An empirically based review of literature discussing the psychological uses of movies by cinema patrons including leisure time activity and satisfaction of inner needs; choice of movies and patrons' reactions to them are based on a diversity of elements and are manifested in a number of ways.

261. Desi, Abel. "A Film es a Mindennapi Elet" (The Film and Everyday Life). Uzenet 9 (1976): 490-496.

262. Desrues. H. "Portrait Robot du Spectateur de Cinéma." Image et Son no. 345 (December 1979): 16-18.
Summary of studies conducted by the Centre National de la Cinematographie and the Centre d'Etude des Supports de Publicité profiling the French movie-goer.

263. Deutschmann, Paul J. "The Mass Media in an Underdeveloped Village." Journalism Quarterly 40 (Winter 1963): 27-35.
Persons living in a small Andean village in Colombia were interviewed to determine their media use habits and opportunities for use; 26 percent of literate and 17 percent of illiterate persons had attended movies in the previous months; discussion of media audience building in Colombia as similar to the U.S. is presented.

264. _____, John T. McNelly, and Huber Ellingsworth. "Mass Media Use by Sub-Elites in 11 Latin American Countries." Journalism Quarterly 38 (Autumn 1961): 460-472.
Frequency of movie attendance was slightly greater in non-television countries (13 percent) than TV countries (11 percent).

265. "Die Kinder und das Filmverbrechen" (Children and Crime in the Cinema). Korrespondenz für Filmkunst 2: 4-5.

266. Diehl, Mrs. Ambrose A. "The Moral Effect of the Cinema on Individuals." International Review of Educational Cinematography 3 (1931): 1123-1137.
Advocates the need for substantive research to determine the effects of movies.

267. Dimas, Chris. "The Effect of Motion Pictures Portraying Black Models on the Self-Concept of Black Elementary School Children." Unpublished Ph. D. dissertation, Syracuse University, 1970.
Black students who viewed films portraying black actors and actresses indicated certain aspects of the self (individuation, esteem, identification) more positively than did black students who viewed films portraying white models.

268. Disman, M. "Über den Versuch einer Feststellung des Einflusses von Theater und Kino auf die Schuljugend im Alter von 11-14 Jahren (Zusammenfassung)" (An Attempt to Determine the Influence of the Theater and Movies on School Children Between the Ages of 11 and 14: [Summary]). Compte Rendu, 8th Conference Internationale Psychotechnique, Prague, 1935, pp. 743-744.

269. Dodman, N. D. "The Cinema Attendance of Adolescents." Proceedings of the British Association, September 1948.

270. Doscher, Luelyne. "The Significance of Audience Measurement in Motion Pictures." Journal of Social Issues 3 (Summer 1947): 51-57.
Discussion of the uses of such research and the assumptions about the audiences which underlie these researches.

271. Downs, Anthony. "Drive-Ins have Arrived." Journal of Property Management 18 (March 1953): 149-162.
A nonempirical discussion and analysis of who goes to the drive-ins and why, early drive-ins and how the type grew, and where the drive-in fits into the movie industry.

272. Drama Committee of the Twentieth Century Club. "The Amusement Situation in the City of Boston." Twentieth Century Club, 1910.
Presents data on the seating capacity and attendance prices for a variety of leisure activities.

273. Drillich, P. A. "Een Filmdiscussiegroep in een Inrichting" (A Study-Group on the Cinema in an Institution). De Koepel, November 1955, pp. 386-390.
Report of an experiment designed to encourage 13 to 21 year old girls to adopt a critical approach to films.

274. Driscoll, John. "Some Psychological Bases for Split-Screen Utilization." Journal of the University Film Association 25 (1973, no. 1): 6-7.
Classes of third and sixth grade pupils were used in an experiment which showed that "factual learning on the film seen and heard was little impaired by the audible presence of the rather irrelevant soundtrack of another film."

275. Dronberger, Ilse. "Student Attitudes Toward the Foreign Film." Journal of University Film Producers Association 17 (1965): 6-9, 19-22.
Reports reactions to a series of foreign films shown in a midwest community.

276. Dudley, O. "The Leisure Activities of Secondary Children." Unpublished M. A. thesis, University of London, 1952.

277. Dumazedier, Joffre. "Loisir Cinématographique et Culture Populaire" (Cinematographical Leisure Activities and Popular Culture). Revue de l'Institute de Sociologie Solvay 3 (1959): 349-370.
    Comparative data between the French film industry and other countries; reviews research on attitudes and expectations regarding the cinema, reasons for attendance, and the decision process of film selection.

278. Dunbar, Olivia Howard. "The Lure of the Films." Harper's Weekly, January 18, 1913, pp. 20, 22.
    A speculative analysis on the attractiveness of movies suggesting that films make no demands on their audience.

279. Dunkerley, G. "An Experiment with Films: Parts I and II." Journal of Education 73 (1941): 306-308, 348-349.

280. Dyer, Ernest. "What do They Like?" Sight and Sound 7 (Summer 1938): 78-79.
    Results of a questionnaire distributed to members of a film society (n=168); feature-length and short-film-type preferences are reported.

281. Dysinger, Wendall S. and Christian A. Ruckmick. "The Emotional Responses of Children to the Motion Picture Situation." Unpublished Ph.D. dissertation, University of Iowa, 1934.
    Observation in theaters and use of physiological measurements in a lab environment (psychogalvanograph and pneumo-cardiograph); differences by age are reported.

282. Eastman, Fred. "Your Child and the Movies." Christian Century 50 (May 3, 1933): 591-593; (May 10, 1933): 620-622; (May 17, 1933): 653-655; (May 24, 1933): 688-690; (May 31, 1933): 718-720; (June 7, 1933): 750-752; (June 14, 1933): 779-781.
    Reports on and reviews the soon-to-be-published Payne Fund studies.

283. Eaton, Reba E. Motion Picture Preferences of Passaic High School. New York: Teachers College, Columbia University, 1929.

284. Eaton, Walter Prichard. "The Menace of the Movies." American Magazine, September 1913, pp. 55-60.
    Speculation on the movies' influence in drawing audiences from the theater.

285. Edman, Marion. "Attendance of School Pupils and Adults at Moving Pictures." School Review 48 (December 1940): 753-763.

286. Eichel, Charles G. "Experiment to Determine the Most Effective Method of Teaching Current History." Unpublished Ph.D. dissertation, New York University, 1939.
    Sixth grade pupils learned and retained more information in the sound film condition (using the March of Time) than in the textbook and current news periodical condition.

287. _____. "Experiment to Determine the Most Effective Method of

Teaching Current History." Journal of Experimental Education 9 (September 1940): 37-40.
A summary of the author's dissertation.

288. Eimers, Robert Conrad. "The Impact of Film Violence on Viewer Mood and Masculine-Feminine Self-Concept." Unpublished Ph. D. dissertation, University of Rochester, 1977.
Undergraduates (n=326) exposed to the violent film showed greater mood change than subjects in the control group; also measured was change in masculine and feminine self-concept, film evaluation, and beliefs about the film.

289. Einsiedel, Edna F., Kandice Salomone, and Fred Schneider. "A Field Experiment on Immediate and Delayed Effects of Aggressive-Erotic, Mild- and Hard-Core Erotic Films on Attitudes Toward Sexual Violence." Paper presented at the International Communication Association conference, May 1982, Boston, MA.
82 college students participated in the study; results showed that on three measures of acceptance of rape myths and other related dimensions males scored higher than females.

290. Eiserer, Paul E. "The Relative Effectiveness of Motion and Still Pictures as Stimuli for Eliciting Fantasy Stories About Adolescent-Parent Relationships." Genetic Psychology Monographs 39 (1949): 205-278.
Results of an experiment suggest that films can be used as effective projective instruments for personality study.

291. "Electric Movie 'Reviewers' Record Reaction to Film." Popular Mechanics 87 (May 1947): 149.
Describes the "televoting" device used in film pretests.

292. Elias, James. "Exposure of Adults to Erotic Materials." Technical Reports of the U.S. Commission on Obscenity and Pornography, vol. 9, pp. 273-312. Washington, D.C.: U.S. Government Printing Office, 1970.
Over three-fourths of those in the sample reported attending an "adults only" movie when they were underage.

293. Elkin, Frederick. "The Value Implications of Popular Films." Sociology and Social Research 38 (May-June 1954): 320-322.
A nonempirical paper advocating that norms and values are unintentionally suggested by movies and that since viewers are not aware of these norms and values a significant impact may be possible.

294. Ellingsworth, Huber W. "Cinema Attendance of a Sub-Elite Latin American Group." Quarterly Journal of Speech 49 (October 1963): 262-265.
Results of interviews and questionnaires from 309 individuals; reports media use, frequency of film attendance, relationship between film attendance and education and TV use, and value of movies as a source of information for introducing change.

295. Elliott, Frank P. "Memory for Trade Names Presented in Screen, Radio, and Television Advertisements." Journal of Applied Psychology 21 (1937): 653-667.
An experiment involving 67 relief workers and 76 undergraduates; data are presented by age, sex, and level of intelligence.

296. Elliott, William R. and William J. Schenck-Hamlin. "Film, Politics and the Press: The Influence of 'All the President's Men.'" Journalism Quarterly 56 (Autumn 1979): 546-553.
Greater influence on attitudes toward the press than on political attitudes was found for respondents who saw All the President's Men; authors conclude that "a film can have an impact on the attitudes of its audience but the direction of the impact will depend on what the audience brings to the film situation."

297. Elton, Arthur. "Filmens Rollei den Sociale Oplysning" (The Role of Films in Creating Social Public Opinion). Menneske og Miljo 1 (1946): 306-307.
Review of research on the use of films for molding public opinion in the U.S., Canada, Denmark, England, and Russia.

298. Emery, Frederick E. "Psychological Effects of the Western Film: A Study in Television Viewing." Human Relations 12 (1959): 195-214.

299. ———— and David Martin. "Psychological Effects of the 'Western' Film: A Study in Television Viewing." Melbourne: University of Melbourne, Department of Audio-Visual Aids, 1957.
Analysis of the effects of The Lone Hand on 43 boys aged 10 and 13; Rosenweig's frustration test and the Thematic Apperception Test were utilized.

300. "English Children and the 'Movies.'" Social Service Review 24 (September 1950): 400.
Brief report on the British Departmental Committee on Children and the Cinema's white paper which stated that movies had "no primary responsibility for juvenile delinquency and moral laxity."

301. "English Children and the 'Movies.'" Social Service Review 26 (March 1952): 87.
Brief report on a pamphlet issued by the London County Council for the Guidance of School Teachers which inquired into the movie-going habits of nearly 15,000 children; frequency of attendance and reactions to films reported.

302. "Enquête sur les Effets du Cinéma sur la Vue" (An Investigation on the Effects of the Cinema on Vision). Revue Internationale du Cinema Education 2 (May 1930): 613-632.
"The bad effects of the cinema on vision, from the ophthalmological and nervous point of view, are not due to cinematography in itself but to the phenomenon of intermittence, to the excessive rapidity with which the films are shown, to the use of worn films and apparatus in poor repair, and to shifts in illumination."

303. Erofeev, P. P. and G. M. Livsic (eds.). "Kino i Gorodskoj Zritel" (Cinema and the Urban Spectator). Moskva, Institut Teorii i Istorii Kino Goskino SSSR, 1978.

304. Erp, Sue Hopper. "A Study of Reactions to the Film 'Confrontations of Death.'" Unpublished Ph.D. dissertation, University of Oregon, 1973.
Investigated attitudes of adults, including undergraduates, toward education and counseling regarding death and dying; reactions to a film were recorded by the Digital Display Program Analyzer.

305. Ervine, St. John. "The Cinema and the Child." Fortnightly Review 137 (April 1932): 426-443.
Reviews literature on the effects of movies; reports frequency of attendance, film-type preferences, effects on eyes, and methods for censorship and control.

306. Essman, Philip. "Comparative Study of Presentation in the Media of Radio, Motion Pictures, and Television." Unpublished M.A. thesis, University of California, Los Angeles, 1949.

307. Eswara, H. S. and Nadig Krishnamurthy. "How School Achievement Relates to Mass Media Use." Journalism Quarterly 55 (Winter 1978): 785-788.
With regard to movie attendance (other media were also examined), low achievers attend more frequently than do high achievers.

308. Evans, Frederick. "War and Child Opinion." Sight and Sound 4 (Autumn 1935): 111-113.
Results of two questionnaires given to 200 children.

309. _____. "War Films and Child Opinion." Discovery Reports 10 (July 1939): 345-360.
Replies to a questionnaire suggest that children are mostly resistant to war propaganda.

310. "Eye Strain in Motion Picture Theaters." American Journal of Public Health 11 (October 1921): 936-937.
Report of the results of a British committee's investigation.

311. Fabregat Cuneo, Roberto. "El Proceso del Cine en el Mundo y en la Cultura y la Deformación de los Temas Culturales al Través del Cine" (The Process of the Cinema in the World and in Culture and the Development of Cultural Themes by Means of the Cinema). Revista Mexicana de Sociología 19 (1957): 387-404.

312. Fabregat Cuneo, Roberto. "Principales Influencias del Cine sobre el Público" (Main Influences of the Cinema on the Public). Revista Mexicana de Sociologia 20 (January-February 1958): 27-55.
A theoretical discussion of the influence of the movies on suggestion, imitation, and educational consequences.

313. Falewicz, Jan. "Upodobania Filmowe Ludnosci Miejskie" (Film Tastes of Urban Populations). Kultura i Spoleczenstwo 8 (July-September 1964): 167-178.
Reports results of a survey of urban Polish movie fans; includes frequency of attendance and reasons for attending movies.

314. _____. "Effect of Criticism on Urban Film Taste." Polish Sociological Bulletin 9 (1964): 90-95.
Through a poll of 1,832 adult urban movie-goers, the study investigated motivations, choice justifications, and evaluation related to movie tastes and habits; film criticism tended to have in indirect effect on the public through opinion leaders.

315. Farmer, Ronald J. "The Effect of Selected Film Sequences on Individuals Toward Nature and Art Forms." Unpublished Ph.D. dissertation, Pennsylvania State University, 1958.

Film Audience 36

316. Favre L. "La Musique des Couleurs et le Cinéma" (The Music of Colors and the Cinema). Bulletin de l'Institut Général Psychologie 27 (1927, nos. 1-3): 78-92.
An analysis of the scientific use and regulation of light waves so as to establish a "music of colors"; describes affective correlates of colors (e. g., warm colors corresponding to calm and sadness).

317. Fearing, Franklin. "Psychology and the Films." Hollywood Quarterly 2 (1946-1947): 118-121.
A nonempirical analysis of films treating psychological themes and the need for psychological research on movie audiences.

318. _____. "The Effects of Radio and Motion Pictures on Children's Behavior." National Probation and Parole Association Yearbook (1947): 78-92.
Review of research including the Payne Fund work and movies' effect on attitudes.

319. _____. "Some Sources of Confusion." Journal of Social Issues 3 (Summer 1947): 2-7.
Presents four issues--movies and radio as entertainment, the "mass audience," effects of mass media, and the social responsibility of the media--on which there exists considerable debate and confusion.

320. _____. "Influence of the Movies on Attitude and Behavior." Annals of the American Academy of Political and Social Science 254 (November 1947): 70-79.
A review of research with directions for future research.

321. _____. "Motion Pictures as a Medium of Instruction and Communication." University of California Publications in Culture and Society 2 (1950, no. 3): 101-202.
Study of the extent to which two films modified the attitudes of, or imparted knowledge to, a group of 500 male naval cadets.

322. _____. "A Word of Caution for the Intelligent Consumer of Motion Pictures." Quarterly of Film, Radio and Television 6 (1952): 129-142.
A review and analysis of the "effects of film" literature including attitudinal effects and the consequences of violence.

323. Federation of British Film-Makers. "Cinema Going in Greater London." London, 1963.
Results of a survey; data are summarized in "The London Filmgoer," Sight and Sound.

324. Federation of Children's Welfare Organizations of Yugoslavia. "Filmi Dete: Clanci, Dokumenti i Informacije" (The Cinema and Children: Articles, Documents and Information). Belgrade: Commission on the Cinema and Children of the Federation of Children's Welfare Organizations of Yugoslavia, 1957, 88 pages (stencilled).
Contains reprints of foreign works as well as a bibliography.

325. Federici, N. "Osservazioni sulle Preferenze del Pubblico Italiano per Films di Diverso Gènere" (Observations on the Preferences of the Italian Public for Films of Various Kinds). Annali della Facoltà di Economia e Commercio 16 (June 1962): 191-205.

326. Feldens, Franz von. "Die 13-14 Jährigen und das Theater" (Thirteen- and Fourteen-Year-Olds and the Theater). Zeitschrift für Pädagogische Psychologie 38 (1937): 173-181.
Results of questionnaires returned by 2,899 boys and girls in public schools; purpose of the study was to determine whether the literacy tastes of children also hold for the theater; discussion of preferences for movies compared to theater.

327. Fenin, George N. "Motion Pictures and the Public." Film Culture 1 (January 1955): 15-18.
A nonempirical discussion of the film audience as it interacts with the medium; author deplores the fact that the public's reaction to cinema has not been investigated.

328. Ferguson, I. M. "Movies for Children." Minnesotan 3 (August 1917): 30-31.

329. Ferland, Yvon and Audrey Voitkus. "Cinema Attendance Habits in Canada." Canadian Statistical Review 53 (May 1978): vi-xiv.
Demographic characteristics are presented.

330. Ferrarotti, Franco. "L'Incidenza del Cinema sul Costume e sulle Norme di Comportamento" (The Influence of the Cinema on Habits and Norms of Behavior). Lo Spettacolo 16 (October-December 1966): 241-261.
A review of literature.

331. _____. "Cinema e Società: Un Rapporto Ambiguo, da Approfondire" (Cinema and Society: An Ambiguous Relationship Elucidated). La Critica Sociologica 1 (Autumn 1967): 88-99.
Results of a questionnaire completed by 62 persons; frequency of attendance, demographic characteristics, and reasons for the popularity of Italian westerns are reported.

332. Fervers, Carl. "Zur Psychologie des Filmerlebens" (The Psychology of the Film Experience). Zeitschrift für Experimentelle und Angewandte Psychologie 6 (1959): 600-607.

333. Field, Mary. "Progrès des Films pour Enfants en Angleterre" (Progress in Films for Children in England). Revue Internationale du Cinéma 3 (1949).

334. _____. "Unfinished Project." Sight and Sound 18 (Spring 1949): 8-11.
Discussion of Children's Entertainment Films' methods for studying the reactions of audiences to movies.

335. _____. "Children's Entertainment Films: Good Company." Films in 1951, Festival of Britain, 1951 (published by Sight and Sound): pp. 59-60.
Discussion of the development of films for children, research methods used to study children, and a brief review of the research.

336. _____. "Children's Taste in Films." Quarterly of Film, Radio and Television 11 (1956-1957): 14-23.
A review of literature although references are not provided.

337. _____. "Children in Cinema." Films and Filming 4 (April 1958): 9-10.

An anecdotal discussion of how children interact with movies including the possibility that films may provide "training in good social behavior."

338. _____. "Children and the Entertainment Film." Sight and Sound 15 (Summer 1961): 46-47.
Description of an experiment investigating the suitability of children's films for children.

339. "51% of French Never Attend." Variety, May 12, 1976, p. 269.
Frequency of attendance by age, sex, and education.

340. "Film and Public: Chance of a Lifetime." Sight and Sound 19 (January 1951): 349-350.
Results of a survey of 100 adults' reactions to a film; also presented are their reasons for attendance.

341. "Film es Kozonsege" (Film and its Audience). Filmkultura 4 (1977): 40-56; 5 (1977): 89-99.

342. "Film Subject Matter Looms Large in Stay-Away; Ticket Prices are Related to Age; Income Strata." Variety, November 18, 1981, pp. 5, 32.
Results of a survey of seven metropolitan centers regarding why people do not go to the movies.

343. "Films and Fans." The Economist 125 (December 5, 1936): 456-457.
Discussion of import quotas and their relation to movie-goers.

344. Finegan, Thomas E. "The Results of the Experiment with Eastman Classroom Films." International Review of Educational Cinematography 1 (1929): 131-147.
A large scale study conducted in 12 cities and involving some 11,000 pupils; subjects in the film condition showed superior results to those in the control group.

345. Fisher, William A. and Donn Byrne. "Individual Differences in Affective, Evaluative, and Behavioral Responses to an Erotic Film." Journal of Applied Social Psychology 8 (1978): 355-365.
Individuals who rated a film as pornographic reported more restrictive sexual socialization experiences and more negative attitudes toward sex than individuals who rated the same film as relatively nonpornographic.

346. Fiske, Marjorie and Leo Handel. "Motion Picture Research: Content and Audience Analysis." Journal of Marketing 11 (October 1946): 129-134.
A review of research and methodology on content analysis and the structure of the movie audience.

347. _____. "Motion Picture Research: Response Analysis." Journal of Marketing 11 (January 1947): 273-280.
A review of research conducted on such topics as the sneak preview, reactions to specific aspects of a movie (e.g., title), effectiveness of advertising, audience motivation and gratification, and the Payne Fund studies.

348. _____. "New Techniques for Studying the Effectiveness of Films." Journal of Marketing 11 (April 1947): 390-393.

Discussion of the purposes, procedures, and benefits of the focussed interview and Lazarsfeld-Stanton Program Analyzer.

349. "500 New Screens Due." Variety, September 30, 1981, pp. 5, 40.
A report on Pacific Theatres vice president Robert Selig's address to the Motion Picture and TV Controllers Association; brief mention of the demographic characteristics of the drive-in theater audience and their motives for attending.

350. Flik, Gotthilf. "Untersuchungen über den Einfluss des Films auf kriminellgewordene Jugendliche" (Investigations on the Influence of the Movie Upon Youth Turned Criminal). Psychologische Rundschau 5 (1954): 1-21.
Results of questionnaires distributed to 178 juvenile delinquents aged 14-21 concerning the influence of their attendance at movies on their crimes; one conclusion states that crime was not less before movies were attended by the juveniles.

351. Flowerman, Samuel H. "Mass Propaganda in the War Against Bigotry." Journal of Abnormal and Social Psychology 42 (October 1947): 429-439.
Theoretical analysis of attitude change as caused by the mass media.

352. _____ and Marie Jahoda. "The Study of Man--Can We Fight Prejudice Scientifically." Commentary 3 (December 1946): 583-587.
Nonempirical discussion including the use of mass media in the "fight."

353. Fohey, Joseph M. "The Bilateral Effect of Film Context." Unpublished M.A. thesis, University of Iowa, 1966.

354. Ford, Richard. "What One Public Says it Likes: Comments on the Bernstein Questionnaire." Sight and Sound 6 (Summer 1937): 70.
Report on the results of a British survey involving 160,000 respondents; data on favorite film stars, effect of stars on attendance behavior, film-type preferences, reactions to advertising films, and frequency of attendance.

355. "Fortune Survey: Moving Pictures." Fortune 13 (April 1936): 222.
Reports on frequency of attendance among adults and children, attendance relative to economic status and race, and whether people attend "any good film" or wait to see only certain films.

356. "Fortune Survey: Movies and Movie Stars." Fortune 16 (July 1937): 103-104.
Responses to the "favorite movie star" question reported by sex; preferences for double or single features and shorts reported.

357. "Fortune Survey: The Movies." Fortune 20 (November 1939): 176.
Favorite actors and actresses and their relative rank; also asked if respondents' had to choose between going to the movies and listening to the radio which would be given up and found that movies were preferred.

358. "Fortune Survey: The People's Taste in Movies, Books, and Radio." Fortune 39 (March 1949): 39-40, 43-44.
Data reported include comparisons between these media in terms of evaluation of content, frequency of attendance, why people don't go to the movies, and film-type preferences.

359. Foulkes, David and Allan Rechtschaffen. "Presleep Determinants of Dream Content: Effects of Two Films." Perceptual and Motor Skills 19 (1964): 983-1005.
Following viewing of a violent film rapid eye movement was longer, content of dreams was more imaginative, vivid, and emotional than following viewing a nonviolent film; content of dreams was judged not significantly different with regard to pleasantness of film content.

360. Fraisse, P. and G. de Montmollin. "Sur la Mémoire des Films" (The Recollection of Films.) Revue Internationale de Filmologie 3 (January-March 1952): 37-69.
After viewing several short films 100 students recorded accounts of what they had seen; results suggest that, among other things, film viewers are not passive when watching a movie.

361. Frank, Josette. "Chills and Thrills in Radio, Movies and Comics." Child Study, Spring 1948, pp. 42-48.
Report of the opinions of psychiatrists on the effect of these media on children.

362. Fredericksen, Don. "Film Study, Literary Criticism, and Science: A Polemical Response to Richard Dyer MacCann." Journal of the University Film Association 29 (Spring 1977): 21-29.

363. Freeman, Frank N. "The Technique Used in the Study of the Effect of Motion Pictures on the Care of the Teeth." Journal of Educational Sociology 6 (January 1933): 309-311.
Discussion of methodological concerns.

364. _____ and Carolyn Hoefer. "An Experimental Study of the Influence of Motion Picture Films on Behavior." Journal of Educational Psychology 22 (1931): 411-425.
Fifth and sixth grade children's responses to a questionnaire; results showed that the films used had no appreciable influence on the acquisition of information.

365. Freidson, Eliot L. "An Audience and Its Taste: A Study of 79 Children." Unpublished Ph.D. dissertation, University of Chicago, 1952.
A study of the impact of movies, television, radio, and comics on 79 children; amount of time spent with each medium, content preferences, opinions and stereotypes regarding these media are reported.

366. _____. "Adult Discount: An Aspect of Children's Changing Taste." Child Development 24 (March 1953): 39-49.
Through interviews with children the author concludes that "the notion of adult discount suggests why older children are no longer moved by what excites younger children."

367. _____. "Communications Research and the Concept of the Mass." American Sociological Review 18 (June 1953): 313-317.
"It is possible to conclude that the audience, from the point of view of its members, at least, is not anonymous, heterogeneous, unorganized and spatially separated"; methodological implications are also discussed.

368. _____. "The Relation of the Social Situation of Contact to the Media

in Mass Communication." Public Opinion Quarterly 17 (Summer 1953): 230-238.
Examines the social situation of contact--alone, with peers, and with family--to comics, television, and movies among second, fourth, and sixth grade pupils.

369. _____. "Consumption of Mass Media by Polish-American Children." Quarterly of Film, Radio and Television 9 (1954-1955): 92-101.
A summary of the author's dissertation.

370. "Frekwencja w Kinematografach natle Roezwoju Konjunktury" (Moving Picture Patronage and General Business Conditions). Konjunktura Gospodarcza 3 (February 1930): 72-73.

371. Frey, R. Scott, Craig A. Piernot, and Dale G. Elhardt. "An Analysis of Riesman's Historical Thesis Through American Film Titles." Journal of Social Psychology 113 (February 1981): 57-64.
Analysis of 2,840 titles of films earning $1 million or more during 1942-1975 to test the thesis of a shift in American social character from inner- to other-directedness; results do not support the predicted shift.

372. Friedman, Norman L. "Some Sociological Notes on the Boom in Film Interest." Youth and Society 2 (March 1971): 323-332.
A nonempirical explanation for the popularity of movies.

373. Friedmann, G. "Sociologie et Filmologie" (Sociology and Filmology). Revue Internationale de Filmologie 3 (1952): 226-227.
Brief discussion of avenues for research.

374. Friedmann, Georges and Edgar Morin. "Sociologie du Cinema" (Sociology of the Cinema). Revue Internationale de Filmologie 3 (April-June 1952): 95-111.
Discussion of the social, historical, and anthropological aspects of motion pictures.

375. Fritz, John Otto. "Film Persuasion in Education and Social Controversies: A Theoretical Analysis of the Components Manifest in Viewer-Film Involvement as They Affect the Viewer's Urge to Further Inquiry into Social Controversies." Unpublished Ed.D. dissertation, Indiana University, 1957.
A nonempirical analysis and discussion.

376. Frutchey, F. P. "Measuring Motion-Picture Preferences." Educational Research Bulletin 14 (March 13, 1935): 67-74.
Discussion of methodological concerns; reports a test comparing a rating scale and a paired-comparison test.

377. _____. "Collecting Evidences of Children's Preferences." Educational Research Bulletin 14 (October 16, 1935): 173-178, 198.
Discussion of methodological issues; comparison between paired comparison and observational techniques.

378. _____. "Can Youth's Appreciation of Motion Pictures Be Improved?" Educational Research Bulletin 16 (April 1937): 97-102.
A review of literature concluding that the teaching of film appreciation has positive results.

379. _____ and Edgar Dale. "Testing Some Objectives of Motion-Picture Appreciation." Educational Research Bulletin 14 (February 13, 1935): 34-37.

380. _____ and Edgar Dale. "Evaluating Motion Pictures." Educational Research Bulletin 15 (September 16, 1936): 163-165.
Discussion of the development of a measuring instrument.

381. Fukasz, G. "Filmnezes Szabad Szombatokon." Filmkultura 10 (March-April 1974): 74-78.
Discussion of movie-going habits of Hungarians.

382. Fulchignoni, Enrico. "Filmology and Infantile Psychology." Bianco e Nero 10 (1949).

383. _____. "Sobre el Valor Psicológico de la Imagen Cinematográfica" (On the Psychological Significance of Cinematic Images). Revista de Psicología General y Applicada 4 (1949): 11-38.
Nonempirical analysis suggesting that the principles of depth psychology may cause the psychological effects of movies.

384. _____. "Filmologia e Psicologia Infantile" (Filmology and Infantile Psychology). Revue Internationale du Cinéma 4 (1949): 26-33.
Discussion of differences in perception of films by adults and children.

385. _____. (The Film and the Projective Methods.) Archivo di Psicologia, Neurologia e Psichiatria 9 (April 1950).

386. _____. "Filomologia e Psicologia Infantil" (Filmology and Child Psychology). Arquivos Brasileiros de Psicotecnica 2 (1950): 59-66.
Discussion of the psychological influence of movies on children in terms of children's perception and affective reactions to films; suggests further study investigating the personality of movie-goers.

387. _____. "Cinéma et Psychologie" (Cinema and Psychology). Revue de Psychologie Appliquée 1 (1951): 61-72.
Discussion of contemporary research on the differences between adult's and children's affective reactions to movies.

388. Fulk, Joseph R. "The Effect on Education and Morals of the Moving-Picture Shows." Proceedings of the National Education Association Annual Meeting (1921): 456-461.
Summary of an audience study conducted in Nebraska towns written in an advocacy style and concluding that the movies were doing more harm than good.

389. "Further Findings from Audienscope Pre-Release Survey." Film Bulletin 46 (January-February 1977): 5.

390. G., W. O. "A Policeman Goes to the Pictures." The Police Journal 17 (1944): 59-66.
A selected review of scientific literature leading to the author's assertion that movies "would appear to have some considerable influence on social conduct"--especially delinquency.

391. Gaer, Felice D. "The Soviet Film Audience: A Confidential View." Problems of Communication 23 (January 1974): 56-70.
Access to a 1966 "semisecret" pamphlet prepared by the Moscow Film Section of the Department of Culture provides the data base for this discussion; included in the audience analyses are Soviet films rated by first preference, foreign films rated by first preference, motives for movie-going, and influences on choice of movie fare.

392. Galifret, Y. and J. Segal. "Cinéma et Physiologie des Sensations" (Cinema and the Physiology of the Sensation). Revue Internationale de Filmologie 2 (October 1948): 289-293.
A descriptive, nonempirical report.

393. Galletto, Albino. "Cinema e Ragazzi" (Cinema and Children). Ragazzi Aspiranti 3 (1949): 105-109.
Analysis of reactions to movies with suggestions regarding teachers' attitudes and actions.

394. "Gallup Gadget." Business Week, February 3, 1945, p. 80.
Discussion of Audience Research, Inc.'s method for evaluating films.

395. "Gallup Gadget Charts Movie Appeal." Science Digest 17 (April 1945): 6.
Report on Gallup's Audience Research, Inc. and their film evaluation device which is similar to CBS' "program analyzer."

396. Gallup Looks at the Movies. Scholarly Resources Inc., 104 Greenhill Avenue, Wilmington, Delaware.
Microfilm containing data from Audience Research, Inc., a Gallup organization directed by David Ogilvy; among the topics covered in the Audience Research Reports were star popularity, movie titles, effectiveness of advertising and publicity, potential profitability of novels, public acceptance of musicals and comedies, reactions to 3-D and wide-screen films.

397. "Gallup Survey Reports Movie Popularity Up Since '66 Poll." Independent Film Journal, March 18, 1974, p. 53.

398. Galuszka, M. and K. Kowalewicz. "Szkic do Badan Potocznego Odbioru Filmu." Kino 12 (November 1977): 29-31.
Discussion of the problems and research aspects of the sociology of the cinema.

399. Gannon, John Patrick. "The Traumatic Commercial Film Experience: An Extension of Laboratory Findings on Stress in a Naturalistic Setting." Unpublished Ph.D. dissertation, California School of Professional Psychology, 1979.
The effects of different levels of stress and identification on affective responses of 90 individuals were assessed in a repeated measures design.

400. Gans, Herbert J. "Hollywood Films on the British Screen: An Analysis of the Function of American Popular Culture Abroad." Social Problems 9 (1962): 324-328.
Reports the results of an exploratory study in which "more than fifty officials in British and American film and television indus-

tries" were interviewed; economic and cultural factors explained the success of American films in Britain.

401. _____. "The Rise of the Problem-Film: An Analysis of Changes in Hollywood Films and the American Audience." Social Problems 11 (1964); 327-336.
A nonempirical analysis.

402. Garcia, Fernandez M. "El Espectador Cinematográfico en España" (The Cinema Spectator in Spain). Estudios de Informacion 13 (January-March 1970): 21-38.

403. Garcia Yague, Jean. "Influencia del Cine en la Juventud" (Influence of the Cinema on Youth). Rumbos, August 1956, pp. 257-265.
Examination of the psycho-social effects of movies on children over seven years of age.

404. Garrison, Lee C. "The Needs of Motion Picture Audiences." California Management Review 15 (Winter 1972): 144-152.
Provides a review of the empirical research literature on motion picture audience research since Handel's 1950 study (Hollywood Looks at Its Audience).

405. Gastra van Loon, F. M. "Speelt de Film bij het Onstaan of in het Verloop van Psychische Stoornissen van het Kind een Rol?" (Does the Film Play a Part in the Genesis or Progress of Psychic Disturbances of Children?). Maandblad voor de Geestelijke Volksgesonheid 10 (February 1955): 62-72.
Responses by psychiatrists and pediatricians to questions concerning their observations of disturbances in 8 to 18 year olds as a result of the children's cinema-going.

406. Gavioli, Orazio. "Cinema e Ricerca Sociale" (Motion Pictures and Social Research). Nord e Sud 8 (December 1961): 95-118.
Review of policymaking-related literature and, especially, audience research conducted in Italy.

407. Geerts, Claude. "Les Téléspectateurs et le Cinéma" (Televiewers and the Movies). Etudes de Radio-Television 15 (1969): 70-81.
Demographic characteristics of TV and film audiences are discussed with regard to their cinematic preferences; among the findings, actors are more significant than directors, especially for the least educated.

408. Geiger, Joseph Roy. "The Effects of the Motion Picture on the Mind and Morals of the Young." International Journal of Ethics 34 (October 1923): 69-83.
Advocacy piece discussing the relationship between movies and audiences; claims that movies have three features which must challenge the serious consideration of the student of ethics who reflects on the relation (of movies) to the mental and moral welfare of the young.

409. Gel'mont, A. M. "Izucenie Detskogo Kinozritelja" (The Young Spectator's Reactions Studied). Moscow: Roskino, 1933, 64 pages.
Reviews 1920-1930 research; discussion of procedural, methodological and statistical means for conducting audience research on children.

410. Gemelli, Agostino. "Les Causes Psychologiques de l'Intérêt des Projections Cinématographiques" (The Psychological Causes of Interest in Cinema Projection). Journal de Psychologie 25 (1928): 598-606.
A nonempirical essay.

411. Gemelli, Agostino. "Cinema e Psicologia" (Cinema and Psychology). Revue Internationale du Cinéma 5 (1950).

412. Gemelli, Agostino. "Le Film Comme Methode Projective" (The Film as a Projective Device). Acta Psychologica 7 (1950): 190-195.
Nonempirical discussion of a possible application of films.

413. _____. "Le Film, Procédé d'Analyse Projective" (The Film as a Projective Device). Revue Internationale de Filmologie 2 (1950, no. 6): 135-138.

414. George, Francis Blaine. "A Study of the Attitudes of Selected Officers of the California Congress of Parents and Teachers Toward the Relationship of Motion Pictures and Television to Children." Unpublished Ed. D. dissertation, University of Southern California, 1965.
Results of a survey in which parents' attitudes toward the two media were assessed; parents favored industry self-regulation and the establishment and legal enforcement of a movie classification system to prevent children from viewing unsuitable films.

415. Gerhardt, Lydia. "Emotionality, Understanding, and Identification in Pre-School Children's Reactions to Western Films." Unpublished M. A. thesis, University of Wisconsin at Madison, 1958.

416. "German Drive-Ins Boom." Variety, July 27, 1977, p. 39.
Reports that drive-ins outdrew walk-ins.

417. Gesswein, Betty. "Children's Choice in Pictures." Unpublished M. A. thesis, 1937.

418. "Getting Them Back to the Movies." Business Week, October 22, 1955, pp. 58, 60, 63.
Discussion of the "new audience" and Hollywood's production, marketing, and exhibition strategies for attracting this audience.

419. Giacomelli, Ferruccio. "Il Film e la Delinquenza Giovanile" (The Film and Juvenile Delinquency). Unpublished thesis, Faculty of Medicine of Perugia, 1956.
Review of the literature with the conclusion that the cinema's influence on criminal behavior has not been unequivocally established.

420. Gibson, Harold J. (Mrs.) and Vaskey Nahabedian. "A Survey of the Reading, Radio and Motion Picture Habits of Royal Oak Public School Students and Their Parents." Royal Oak, Michigan: Royal Oak Public School, 1949, 21 pages.
Students go to the movies more frequently than their parents; parents influence pupils' film choice; film-type preferences of pupils are detailed; how film selection is made by students is detailed.

421. Gillette, Don Carle. "Movies Defy Polls and Projections." Boxoffice 108 (November 10, 1975): 3.
Guest editorial in which Gillette discusses the attendance survey conducted by the Opinion Re earch Corporation for the MPAA.

422. _____. "Predicting Film Potentials." Boxoffice, 109 (February 14, 1977): 2.

423. Gilstad, David S. "An Evaluation of American Feature Film Age Suitability, Quality, and Popularity: 1965-1967." Unpublished M. S. thesis, Ohio University, 1968.
One-third of the films analyzed were considered unsuitable for "young people"; the opinion of critics and audience, for the most part, found the films to be "fair"-to-"good" in quality, with only 10 percent rated as "poor"; a consistent pattern of higher popularity accompanying higher quality was found.

424. Giltrow, David Roger. "Young Tanzanians and the Cinema: A Study of the Effects of Selected Basic Motion Picture Elements and Population Characteristics on Filmic Comprehension of Tanzanian Adolescent Primary School Children." Unpublished Ph. D. dissertation, Syracuse University, 1973.
Researches the question: which movie variables are most completely comprehended and which population variables influence comprehension; 1,276 11 to 19 year olds wrote responses to a film and these responses were content analyzed.

425. Giraud, Jean. "Quelques Aspects du Rapport Entre le Cinéma et un Type d'Adolescents: l'Elève du Centre d'Apprentissage" (Some Aspects of the Relationship Between the Cinema and a Certain Type of Adolescent: The Trade-School Pupil); Paper presented at the Second International Congress of Filmology, Paris, 1955.
Reports frequency of attendance, habits, and preferences for movies among students.

426. Girodo, M. "Film-Induced Arousal, Information Search, and the Attribution Process." Journal of Personality and Social Psychology 25 (1973): 357-360.
An examination, by experimental method, of misattribution of an internal state and exposure to a movie (Un Chien Andalou).

427. Glogauer, Werner. "Sozialpsychologische Aspekte der Filmwirkung" (Sociopsychological Aspects of the Influence of the Cinema). Jugend und Film 2 (1957): 1-16.
Presentation of topics in need of research.

428. Goldberg, Albert Leonard. "The Effects of Two Types of Sound Motion Pictures on Attitudes of Adults Toward Minority Groups." Unpublished Ed. D. dissertation Indiana University, 1955.
A pretest-posttest experiment found that among the 304 adult subjects participating, a significant attitude change occurred for the black and white "realistic" film but not for the color, abstract design film; data were also analyzed by age, education, religion, and sex of the subjects.

429. _____. "The Effects of Two Types of Sound Motion Pictures on the Attitudes of Adults Toward Minorities." Journal of Educational Sociology 29 (May 1956): 386-391.
A summary of the author's dissertation.

430. Goldberg, Herman D. "The Role of 'Cutting' in the Perception of the Motion Picture." Journal of Applied Psychology 35 (February 1951): 70-71.
Through use of 147 undergraduates' responses to a questionnaire the meaning of a movie was analyzed under two different conditions.

431. Goldmann, Annie. "Quelques Problemès de Sociologie du Cinéma" (Problems in the Sociology of Cinema). Sociologie et Societés 8 (April 1976): 71-80.
Discussion of issues in need of research attention.

432. Goldstein, Jeffrey H., Ralph L. Rosnow, Tamas Raday, Irwin Silverman, and George D. Gaskell. "Punitiveness in Responses to Films Varying in Content: A Cross-National Field Study of Aggression." European Journal of Social Psychology 5 (1975): 149-165.
Punitiveness in male movie-goers in four cities was measured before or after they attended films varying in content; at aggressive films there was an increase in punitiveness, while a reduction in punitiveness was found at neutral movies; sexual films led to smaller increases in punitiveness than aggressive pictures.

433. Goldstein, Michael J., Robert B. Jones, Theodore L. Clemens, Glenn W. Flagg, and Franz C. Alexander. "Coping Style as a Factor in Psychophysiological Response to a Tension-Arousing Film." Journal of Personality and Social Psychology 1 (April 1965): 290-302.
A group of psychiatric outpatients and a group of volunteers who were not seeking psychiatric help were exposed twice to Wages of Fear at one-week intervals.

434. Goldstein, M.J. and H. Kant. "Exposure to Pornography and Sexual Behavior in Deviant and Normal Groups." Technical Reports of the U.S. Commission on Obscenity and Pornography, vol. 7. Washington, D.C.: U.S. Government Printing Office, 1970.
Interview responses of 52 customers of adult bookstores and adult movie theaters were compared with responses (to the same interview questions) from 53 control subjects; the two groups were fairly similar in terms of a variety of demographic variables except that the consumers of erotic materials tended to be better educated and had higher level occupations.

435. Goldwyn, Samuel. "Hollywood Is Sick." Saturday Evening Post 213 (July 13, 1940): 18-19, 44, 48-49.
A partisan discussion of the public's preference for the double bill at movies based on data gathered by the Gallup organization; results of preliminary surveys show that "three out of every four potential movie patrons do not want double bills."

436. Goncalves, S. "Consideracões sobre a Crianca e o Cinema" (Considerations Concerning the Child and the Cinema). Crianca Portuguesa 2 (1943); 137-146.
Summary of various studies which have examined the influence of movies on children; film-type preferences are discussed and film suitability for viewing guidelines are suggested.

437. Gontermann, H.E. "Kind und Kino. Neue Betrachtungsmethoden" (The Children and the Cinema. A New Method of Observation). Padagogische Welt 4 (1950): 432.

438. Gonzalez, Paulino and Antonio Ramos. (Thematic Expectations in Movies Viewed by Young Workers Integrated in Formal Groups). Revista del Instituto de la Juventud 42 (August 1972): 9-31.
Examination of film-type preferences as related to age, school grade level, status, and socio-economic level.

439. Goodman, David J. "Comparative Effectiveness of Pictorial Teaching

Aids: An Experimental Investigation in Safety Education at the Elementary-School Level." Unpublished Ph.D. dissertation, New York University, 1942.
Silent films were most effective while sound and silent film slides were both superior to sound movies in all but one instance.

440. _____. "Experimental Research in Audio-Visual Education." Educational Screen 22 (February 1943): 65, 75.
An abstract of Janey Evelyn Haneline's M.S. thesis is presented.

441. _____. "Comparative Effectiveness of Pictorial Teaching Aids: An Experimental Investigation in Safety Education at the Elementary-School Level." Journal of Experimental Education 12 (September 1943): 20-25.
A summary of the author's dissertation.

442. Goodman, Ezra. "Are the Movies a Menace?" Coronet, July 1948, pp. 35-50.
A review of 12 charges against Hollywood and response to these charges by social commentators and some empirical literature.

443. Gorney, Sondra. "The Puppet and the Moppet." Hollywood Quarterly 1 (1945-1946): 371-375.
A non-quantitative discussion of film content appropriate for children.

444. Gould, Kenneth M. "Cinepatriotism." Social Forces 7 (September 1928): 120-129.
An advocacy piece in which it is suggested that "provincialism and authoritarianism are the twin idols of the movie ritual."

445. Gratiot-Alphandery, H. "Jeunes Spectateurs" (Young Audience). Revue Internationale de Filmologie 2 (1951, nos. 7-8): 257-263.
Results of a questionnaire assessing the reactions of 210 four to six year olds.

446. _____. "L'Enfant et le Film" (The Child and the Film). Revue Internationale de Filmologie 3 (1952): 222-223.
Discussion of areas for investigation.

447. Grau, Robert. "The 'Talking' Picture and the Drama." Scientific American, August 12, 1911, pp. 155-156.
An optimistic view of the movies, the talkies, and the audience.

448. Gray, Barbara. "The Social Effects of the Film." Sociological Review 42 (1950): 135-144.
Review of literature concerning the effect of film on children's emotions, imitation behavior, and delinquency; demographic attributes of audience composition are presented.

449. _____. "The Social Effects of the Film." Sociological Review 42 (1950): 12.
Survey of 300 Birmingham children; reports frequency of attendance, attendance unit and attendance unit preferences, and the relationship between movie-going and juvenile delinquency.

450. _____. "Enfants et Adolescents Devant les Films" (Children and Adolescents at the Cinema). Revue Internationale de Filmologie 3 (1952); 193-210.

A review of research on the influence of movies; reports frequency of attendance, film-type preferences, and social and emotional effects.

451. Greadington, Barbara A. Gant. "The Effect of Black Films on the Self-Esteem of Black Adolescents." Unpublished Ph.D. dissertation, University of Miami, 1977.
A single exposure to films portraying black performers in stereotypic and nonstereotypic roles did not significantly affect the self-esteem of black adolescents.

452. Gredler, Yvonne Singleton. "The Effects of Film and Discussion on Facilitating Shift in Kohlberg's Stages of Moral Development Among Adolescents." Unpublished Ph.D. dissertation, University of South Carolina, 1976.
An experiment involving 108 middle school pupils; results showed that exposure through film and discussion led to greater gains than discussion alone.

453. Greene, Nelson L. "Motion Pictures in the Classroom." Annals of the American Academy of Political and Social Science 217 (November 1926): 122-130.
A discussion of the use, advantages, and disadvantages of movies in school.

454. Greenwald, D. "Galvanic Changes in Clinical Patients Resulting from the Motion Picture Situation." Unpublished M.A. thesis, State University of Iowa, 1933.
Psychogalvanic recordings of 50 psychopathic individuals were made and the results compared to those of a previous study involving normal individuals; marked variations from the normal in amplitude and frequency of response were found.

455. Greenwald, D.U. "Some Galvanic Responses of Psychopathic Individuals." Proceedings of the Iowa Academy of Science 40 (1933): 194-195.
A summary of the author's M.A. thesis.

456. Gregorio, Domenico De. "Cinema and Television Audiences in Italy." Gazette 11 (1965, no. 1): 68-81.
A literature review comparing the size and preferences of cinema and television audiences in Italy.

457. Gregory, John Robert. "Some Psychological Aspects of Motion Picture Montage." Unpublished Ph.D. dissertation, University of Illinois, 1961.
Results suggest that the dynamics of cognitive interaction occurring when film shots are placed in succession is valid.

458. Griffith, Hubert. "Films and the British Public." Nineteenth Century 112 (August 1932): 190-200.
Recounts the experience of a drama critic who observed the making of one film; occasional anecdotal asides concerning audiences and their film tastes.

459. Gritcin, V.N. "Molodez i Kino. Opyt Analiza Cennostnyh Orientacij Molodez na Kinematograf" (Youth and Pictures. An Analytical Essay of Youth Valuable Orientations with Cinema). Sociologiceskie Problemy Kul'tury (1976): 61-77.

460. Groder, Ursula. "Das Filmerlebnis und seine Pädagogische Vertiefung. Erfahrungsberichte zum Film 'Es est Mitternacht, Dr. Schweitzer' " (Cinematographic Experience and its Educational Elaboration. A Record of Activities Organized in Connection with the Film "It's Midnight, Dr. Schweitzer"). Film, Jugend, Schule 14 (July 1955). Survey of 17 teachers and the activities they used as well as their perception of pupils' understanding of the film.

461. Grofer, Edward. "Attitude Changes Effected by an Industrially Produced Education Film." Unpublished M.A. thesis, University of Iowa, 1959.

462. Guillemaut, J. "Cinéma et Délinquance" (Movies and Delinquency). Annales Medico-Psychologiques 2 (1967): 808 (Report presented at the Journée Nationale de Pedo-Psychiatrie, October 1967). Asserts that by themselves films do not cause juvenile delinquency and that, in fact, movies may have a reeducative potential that may help prevent delinquency.

463. Gundlach, Ralph H. "The Movies: Stereotypes or Realities?" Journal of Social Issues 3 (Summer 1947): 26-32. Content analysis demonstrates that most motion pictures tend to romanticize life by one of three themes; implications for the viewer are suggested.

464. Hadsell, Reign S. "Effects of Films and Reading and Test Materials on Attitudes Toward Due Process of Law." Unpublished Ph.D. dissertation, Yale University, 1954.

465. Haefner, D.P. "Some Effects of Guilt-Arousing and Fear-Arousing Persuasive Communications on Opinion Change." Technical Report No. 1, Office of Naval Research, University of Rochester, 1956. Contract no. Non-668. Different movie soundtracks that were designed to incite fear or guilt produced changes on other mood factors as well.

466. Hafeez, M.A. "Psychology of Films." Journal of Education and Psychology 8 (1950): 14-22. An advocacy piece suggesting that movies lean toward the "bad" side and that contemporary pictures are aimed at "crude emotions."

467. Hahn, H. "On the Application of Psychotechnical Valuation to a Publicity Film." Sovetskaia Psikhotekhnika 5 (1932): 63-64. A film advertising pharmaceutical products was shown to 100 persons; analysis of the data showed that the film was not influential in adding to the "good name" of the product.

468. Hale, Gordon A., Leon K. Miller, and Harold W. Stevenson. "Incidental Learning of Film Content: A Developmental Study." Child Development 39 (1968): 69-77. Incidental learning from a motion picture increased between 3-6th graders; girls had higher scores than boys in all grades.

469. Haley, Jay. "The Appeal of the Moving Picture." Quarterly of Film, Radio and Television 6 (1952): 361-374. An analysis of the reasons for the popularity of movies; reviews

470. Hall, John. "Who Goes to the Cinema?" New Society, November 25, 1976, p. 411.
Review of attendance data in Great Britain including reasons for attendance and non-attendance.

471. Hall, Mordaunt. "The Theatergoer's Reaction to the Audible Picture as It Was and Now." Journal of the Society of Motion Picture Engineers 24 (May 1935): 424-431.
An impressionistic account.

472. Hamilton, James W. "Cinematic Neurosis: A Brief Case Report." Journal of the American Academy of the Psychoanalysis 6 (1978): 569-572.
Presents case material concerning a patient who overidentified with the central character in The Exorcist.

473. Handel, Leo A. "Studies of the Motion Picture Audience." New York: Motion Picture Research Bureau, 1942.

474. _____. "This Thing Called Audience Research." Hollywood Reporter, 1946 Anniversary Edition, n. p.
Discussion of the development and function of audience research in the film industry.

475. _____. "Radio, Movies, Publications Increase Each Other's Audience." Printers' Ink, July 19, 1946, pp. 42-43.
Summary of research showing a positive correlation between radio listening, reading, and movie-going; data are presented for all adults and by sex.

476. _____. "The Social Obligation of Motion Pictures." International Journal of Opinion and Attitude Research 4 (December 1947): 93-98.
A review of and response to Ruth A. Inglis' Freedom of the Movies.

477. _____. "A Study to Determine the Drawing Power of Male and Female Stars Upon Movie-Goers of Their Own Sex." International Journal of Opinion and Attitude Research 5 (Summer 1948): 215-220.
Results of a study involving 100 persons who were interviewed by a psychologist; 65 percent showed a preference for stars of their own sex which is explained in terms of "self-identification."

478. _____. "Hollywood Market Research." Quarterly of Film, Radio and Television 7 (Spring 1953): 304-310.
Discussion of reasons why Hollywood has done so little audience research and a review of some of the few studies.

479. Haneline, Janey Evelyn. "The Effect of Two Sound Slide-Films on the Development of Desirable Social Attitudes." Unpublished M. A. thesis, George Peabody College for Teachers, 1940.
Experimental study involving 122 high school pupils; results suggest the effectiveness of films for teaching desirable social attitudes.

480. Hansen, John Elmore. "The Effect of Educational Motion Pictures Up-

on the Retention of Informational Learning." *Journal of Experimental Education* 2 (September 1933): 1-4.
An experiment in which it was found that nearly 200 seventh to twelfth graders gained and retained knowledge presented by a film.

481. _____. "A Study of the Comparative Effectiveness of Three Methods of Using Motion Pictures in Teaching (I)." *Educational Screen* 19 (February 1940): 55-57, 74-76.
Reviews the literature and lays out the procedures for a study inquiring as to the factual information gained from films and pupils' ability to apply the knowledge to new situations.

482. _____. "A Study of the Comparative Effectiveness of Three Methods of Using Motion Pictures in Teaching (II)." *Educational Screen* 19 (March 1940): 97-98.
Results of the experiment are reported.

483. Harap, Henry. "The Motion Picture as Communication." *Social Education* 7 (1943): 19-21.
Informal discussion of emotional response to movies and their effect on conduct and attitudes.

484. Hardgrave, R. L., Jr. "Film and Society in Tamilnadu." *Monthly Public Opinion Surveys* 15 (March-April 1970).

485. Harivelle, J. "L'Enfant au Cinéma; Spectateur et Sujet d'Étude" (The Child at the Cinema; Spectator and Subject of Study). *Le Populaire du Centre*, January 1952.

486. Hart, W. A. "Een Inleidend Onderzoek tot het Probleem Film en Jeugd" (A Preliminary Investigation of the Problem of Film and Youth). *Nederlands Tijdschrift voor de Psychologie en haar Grensgebieden* 8 (1953); 163-200.
Frequency of movie attendance and film-type preferences among 1,000 Dutch school children.

487. Haskett, Hazel Berniece. "An Exploration of the Concepts of Secondary School Boys and Girls Concerning the Roles of Parents in Family Living as Indicated by Their Responses to Certain Family Situations in Selected Motion Pictures." Unpublished Ed. D. dissertation, New York University, 1952.
Two questionnaires elicited students' reactions to film portrayals of family life and sex role behavior.

488. Hauser, Arnold. "Notes on the Sociology of the Film." *Life and Letters Today*, December 1938, pp. 80-87.
A nonempirical analysis.

489. Hauser, Philip M. "How do Motion Pictures Affect the Conduct of Children?" *Journal of Educational Sociology* 6 (December 1932): 231-237.
Description of the study, sample, and methods of gathering data; results are not presented.

490. Hawel, W. "Untersuchung Zweier Verschiedener Filmdarbietungen als Psychologische Ursache für Emotionalen Stress" (Investigation of Two Different Film Presentations as the Psychological Cause of Emotional Stress). *Psychologie und Praxis* 14 (July 1970): 125-133.

A black and white film with murder as part of its content evoked greater and longer-lasting emotional stress than a color film containing mood scenes which produced a euphoric effect.

491. Hawkins, Robert P. "Learning of Peripheral Content in Films: A Developmental Study." Child Development 44 (March 1973): 214-217.
Third, 5th, 7th, and 9th grade children were tested on knowledge of film content; learning of content incidental to the plot of the film declined at grade 9 for an adult film but increased for a children's film; high interest in the film was associated with greater peripheral learning.

492. Heiby, Elaine and James D. Becker. "Effect of Filmed Modeling on the Self-Reported Frequency of Masturbation." Archives of Sexual Behavior 9 (April 1980): 115-121.
A pretest-posttest study with a control group; effects of a female masturbation modeling film on the attitudes and frequency of masturbation among 24 female undergraduates.

493. Heindel, R. Heathcote. "American Attitudes of British School Children." School and Society 46 (December 25, 1937): 838-840.
Results of a study involving 1,000 responses to a questionnaire inquiring as to pupils' sources of information about the U.S.; findings indicate that the cinema was the most frequently mentioned source of information.

494. Heinrich, Karl. "Traumfabrik und Jugendträume. Eine Filmpsychologische Studie" (Dream Factors and Juvenile Dreams. A Psychological Study of the Film). Film-Bild-Ton 6 and 7 (1953): 221-227, 258-264.
Study of compositions written by 363 pupils as inspired by three movie posters depicting three types of films.

495. Heisler, Florence A. "Characteristics of Elementary-School Children Who Read Comic Books, Attend the Movies, and Prefer Serial Radio Programs." Unpublished Ph.D. dissertation, New York University, 1944.

496. _____. "A Comparison of the Movie and Non-Movie Goers of the Elementary School." Journal of Educational Research 41 (March 1948): 541-546.
Survey of 600 second to eighth graders; reports frequency of attendance by grade and respondents' score on mental maturity, achievement, and personality measures.

497. _____. "A Comparison Between Those Elementary School Children Who Attend Moving Pictures, Read Comic Books and Listen to Serial Radio Programs to an Excess, with Those Who Indulge in These Activities Seldom or not at All." Journal of Educational Research 42 (November 1948): 182-190.
Comparison of 600 first through eighth graders on dimensions such as chronological and mental age, educational achievment, family socio-economic status, social adjustment, and personal adjustment.

498. Heisler, Gerald H. "The Effects of Vicariously Experiencing Supernatural-Violent Events: A Case Study of The Exorcist's Impact." Journal of Individual Psychology 31 (November 1975): 158-170.

Subjects who saw The Exorcist, as compared to subjects who saw no movie and subjects who saw another popular film, left the theater believing significantly more in mystical events, were more pessimistic about their ability to change events in their lives, and were more fearful of things they did not understand.

499. Helier, Daniel. "Kinden Bioscoop. De Juiste Verhouding" (Children and the Cinema. The Golden Mean). Het Kind 1 (January-February 1952): 31-44.
Summary of reports which have researched attendance habits and the influence of movies on children.

500. Hellwing, Albert. "Cinematógrafo y Criminología" (Moving Pictures and Criminology). Revista de Criminología, Psiquiatría y Medicina Legal 17 (1930): 224-237.
A literature review.

501. Hennebelle, M. and G. Hennebelle. "Cinéma et Société au Maghreb." Annales Africaines Nord 12 (1973): 131-150.

502. Henry, Ralph L. "The Cultural Influence of the Talkies." School and Society 29 (February 29, 1929): 149-150.
An advocacy piece offering a pessimistic prediction.

503. Herbener, Gerald Frederick. "Perceived Similarities Between the Personalities of Viewers and Characters of Television and Film Drama." Unpublished Ph.D. dissertation, Ohio University, 1974.
Responses to a questionnaire by 28 individuals; investigated the attribution process of viewers to media characters.

504. Herman, Ginette and Jacques-Philippe Leyens. "Rating Films on TV." Journal of Communication 27 (Autumn 1977): 48-53.
Results of a four year study investigating movies on Belgian television that carry advisory warnings regarding film content; films with warnings were viewed more often than those without warnings.

505. Hernandez, Andres R. "Filmmaking and Politics: The Cuban Experience." American Behavioral Scientist 17 (January-February 1974): 360-392.
Includes a brief discussion of the movie audience in Cuba.

506. Hershey, Lenore. "What Women Think of the Movies." McCall's 94 (May 1967): 28, 124.
Responses by 12,000 McCall's readers to a survey; movie-going habits, film favorites, and complaints about movies are reported.

507. Hess, Philip Joseph. "An Experimental Study of the Relationship Between a Conscious and an Unconscious Measure of Audience Response to a Motion Picture Film." Unpublished M.A. thesis, State University of Iowa, 1960.
Experiment comparing the push button with the electrodermal (galvanic skin) response methods involving 32 female undergraduates.

508. Hester, Al. "Opinions Concerning Motion Pictures and Their Influence in a Large Mexican City." Paper presented at the Popular Culture Association conference, April 1980, Detroit, MI.
A pilot study exploring movie-going habits, film-type preferences, and opinions concerning movies and their effects on behavior; a 60-question survey was used.

509. Heucke, Almut. "Zur Gefühlsansprechbarkeit von Verwahrlosten Weiblichen Jugendlichen: Ein Studie auf Grund von Filmgesprächen in einem Mädchenheim" (Emotional Sensitivity of Neglected Female Adolescents: A Study Based on Talks About Movies in a Girls' Home). Praxis der Kinderpsychologie und Kinderpsychiatrie 20 (March 1971): 67-71.
Examined the emotional sensitivity of six 18-19 year old girls; findings indicated that the girls were more or less emotionally moved by the four films shown to them.

510. Heuyer, Georges. "Apport de la Psychiatrie à la Filmologie" (Contributions of Psychiatry to Filmology). Revue Internationale de Filmologie 3 (1952): 216-217.
Brief note on the psychological effects of movies.

511. _____. "Observation sur les Enfants Inadaptés" (Observation of Maladjusted Children). Revue Internationale de Filmologie 3 (1952): 217-219.
Study of children aged 7 to 17; reactions to comedies and cartoons, the relationship between affective states and their reactions, and their comprehension of films.

512. _____. "Influence Immédiatement Décelable du Film à Partir de 10 Ans. Recontre Internationale d'Experts sur les Aspects Psychologiques, Techniques et Sociaux des Problèmes du Cinéma et de la Jeunesse, Luxembourg" (The Immediately Discernable Influence of the Cinema from the Age of 10 Upwards. International Meeting of Experts to Consider the Psychological, Technical and Social Aspects of Problems Concerning the Cinema and Young People, Luxembourg). Geneva: Fraternité Mondiale, 1955, 12 pages (stencilled).
Discussion of children's understanding of and affective responses to movies; suggests physiological measurements are needed so as to better understand psychological responses to films.

513. _____. "Cinéma et Affectivité" (Cinema and Emotion). L'Ecole des Parents, January 1956, pp. 15-27.
Summary of studies conducted by the author and his colleagues; reviews findings on psychiatric patients' (children) understanding of film content and reactions to different types of films.

514. _____ and Serge Lebovici. "Troubles du Caractère et Cinéma" (Character Disturbances and the Cinema). Psyche, Revue Internationale des Sciences de l'Homme et de Psychanalyse 11 (1947): 1, 106.
An examination of the relationship between children's emotional disturbances and movies they have seen.

515. _____. "Influence Immédiatement Décelable du Film à Partir de l'Age de 10 Ans" (Immediately Detectable Influence of Film from Age 10 Years On). Presse Médicale 50 (1955): 1058-1060.

516. _____, and G. Amado. "Enquête Filmologique chez les Enfants et Adolescents Inadaptés" (Film Survey of Maladjusted Children and Adolescents). Revue Internationale de Filmologie 2 (1949, no. 5): 57-64.
Responses to a questionnaire by psychiatric clinic patients.

517. _____, Serge Lebovici, and L. Bertagna. "Sur Quelques Réactions

d'Enfants Inadaptés" (Some Reactions of Maladjusted Children). Revue Internationale de Filmologie 3 (January-March 1952): 71-79. Reactions of 22 7 to 17 year olds to comedy, cartoon, adventure, gangster, and animal films; children were psychiatric patients; reactions measured by observation during the films and by questions asked afterwards.

518. _____, Serge Lebovici, and L. Bertagna. "Recherches Experimentales Filmologiques; Comprehension et Réactions des Enfants Débiles et Caractérials" (Experimental Studies of Motion Pictures; Comprehension and Reactions of Feebleminded and Character Disturbed Children). Revue Française de Psychanalyse 3 (1955): 1-4.

519. Hibben, Paxton. "The Movies in Russia." The Nation 121 (November 11, 1925): 539-540.
An impressionistic account of the Soviet film industry with brief mention of the audience.

520. Hickey, Florence E. "Children's Interests in Moving Pictures, Radio Programs, and Voluntary Book Reading." Unpublished M.S. thesis, Boston University, 1948.
Survey of 324 fourth, fifth, and sixth graders; data are presented by grade level, chronological and mental age, reading level, and sex; frequency of attendance and interest in numerous film-types reported.

521. Hirsch, Richard S. "Moving Attitudes with Moving Pictures." Educational Screen 28 (December 1949): 446-447, 460.
High school students' attitude toward Shakespearean plays measured by a pretest-posttest questionnaire; following exposure to Shakespearean films the experimental group's attitude shifted to a significantly more positive position.

522. Hoffman, Bernd-Wolfgang. "An Experimental Study of Learning and Attitude Change Through Film and of Effects of Music-Montage Interludes in a Film." Unpublished M.S. thesis, University of Wisconsin, 1979.
A pretest-posttest involving 161 high school students; music-montage had no general effect on attitudes and did not influence learning from films.

523. Hoffmann, A. "Das Filmerlebnis" (The Cinema Experience). Zeitschrift für Pädagogische Psychologie und Jugendkunde 39 (1938): 188-203.

524. Hoffmann, Hermann. "Das Problem der Reizüberflutung. Bericht über die Ergebnisse einer Testvorführung des Films 'Die Feuerspringer von Montana'" (The Problem of Excessively Sensational Films. Results of an Experimental Screening of the Film "Die Feuerspringer von Montana"). Film, Jugend, Schule 9 (July 1954).
Study of the psychological effects of a film on 28 10 to 14 year olds; analyses made on the basis of compositions and drawings made by the children.

525. Holaday, Perry Ward. "The Effect of Motion Pictures on the Intellectual Content of Children." Unpublished Ph.D. dissertation, State University of Iowa, 1930.
Pretest-posttest experiment; concludes that general knowledge of

both children and adults is increased by movies; reports data on memory of specific incidents in the film and types of action best remembered.

526. Holdridge, David Ross. "High Versus Low Camera Angle in Film Production as a Factor Influencing Viewers' Predictions of Performance." Unpublished Ph. D. dissertation, Syracuse University, 1974.
Personal attributes, characteristics, and gestures of an actor were the most important factors influencing observers' perception of the actors' performance in three competitive activities; camera angle was less important than the above variables.

527. Hoover, William Franklin. "Replicating Photographic Lighting Effects to Elicit Certain Conditioned Responses in Motion Picture Audiences." Unpublished Ed. D. dissertation, Wayne State University, 1970.
Purpose of the study was to develop a methodology for using audience opinion to dictate lighting arrangement to achieve various lighting effects; teenagers made up the sample.

528. Horn, A. "The Influence of Age Upon Movie Scores in a Rural Community." Unpublished M. A. thesis, Columbia University, 1927.

529. Horton, Donald and R. Richard Wohl. "Mass Communication and Para-Social Interaction." Psychiatry 19 (1956): 215-229.
Discussion and analysis of the illusion of face-to-face relationships between spectator and mass media performer; presentation of the role of the audience, coaching of audience attitudes, conditions for acceptance of the para-social role by the audience, and the values of this interaction for the audience.

530. Houston, Penelope. "Box Office." Sight and Sound 44 (Winter 1974/75): 23.
Brief note reporting an increase in attendance in Britain and suggesting reasons for this.

531. "How Children are Entertained." Journal of Education, February 25, 1915, pp. 207, 212.
Discussion of frequency of attendance among Portland children; speculation regarding the movies as social centers and the influence of movies on the children's lives; advocates that theaters should offer "films of high educational value."

532. "How the New TV Forms Affect Movie-going." Media Science Newsletter 3 (May 15-31, 1979): 2.

533. "How People Spend Their Time." Broadcasting, January 6, 1958, p. 36.
Results of a Sindlinger and Co. survey of persons 12 years of age and older; number of hours spent attending to various media reported.

534. Howe, Frederic C. "Leisure." Survey 31 (January 5, 1914): 415-416.
An editorial by the director of the People's Institute (NY) advocating that leisure activities "must be controlled by the community" rather than by commercial forces.

535. _____. "What to do with the Motion-Picture Show: Shall it be Censored?" Outlook, June 20, 1914, pp. 412-416.
Anecdotal reports on the effect of movies on audiences; lengthy discussion of the organization, standards of judgment, and difficulty in applying these standards by the National Board of Censorship of Motion Pictures.

536. Howitt, Dennis and Guy Cumberbatch. "Affective Feeling for a Film Character and Evaluation of an Anti-Social Act." British Journal of Social and Clinical Psychology 11 (June 1972): 102-108.
Results of an experiment using self-report measures of adolescent boys and girls showed that positive affect for a film character did not influence the subjects to be more favorably disposed toward the anti-social behavior of the character.

537. Hoyt, Howard Rush. "Audience Reaction to Selected Film Techniques with Respect to Demographic Background." Unpublished M.S. thesis, University of Oregon, 1972.
An experiment involving 51 undergraduates; use of an audience analyzer and questionnaire; variables include: age, sex, movie-going habits, and liberal attitudinal predisposition.

538. Hudson, David D. "The Effects of Censorship and Uniqueness Motivation on the Valuation of Sexually Explicit Messages." Paper presented at the Speech Communication Association conference, November 1980, New York, NY.
An experiment involving undergraduates; sexually explicit films were valued less in conditions of restriction than in conditions of approval.

539. Hudson, Octavia. "Audience Racial Composition and Interaction as Determinants of the Appeal of Black Films to Whites." Unpublished Ph.D. dissertation, Harvard University, 1979.
Observation of audiences and questionnaires used with 170 moviegoers at suburban and metropolitan theaters to explore the hypothesis that movie-going may be a possible means for whites to satisfy an individual need to evaluate ambiguous opinions.

540. Hughes, A. G. "London Children and the Cinema." London City Council, 1951.

541. Hughes, Bertha B. "Results of a Motion-Picture Survey." Educational Screen 2 (September 1923): 324-329.
5,000 school children in grades five through high school participated; data reported include frequency of attendance, film-type preferences, favorite actors, attendance unit, and reasons for attendance.

542. Hulett, J. E., Jr. "Estimating the Net Effect of a Commercial Motion Picture Upon the Trend of Local Public Opinion." American Sociological Review 14 (April 1949): 263-275.
Using a modified panel technique the trend of public opinion regarding medical treatment for polio as portrayed in Sister Kenny was measured; results indicated that the film was an ineffectual propaganda instrument.

543. _____. "Comments on Mr. Zeisel's Note." American Sociological Review 14 (August 1949): 551-552.
A rejoinder to Hans Zeisel's reanalysis of the original data.

544. Hull, Charles and Harold Stark. "The Response of the Deaf or Blind Child to Talking Motion Pictures." American Annals of the Deaf 87 (September 1942): 318-330.
The reactions of children 14 to 18 years old to seven commerical movies were gathered by means of a questionnaire; data reported include learning from the films, affective response to the films, and analysis of filmic messages.

545. Humphrey, John. "Emotional Reactions to Abstract Motion on Film." Unpublished M. A. thesis, University of Southern California, 1950.

546. _____. "Emotional Reactions to Abstract Motion on Film." Journal of the University Film Association 6 (Spring 1950): 11-12.

547. Hungerford, Chris. "A Survey of Los Angeles Theater Attendance of Two Motion Pictures Which were Advertised on Television." Unpublished M. A. thesis, University of Southern California, 1955.
A survey was distributed to patrons attending two movies at eleven theaters over a one week period; drive-in theater audiences were affected to a larger extent than house theater audiences by television commercials.

548. Ikuta, M. "Mass Communication no Baitai to Shite no Eiga-sono Tokushitsu Nitsuite" (The Motion Picture as a Medium of Mass Communication). Hogaku Kenkyu 29 (September 1956): 1-18.

549. Ines, Doroteo. "Influence of Motion Pictures Upon Sunday School Children (Ages 11-17) of Christian Churches in Los Angeles, California." Unpublished M. A. thesis, University of Southern California, 1938.

550. International Educational Cinematographic Institute. "The Social Aspects of the Cinema." Monograph no. 5. Rome: I. E. C. I., 1928.

551. _____. "The Effect of the Cinema on the Sight." Monograph no. 10. Rome: I. E. C. I., 1929.

552. _____. "The Cinematograph and Hygiene." Monograph no. 15. Rome: I. E. C. I., 1930.

553. "International Survey, Conference of Filmology." Revue Internationale de Filmologie 2 (1949, no. 5): 13-20.
Reports on key issues in the study of film-audience relations.

554. Institut International de Cooperation Intellectuelle. "Le Cinéma et le Gout du Public, Eléments d'Enquête Internationale" (The Cinema and the Public, Preliminary Results of an International Inquiry). Paris: I. I. C. I., 1940.

555. Irgens, Hans R. "Filmseende och Mognad" (Reactions to Films and Maturity). Unpublished M. A. thesis, Goteborg, 1958.
Pilot study in which the affective responses of 42 high school students to Avant le Déluge were measured.

556. Itkyal, N. L. "Report on Cinema and the Public: A Pilot Survey of Audience Reaction in Greater Bombay." Bombay: Central Board of Film Censors, 1958 (stencilled).

557. "It's Film Plot, Not Star, That Attracts Moviegoers." Science Digest 43 (May 1958): 21.
Results of a nationwide study of the habits of movie-goers conducted by the Opinion Research Corp.; demographic data, frequency of attendance, reasons for attendance, and the salience of selected variables to film choice decisions.

558. Iuritski, N. "Znachenie Kino Dlia Detei" (The Significance of the Cinema to Children). Semia i Shkola 7 (July 1948): 27-28.
An advocacy piece suggesting that children's identification with film characters can be beneficial to character building with proper guidance.

559. Jacob, Jean N. "La Compréhension du Langage Cinématographique par les Enfants" (Childrens' Comprehension of Movie Language). International Review of Applied Psychology 18 (1969): 199-227.
Using 9-11 year old boys with various socioeconomic backgrounds this study found significant differences in understanding of film language between the subjects.

560. Janowitz, Morris and Robert Schulze. "Trends in Mass Communications Research." World Congress of Sociology, Transactions 3 (1959): 129-149.
Literature review using Lasswell's "who says what to whom with what effects" as its organizational scheme.

561. Janssen, C. "Notities uit de Provincie." Skoop 15 (September 1979): 22.
Geographical segmentation of audience attendance in the Netherlands during 1978.

562. Japan, Ministry of Education. "Seishonen no Eiga-Kogyo Kanran-jokyo Chosa Gaiyo, Jo" (Summary of Surveys on Film-viewing by Children and Adolescents, vol. 1). Tokyo: Ministry of Education, Social Education Bureau, 1929. (Data for Research on Educational Films, series 3).
Summary of data collected by survey in 1927 of primary and secondary students in Tokyo and Osaka; cinema attendance was ascertained and analyzed by sex and year in school.

563. _____. "Seishonen no Eiga-Kogyo Kanran-jokyo Chosa Gaiyo, Chu" (Summary of Surveys on Film-viewing by Children and Adolescents, vol. 2). Tokyo: Ministry of Education, Social Education Bureau, 1930. (Data for Research on Educational Films, series 4).
Additional statistical data obtained in the 1927 surveys are presented including: types of theaters attended, film-type preferences, actors, and actresses preferred, and reasons for not going to the movies.

564. _____. "Seishonen no Eiga-Kogyo Kanran-jokyo Chosa Gaiyo, Ge" (Summary of Surveys on Film-viewing by Children and Adolescents, vol. 3). Tokyo: Ministry of Education, Social Education Bureau,

Random sample consisting of 3,107 individuals in which questionnaires and personal interviews were employed; frequency of attendance is reported in addition to film-type preferences; data are cross-tabulated by demographic characteristics.

1932. (Data for Research on Educational Films, series 8). Comparative analyses of the 1927 data.

565. _____. "Seishonen no Eiga-Kogyo Kanran-jokyo Chosa Gaiyo" (Summary of Surveys on Film-viewing by Children and Adolescents). Tokyo: Ministry of Education, Social Education Bureau, 1935. (Data for Research on Educational Films, series 11). Report of a survey conducted in ten Japanese cities in June 1934; similar data gathered as in the 1927 study.

566. Jarvie, I. C. "Film and the Communication of Values." Archives Europeennes de Sociologie 10 (1969): 205-219.
Advocates that movies cannot be blamed as the cause for such things as corruption of the public's taste or incitation to violence.

567. Jayne, Clarence D. "A Study of the Learning and Retention of Materials Presented by Lecture and by Silent Film." Journal of Educational Research 38 (September 1944): 47-58.
An experiment involving 271 high school freshmen; results suggest that increased learning was not due to the film experience alone, but rather to the integration of the film with other teaching procedures.

568. Jersild, A. T. "Radio and Motion Pictures." Yearbook National Social Studies Education 38 (1939, Part I): 153-173.
Survey of the findings of experimental research on radio listening at home and in the classroom, and commercial and educational movies.

569. Jessel, Oskar R. "Münchner Vorstadtkinder und Film" (Suburban Children of Munich and the Cinema). Jugend und Film, November 1956, pp. 1-12.
Responses to a questionnaire by 695 8 to 14 year olds; frequency of attendance, attendance unit, reasons for attendance, and film-type preferences are among the data reported.

570. Jester, Ralph. "Hollywood and Pedagogy." Journal of Educational Sociology 12 (November 1938): 137-141.
An advocacy piece suggesting that movies function very effectively, but haphazardly, as a form of social control, industry executives are largely indifferent to social implications of the medium, and that the industry has initiated a small scale movement to supply material designed for the classroom.

571. Jimenez de Asua, Luis. "Cinematógrafo y Delincuencia" (The Cinema and Delinquency). Revista de Criminología, Psiquiatría y Medicina Legal, May-June 1924, pp. 377-384.
Review of literature concluding that movies, like literature and art, are effective in suggesting crime; discussion of attempts at censorship as a preventative measure.

572. Jindal, Akalanka. "Sociological Research on Films." Sociological Bulletin 9 (September 1960): 56-72.
An overview of various areas in need of research including film and fashion, public taste, film and social disorganization; some literature is also reviewed.

573. Johnson, Brian R. "General Occurrence of Stressful Reactions to Com-

mercial Motion Pictures and Elements in Films Subjectively Identified as Stressors." Psychological Reports 47 (December 1980): 775-786.
Survey interview of two adult populations to determine the frequency with which movies produce clinically significant stress-type reactions.

574. Johnson, Keith F. "Cinema Advertising." Journal of Advertising 10 (1980, no. 4): 11-19.
Review of research; includes discussion of audience recall studies and patron attitude toward cinema advertising.

575. Johnson, Mark. "A Study of the Rendition and Suggestion of Motion in the Animated Film." Unpublished M. A. thesis, University of Southern California, 1977.

576. Johnston, William A. "The Structure of the Motion Picture Industry." Annals of the American Academy of Political and Social Science 128 (September 1926): 20-29.
Largely focused on industry-related aspects such as production and exhibition; brief mention of attendance data.

577. Johnstone, John W. C. "Social Context and Mass Media Reception." Studies in Public Communication 2 (1959): 25-30.
A nonempirical discussion of four levels of social aggregates as they influence interpretation of media messages.

578. Jolivet, Jean. "Le Temps au Cinéma" (Time in Films). Revue Internationale de Filmologie 1 (October 1948): 331-334.
A nonempirical analysis.

579. Jones, Dorothy B. "Quantitative Analysis of Motion Picture Content." Public Opinion Quarterly 6 (Fall 1942): 411-428.
Results of a content analysis with suggestion for the utility of the coding system for audience research.

580. Jones, Harold E. "Attendance at Moving Pictures as Related to Intelligence and Scholarship." Parent-Teacher, March 1928.
Results of a questionnaire completed by 2,200 grade and high school students; describes attendance patterns by age, sex, and rural versus urban home; slight significant relationship between frequency of attendance and both intelligence and scholarship; best and worst students attended somewhat less often; no cumulative effect of frequent attendance upon scholarship.

581. _____. "Children at the Movies: How Motion Pictures Form Social Attitudes." Journal of the American Association of University Women 27 (June 1934): 221-225.
A summary of studies conducted by the author and others.

582. _____. "Motion Pictures and Radio as Factors in Child Behavior." National Probation and Parole Association Yearbook (1947): 66-77.
Review of research on topics such as emotional interest and memory of movies, emotional and physical response to movies, and the effect of violence.

583. _____ and Herbert S. Conrad. "Rural Preferences in Motion Pictures." Journal of Social Psychology 1 (1930): 419-423.

Results of a field study inquiring as to film-type preferences and affective responses to movies.

584. _____, Herbert Conrad, and Aaron Horn. "Psychological Studies of Motion Pictures. II. Observation and Recall as a Function of Age." University of California Publications in Psychology 3 (August 18, 1928): 225-243.
Retention of information peaked for respondents 19 to 25 years and was lowest for 11 to 13 and 45 to 55 year olds.

585. Jones, Vernon. "Influence of Motion Pictures on Moral Attitudes of Children and the Permanence of the Influence." Psychological Bulletin 31 (1934): 725-726.
An experiment involving seventh graders; results indicated that children exposed to a film changed their attitude in the direction advocated by the film; a follow-up retest was conducted six months after the initial treatment.

586. Jorgensen, Rebekah Lee. "The Screening of America: The Use and Influences of American Films and Television Programs by Adolescents in a Romanian Community." Unpublished Ph.D. dissertation, Ohio State University, 1980.
Multiple methods were applied over six months; media decision-making in Bucharest was also examined; the popularity of American media among adolescents and their sources of information about the U.S. are reported.

587. Jowett, Garth S. "The First Motion Picture Audiences." Journal of Popular Film 3 (Winter 1974): 39-54.
Discussion of the reasons for the development of film audience, motives for attendance, and demographic characteristics.

588. Jump, Rev. Herbert A. "The Child's Leisure Hour--How it is Affected by the Motion Picture." Religious Education, October 1911, pp. 349-354.
A nonquantitative discussion of the social function and social influence of the movies; author states that "the motion picture is the cleanest form of popular entertainment being given indoors today."

589. Jurovsky Anton. "Variacie Filmoveho Zazitku u Mladeze" (Influence of Movies on Adolescents). Sbornik Praci Filosoficke Fakulty Brnenske University 11 (1962): 117-133.
Results of a questionnaire completed by 2,820 11 to 18 year olds; interest in movies did not differ by age; film-type preferences and differences by age are reported.

590. Kaiser, Charles and Robert Roessler. "Galvanic Skin Responses to Motion Pictures." Perceptual and Motor Skills 30 (April 1970): 371-374.
Experiment involving 20 male undergraduates; GSR measurements were taken during rest, during a bland, and during a stressful film.

591. Kantor, Bernard R. "Infrared Motion-Picture Technique in Observing Audience Reactions." Journal of the Society of Motion Picture and Television Engineers 64 (November 1955): 626-628.
Detailed description of installation and procedures; specifications for light sources, exposure, and development are noted.

592. Karsten, Anitra. "Lasten Elokuvissa Kayminen" (Cinema Habits of Finnish Children). Lapsi ja Nuoriso 7 (1955).
Study of frequency of attendance, attendance habits, and film-type preferences of school-age children in Helsinki; the study was conducted by the Finnish Central Union for Child Welfare.

593. Karsten, D. "Der Film im Weltbild unserer Jugend" (The Role of the Film in our Youth's Conception of the World). Film Forum, November 1951.

594. "Kartlegging av Kinobesokende i Oslo" (Survey of the Cinema Audience in Oslo). Markedskommunikasjon, 1979.

595. Katz, Elias. "A Brief Survey of the Use of Motion Pictures for the Treatment of Neuropsychiatric Patients." Psychiatric Quarterly 20 (1946): 204-216.
A literature review.

596. Katz, Elihu, Michael Gurevitch, and Hadassah Haas. "On the Use of the Mass Media for Important Things." American Sociological Review 38 (April 1973): 164-181.
In a large Israeli sample, media use was found to vary to serve various needs; films were found to help maintain friendship and served self-gratification and sociability functions.

597. Kaufman, Kenneth Alan. "Why do People Go to the Movies?--A Study of Motion Picture Attendance as a Socially Comfortable Activity." Unpublished M. A. thesis, University of Pennsylvania, 1973.
A weak connection was found between high anxiety, or uncomfortable situations, and the choice of film attendance (other choice alternatives included play, concert, sports events, and opera or ballet).

598. Keilhacker, Margarete. "Berechtigung und Wirksamkeit des Jugendverbotes in der Sicht der Jugend" (Youth Expresses its Viewpoint on Whether the Exclusion of Young People from some Films is Justifiable and Effective). Jugend und Film, January 1956, pp. 1-8.
Opinions by youngsters from two towns concerning the deleterious influence of movies and methods to regulate attendance.

599. Keilhacker, Margarete. "Zum Filmbesuch der 15-18j. Jugendlichen und seiner Methodischen Erfassung" (A Study of Cinema Attendance by 15-18 Year Olds and the Methods Used). Jugend und Film, September 1956, pp. 1-20.
Sample of 519 females from six schools reporting on their favorite films.

600. ———. "Zwei Hauptmotive des Filmbesuch der Fünfzehn- bis Achtzehnjährigen" (The Two Main Reasons for Cinema Attendance of Adolescents Between the Ages of Fifteen and Eighteen). Jugend, Film, Fernsehen 2 (1958): 1-14.
Summary of several studies involving some 3,000 pupils; questionnaire methodology.

601. Keilhacker, Martin. "Unsere Jugend und die Welt des Films" (Our Youth and the World of the Cinema). Vierteljahresschrift für Wissenschaftliche Pädagogik 4 (1951).

602. _____. "Das Filmerlebnis der Jugend" (Youth's Cinema Experience). Pädagogische Welt 6 (1952, no. 6): 259-263.

603. _____. "Le Cinéma et les Réactions des Enfants et des Adolescents" (Cinema and the Reactions of Children and Adolescents). Cahiers de Pedagogie de l'Université de Liège 14 (1955): 67-75.
Review of research on the differences in reactions to films between adolescents and children.

604. _____. "Die Filmeinflüsse bei Kinder und Jugendlichen und die Problematik ihrer Feststellung" (The Influence of the Cinema on Children and Adolescents, and How to Assess It). In Erich Feldman and Walter Hagemann, Der Film als Beeinflussungsmittel (The Cinema as a Means of Influence), papers and reports of the second annual meeting of the German Filmological Society, Emsdetten: Verlag Lechte, 1955.
Discussion of methodological considerations with regard to measuring the influence of movies on children.

605. _____. "Grundzüge des Filmerlebens der Kinder und Jugendlichen in der Ausgehenden Kindheit und Beginnenden Pubertät" (Fundamentals of the Reaction of Children and Adolescents to Films). Filmkunst, 1956, pp. 5-16 (Special number of "Jugend und Film").
Largely a nonempirical analysis; includes a description of research and methods used by the Munich Arbeitskreises.

606. _____. "Der Wirklichkeitscharakter des Filmerlebens bei Kindern und Jugendlichen" (The Character of Reality in the Film Experience of Children and Adolescents). Jugend und Film 1 (1957): 9-22.
A nonempirical comparison of the ways in which adults and children experience films.

607. _____. "Neuere psychologische und pädagogische Forschungsergebnisse auf dem Gebiet 'JugendSchutz und Film'" (Results of Recent Psychological and Pedagogical Research on the Protection of Youth and the Cinema). Jugend und Film 2 (1958): 13-30.
Summary of mostly German research focused largely on the effects of movies on children.

608. Keir, Gertrude. "Psychology and the Film." Penguin Film Review 2 (1949, no. 2): 67-72.
Analysis of the reasons for the emotional impact of movies; discusses Kracauer's From Caligari to Hitler, Payne Fund research, and Meyer's Sociology of Film.

609. Keir, Richard George. "Sex, Individual Differences, and Film Effects on Responses to Sexual Films." Unpublished Ph.D. dissertation, University of Connecticut, 1972.
Males were more aroused and physiologically responsive than females after viewing a film depicting heterosexual coitus or oral-genital sex; film effects, gender differences, and interaction with individual differences were investigated.

610. Keliher, Alice V. "Children and Movies: A Critical Summary of the Scientific Literature." Films 1 (Summer 1940): 40-48.
Literature review covering such topics as attitudinal research, emotional effects of films on children, identification, behavior of delinquents, and film-type preferences.

611. Keliher, Alice V. "Children and the Movies." Child Study 19 (April 1942): 67-69, 96.
Review of literature focusing on what children "are getting or could get from the movies."

612. Kellogg, Arthur. "Minds Made by the Movies." Survey Graphic 22 (May 1933): 245-250, 287-290.
A review of the Payne Fund studies.

613. Kersterton, B. "The Recreational Cinema and the Adolescent." Unpublished Ph. D. dissertation, University of Birmingham, 1945.

614. Kesterton, B. "The Content of Films." Proceedings of the British Association, September 1948.

615. Kindem, Gorham A. "Statistical Analysis of Non-Theatrical Feature Film Exhibition: A Predictive Model for University Film Attendance." Journal of the University Film Association 32 (Fall 1980): 55-59.
Four variables were found to be highly predictive of student film attendance.

616. _____. "Hollywood's Movie Star System and the Film Industry in the 1940's." Paper presented at the 4th International Conference on Culture and Communication, April 1981, Philadelphia, PA.
Statistical examination of the relationship between movie star marquee values and box office success of films released during the 1940s.

617. _____ and Charles Teddlie. "Attacking Prejudice with Comic Satire and Serious Drama." Paper presented at the University Film Association conference, August 1979, Ithaca, NY.
An experiment designed to ascertain which type of film--a comic satire or a serious drama--was more effective in changing ethnic stereotypes and reducing ethnic prejudice; undergraduates served as subjects.

618. Kinder, Melvyn Irvin. "The Effects of Prior Information Desensitization, and Denial on Physiological Reactivity to a Stressful Motion Picture." Unpublished Ph. D. dissertation, University of California, Los Angeles, 1967.
High information was more successful than low information in reducing subjects' reaction to stressful scenes in a motion picture.

619. Kippax, Susan and John P. Murray. "Using the Mass Media: Need Gratification and Perceived Utility." Communication Research 7 (July 1980): 335-360.
Interviews with 206 Australian adults and their responses to a questionnaire; television, newspaper, and books were perceived as the most helpful media sources of need gratification while radio, magazines, and films were perceived as less helpful.

620. Kishler, John Pullman. "The Differential Prediction of Learning from a Motion Picture by Means of Indices of Identification Potential Derived from Attitudes Toward the Main Character." Unpublished Ph. D. dissertation, Pennsylvania State College, 1950.
Pretest-posttest design with recorded group and individual interviews, 814 undergraduates; to explore the effect of audience identification on learning; support was found for prediction of differential learning based on attitude toward a film's main character.

621. _____. "The Effects of Prestige and Identification Factors on Attitude Restructuring and Learning from Sound Films." ERIC ED 053 568 (March 1950).
An experiment to determine the effect of audience attitude toward and identification with the main character of a film on learning from the film Keys of the Kingdom.

622. _____. "Prediction of Differential Learning from a Motion Picture by Means of 'Indices of Identification Potential' Derived from Attitudes Toward the Main Character." American Psychologist 5 (June 1950): 298-299.
Prediction of differential learning based on attitudes toward the main character is possible.

623. Kleitman, N. "The Effect of Motion Pictures on Body Temperature." Science 101 (May 18, 1945): 507-508.
Results showed that "it appears that attending motion picture shows, though looked upon as 'relaxation' in the sense of escape from the humdrum reality of existence, is by no means relaxation in the physiological sense."

624. Klenow, Daniel J. and Jeffrey L. Crane. "Selected Characteristics of the X-Rated Movie Audience: Toward a National Profile of the Recidivist." Sociological Symposium 20 (Fall 1977): 78-83.
Young single males with at least a high school education had the highest propensity for repeated attendance at X-rated films.

625. Knowles, Lyle and Houshang Poorkaj. "Attitudes and Behavior on Viewing Sexual Activities in Public Places." Sociology and Social Research 58 (January 1974): 130-135.
A positive association between permissiveness and frequency of viewing sexually explicit films was found.

626. Knowlton, Daniel C. and J. Warren Tilton. "Auditorium Versus Classroom Showing of Motion Pictures in History Teaching." Journal of Educational Psychology 23 (1932): 663-670.
Results of an experiment involving 144 seventh graders; no evidence was found for superiority of the auditorium setting.

627. Kocsis, Janet M. "Three Studies Examining the Effect of Film Exposure on Dreams." Unpublished M.A. thesis, California State University, Northridge, 1974.
Films were found to influence quality or tone of dreams more than being used as material for dream content; more dream recall, lengthier dreams, and more aggressive dream content was found for subjects who viewed highly charged, emotionally arousing films than subjects who viewed neutral, pleasant films.

628. Kogan, L. N. Chudozestvennyj vkus: Opyt Konkretno-Sociologiceskogo Issledovanija (Taste in Art: Experiences of a Concrete Sociological Study on Taste of Theater and Moviegoers in the Cities in the Ural). Moscow: 1966.

629. Kogan, L. N. Kino i Zritel': Opyt Sociologicekogo Issledovanija Pod Obscej Redakciej (The Cinema and the Movie-Goers: A Comprehensive Sociological Study on Movie-Goers Conducted in Industrial Centers in the Ural). Moscow: Isskustvo-Verlag, 1968.

630. Kracauer, Siegfried. "Cinema et Sociologie" (Cinema and Sociology). Revue Internationale de Filmologie 1 (October 1948): 311-318.
A synopsis of the author's book From Caligari to Hitler.

631. _____. "National Types as Hollywood Presents Them." Public Opinion Quarterly 13 (Spring 1949): 53-72.
Content analysis of the treatment given British and Russian characters by American films since 1933; implications for the effect the characterizations may have an movie-goers are drawn.

632. Kruse, William F. "The Motion Picture and the American School." International Review of Educational Cinematography 4 (1933): 645-654.
Mostly devoted to application of films to the educational setting; brief mention of attitudinal research and the potential propaganda force of theatrical films.

633. Kugelgen, H. von. "Jugendkriminalität Durch Film- und Umwelteinflüsse" (Juvenile Criminality as Influenced by Films and Environment). Erziehungskunst 14 (September 1950): 285-286.
An impressionistic report.

634. Kulik, Adam. "O Ekspererymentalnych Metodach Badania Upodoban Filmowych" (Experimental Methods of Investigating Taste in Films). Psychologia Wychowawcza 4 (1961): 264-280.
A discussion of the uses and limitations of methods for assessing childrens' taste in films; suggestions for improvements are presented.

635. _____ and Janina Wroblowa-Koblewska. "Deuxième Concours International du Film Récréatif pour Enfants. Compte-Rendu et Premières Deductions" (Second International Competition of Children's Entertainment Films. Report and Preliminary Findings). Warsaw: Polish Head Office of Cinematography, 1957 (stenciled).
Large-scale survey of 1,500 7 to 12 year olds inquiring as to their film-type preferences and reactions to 60 different films.

636. Lacis, A. and I. Kejlina. "Deti i Kino" (Children and the Cinema). Moscow: General Directorate of Social Education, Peoples' Commissariat of Instruction of the RSFSR, 1928, 85 pages.
Data gathered from 2,000 Moscow children including dysfunctional aspects of films that are not age-appropriate.

637. Landry, Lionel. "La Psychologie du Cinéma" (The Psychology of the Cinema). Journal de Psychologie Normale et Pathologique 24 (1927): 134-145.
Descriptive analysis of the psychological basis of movies as they affect viewers.

638. Lanphier, Marion F. "An Experiment--The Child's Matinee." Educational Screen 1 (June 1922): 183-186, 198.
Children's preferences for various film content elements were ascertained; not a true experiment as the title suggests.

639. Lanz-Stuparich, Maria. "Les Adolescents et le Cinéma" (Adolescents and the Cinema). In Franziska Baumgarten, La Psychotechnique

dans le Monde Moderne. Paris: Presses Universitaires de France, 1952, pp. 557-561.
Study of attendance habits, film-type preferences, and reactions to movies among 400 13 to 16 year olds; methods included personal interviews, clinical analyses, and questionnaires.

640. Lasky, Jesse. "Does the Public Know What it Wants?" Theatre Magazine, August 1918, pp. 114-115.
The vice president of Famous Players-Lasky offers his opinions on audiences.

641. Lassner, Rudolf. "Sex and Age Determinants of Theatre and Movie Interests." Journal of General Psychology 31 (October 1944): 241-271.
Results of a questionnaire sent to 270 adolescents and adults in Vienna; motives for attendance, film-type preferences, evaluation of film most recently attended, and changes of interest in movies over time are reported.

642. Lazarsfeld, Paul F. "Audience Research in the Movie Field." Annals of the American Academy of Political and Social Science 254 (November 1947): 160-168.
Review of research, including methodological issues and suggestions for future research.

643. _____. "Motion Pictures, Radio Programs, and Youth." In Frances Henne, Alice Brooks, and Ruth Ersted (eds.), Youth, Communication and Libraries (Chicago: American Library Association, 1949), pp. 31-45 (papers presented before the Library Institute at the University of Chicago, August 11-16, 1947).
Data on frequency of attendance by age and education are presented; discussion on the movies' role in sublimation.

644. _____ and Robert K. Merton. "Studies in Radio and Film Propaganda." Transactions of the New York Academy of Science 6 (November 1943): 58-79.
Review of literature including discussion of methodological issues.

645. Lazarus, Richard S., Joseph C. Speisman, Arnold M. Mordkoff, and Leslie A. Davison. "A Laboratory Study of Psychological Stress Produced by a Motion Picture Film." Psychological Monographs 76 (no. 34, whole no. 553, 1962).
Measures of skin resistance, heart rate, interviews, and responses to the Nowlis Adjective Check List all showed "consistent and marked evidence of psychological stress" among undergraduates.

646. League of Nations, Advisory Committee on Social Questions. "The Recreational Cinema and the Young." Geneva: League of Nations Publications, 1938, 34 pages.
Review of literature including frequency of attendance, effect of attendance, and children's film-type preferences.

647. Lebedev, N. "O Konkretno-Sociologiceskih Issledovanijah Kinematografo" (On Cinematographic Concrete Sociological Researches). Kinematograf Segodnja (1971): 255-278.

648. Lebovici, Serge. "Psychanalyse et Cinéma" (Psychoanalysis and Cinema). Revue Internationale de Filmologie 2 (1949, no. 5): 49-55.

Reviews literature and discusses applications regarding the process of viewer identification, attitude, and reactions.

649. Lebovici, Serge. "Réactions Affectives au Film" (Emotional Reactions to Film). Revue Internationale de Filmologie 3 (1952): 221.
Brief note on research studies.

650. Lehman, Harvey, C. and Paul A. Witty. "The Compensatory Function of the Movies." Journal of Applied Psychology 11 (1927): 33-41.
More than 3,000 children in grades 3 to 12 participated in this broad-based study; data are analyzed by sex and race; authors suggest that the reason for the immense popularity of the movies is that "the movie provides vicarious satisfaction for those fundamental desires which life most often inhibits or suppresses."

651. Leighton, Alexander H. and T. Lidz. "The Talking Picture in Psychiatric Teaching and Research." American Journal of Psychiatry 98 (1942): 740-744.

652. Leighton, Alexander H., Edward A. Mason, Joseph C. Kern, and Frederick A. Leighton. "Moving Pictures as an Aid in Community Development." Human Organization 31 (Spring 1972): 11-21.
Results of observational data concerning the use of films as an adjunct to a program of social change.

653. LeMoal, P. "La Santé des Enfants et Leur Equilibre Psychique en face du Cinéma" (The Health and Psychic Equilibrium of Children at the Cinema). Informations Sociales 3 (July 1949): 897-906.

654. ———. "La Santé des Enfants et Leur Equilibre Psychique en face du Cinéma" (The Health and Psychic Equilibrium of Children at the Cinema). Famille 1 (January 1950): 1-8.

655. ——— and M. M. Faugere. "Le Cinéma et l'Enfant" (The Cinema and the Child). Sauvegarde de l'Enfance 2 (November-December 1947): 66-77.
Questionnaires distributed to 1,163 10 to 16 year olds; data gathered include enjoyment of cinema-going, film-type preferences, frequency of attendance, and fright reactions to movies.

656. ——— and Helene de Lalande. "Action du Cinéma sur les Mineures Délinquantes" (The Influence of the Cinema on Delinquent Girls). Paper presented at the 2nd International Congress of Filmology, 1955, Paris.
Survey of 150 13 to 19 year old girls; data on their favorite recreational activities, attitude toward movies, frequency of movie attendance, and film-type preferences are reported.

657. Leonard, Barbara Evelyn. "The People and Appeals of Newspaper Movie Ads: A Content Analysis." Unpublished M. A. thesis, University of Pennsylvania, 1972.
Analysis of verbal and pictorial appeals in a sample of motion picture advertisements from the New York Times indicates that advertisers' concept of the film audience has changed since White and Albert's 1955 study: the current audience "now being a more selective and discerning group who are to be lured to films, not by the fame of the actors, but by the quality of the movies."

658. Leonard, Margaret J. "A Study of the Motion Picture as a Factor in the Life of 242 Girls from Subadequate Families." Social Science Monographs 1 (January 1931): 27-33.
Few pictures were remembered and there remained a good deal of uncertainty as to whether movies had a definite effect on the character of the girls studied.

659. Leroy-Boussion, A. "Etude du Comportement Emotionnel Enfantin au Cours de la Projection d'un Film Comique" (A Study of the Emotional Behavior of Children During the Projection of a Comic Film). Revue Internationale de Filmologie 5 (April-June 1954): 105-123.
Differences in reactions among three age groups of 222 children; data presented by age, sex, intellectual level, and type of home environment.

660. _____. "Le Jeune Spectateur et Son Entourage" (The Young Spectator and His Entourage). Enfance 4 (September-October 1954): 293-316.
Study of the reactions of 4 to 14 year olds to a short comic film as influenced by people surrounding the children.

661. Leroy, Edgar. "L'Enfant et le Cinéma d'Aujourd'hui" (The Child and the Cinema of Today). Revue Internationale de l'Enfant 8 (1929): 704-705.
Advocacy piece asserting that films may be injurious to children psychologically and educationally; author suggests that the state should prohibit children from attending adult films and encourage production of age- (child-) appropriate movies.

662. Leventhal, Howard and William Mace. "The Effect of Laughter on Evaluation of a Slapstick Movie." Journal of Personality 38 (March 1970): 16-30.
Two experiments in which young children were the subjects; findings "suggest that people with high control over the onset and termination of their own expressive behavior ... tend to discount their laughter when making cognitive evaluations."

663. Levinson, Elias. "Effects of Motion Pictures on the Response to Narrative: A Study of the Effects of Film Versions of Certain Short Stories on the Responses of Junior High School Students." Unpublished Ph.D. dissertation, New York University, 1963.
Comprehension, knowledge of word meanings, identification with characters, and enjoyment were measured; data were analyzed by I.Q., age, and sex; results showed that film viewing, either before or after reading, improved response.

664. Levonian, Edward. "Measurement and Analysis of Physiological Response to Film." Report no. 62-66, University of California, Los Angeles, 1962.

665. Levonian, Edward. "The Use of Film in Opinion Measurement." Audiovisual Communication Review 10 (July-August 1962): 250-254.
Results of a study in which films were used to measure college students' opinions about India.

666. _____. "Auditory and Visual Retention in Relation to Arousal." AV Communication Review 16 (Spring 1968): 57-62.
Arousal during learning was measured by galvanic skin response while high school students viewed a film.

667. Levy, Sheldon G. and William F. Fenley. "Audience Size and Likelihood and Intensity of Response During a Humorous Movie." Bulletin of the Psychonomic Society 13 (June 1979): 409-412.
Audiences at 15 showings of M*A*S*H were observed for responses to 25 scenes; evidence suggested that likelihood of response increased with the size of the audience and that social facilitation rather than conformity explains the findings.

668. Leweranz, A. S. "An Analysis of the Academic Achievement and Mental Level of 257 Elementary School Pupils in Relation to Frequency at Motion Picture Theatres." Los Angeles City School District, Psychological and Educational Research Division, 1929 (on file at the University of Southern California library).

669. Lewin, William. "What Shall We Read About the Movies, Radio, and Audio-Visual Methods?" Audio-Visual Guide 16 (September 1949): 29-43.
An annotated listing of 189 books.

670. Lewis, Jerry M. "The Differentiation of Popular Culture Audiences." Journal of Popular Culture 11 (Fall 1977): 425-435.
Survey of more than 400 undergraduates; reports frequency of attendance, opinion leadership, and the influence of movie ratings on attendance.

671. Lewis, William Joseph. "A Comparison of Responses of Adolescents to Narrative and Lyric Literature and Film." Unpublished Ph.D. dissertation, Florida State University, 1972.
Tenth grade students wrote their responses to two literary selections and two films; data were analyzed by age, sex, intelligence, and language abilities; results showed that the students interpret film significantly more than they interpret literature and that they narrate literature more than they narrate film.

672. Liber, B. "Minds and Movies." Medical Record 160 (April 1947): 238-239.
A nonempirical analysis.

673. Linck, David. "The Latino Audience: This Market Translates into Dollars." Boxoffice 118 (February 1982): 32-33.
Informal analysis of the Spanish-speaking movie audience in the U.S.; emphasis on exhibitor strategies.

674. Linden, Michael. "MPAA Interprets ORC Survey" (letter to the editor). Boxoffice 108 (November 24, 1975): 12.
The MPAA's Director of Research responds to D. C. Gillette's guest editorial (November 10) regarding the interpretation of the Opinion Research Corporation's recent poll.

675. Linquist, Rae Andre. "The Evolution of an Image: Marketing Techniques of the American Motion Picture Industry 1946-1969." Unpublished M. T. A. thesis, University of California, Los Angeles, 1969.
Historical treatment of problems encountered and developmental issues.

676. Litman, Barry R. "Predicting TV Ratings for Theatrical Movies." Journalism Quarterly 56 (Autumn 1979): 590-594, 694.

Building on Taylor's work, the findings from this study (which used stepwise multiple regression analysis) indicate that television ratings for theatrical films are best predicted by film rentals and season and day of broadcast; age of the film and critics' ratings of the film were negatively correlated with expected TV ratings.

677. _____. "An Empirical Analysis of Theatrical Movie Popularity." Paper presented at the Popular Culture Association conference, April 1980, Detroit, MI.
Statistical analysis of several variables' predictive power for box office success.

678. _____. "Predicting Success of Theatrical Movies: New Empirical Evidence." Paper presented at the Association for Education in Journalism conference, August 1980, Boston, MA.
Statistical analysis of several variables' predictive power for box office success.

679. Llinas, Pablo A. "Un Homicida Menor de Edad. Influencia del Cinematografo y del Ambiente Hogareno y Social" (An Adolescent Homocide. The Influence of Motion Pictures and of Home and Social Environment). Revista de Medicina Legal de Columbia 6 (1943): 40-45.
Report of a case study.

680. Lohde, G. "Versuche mit Spielfilmen" (An Experiment with Entertainment Films). Welt der Schule 4 (1951).

681. London County Council. "School Children and the Cinema." London County Council, 1932.

682. "The London Filmgoer." Sight and Sound 33 (Autumn 1964): 161-162.
Reports on the Federation of British Film Makers' "Survey of Cinema Going in Greater London"; data presented include frequency of attendance, reasons for attendance, attendance unit, evaluation of current cinema, and reasons for choice of most recent film attended.

683. Long, Arthur Lee. "The Influence of Color on Acquisition and Retention as Evidenced by the Use of Sound Films." Unpublished Ed. D. dissertation, University of Colorado, 1945.
Two groups, totaling nearly 400, of fifth, sixth, eleventh, twelfth graders responded to questionnaire tests; intelligence and achievement tests were also administered; results indicate the influence of color films on retention of information was much superior to black and white films.

684. Long, Howard Rusk. "Rural Communication Patterns: A Study in the Availability and Use of Print, Radio and Film in Shelby County, Missouri." Unpublished Ph. D. dissertation, University of Missouri, 1948.
Data are presented according to age, sex, and economic status of the residents; results suggest that persons who use one medium of mass communication also tend to use the others.

685. Loriga, G. "The Cinema and the Study of Fatigue." International Review of Educational Cinematography 2 (1930): 913-916.
Suggests methods to be employed in the measurement of fatigue as presented by films.

686. Lorimor, E. S. and S. W. Dunn. "Use of the Mass Media in France and Egypt." Public Opinion Quarterly 32 (Winter 1968-1969): 680-687.
Cinema was found to be the least used medium; attendance patterns in both countries was very similar; 71 percent of the respondents in both countries reported no attendance during the preceding week and 27 percent reported having gone once or twice.

687. Los Angeles Times. "A Look at Southern California Movie-Going." Los Angeles: Los Angeles Times Marketing Research, 1972.
A 62 page report of a survey; leisure-time activities and movie attendance, profiles of adult movie-goers and non-movie-goers, general movie-going habits, and sources of information about movies are reported.

688. Los Angeles Times. "Movie Attendance in Los Angeles." Los Angeles: Los Angeles Times Marketing Research, 1977.
A 39 page report of a survey; profile of households with movie-goers and analysis of variables related to most recent movie attended.

689. Louttit, C. M. "Motion Pictures and Youth: A Review." Journal of Applied Psychology 18 (April 1934): 307-316.
A review of the Payne Fund research.

690. Lovedahl, Gerald Grey. "An Assessment of the Effectiveness of a Film Presentation in Changing Audience Attitudes Toward and Knowledge of Industrial Arts." Unpublished Ph. D. dissertation, Ohio State University, 1977.
A separate sample pretest-posttest design was used; results showed that the respondents gained a more favorable attitude toward industrial arts and that they possessed a greater degree of knowledge about the subject after viewing the film.

691. Lovell, Terry. "Sociology and the Cinema." Screen 12 (1971): 15-26.

692. Low, Rachael. "Audience Research." Sight and Sound 15 (Winter 1946-47): 150-151.
Discussion of previous literature; concludes that "however desirable scientific accuracy may be in the interests of sociology, it is to be feared that its enlistment in the cause of commercialism in the cinema can only delay the appearance of higher standards of artistic appreciation."

693. Low, Rachael. "The Implications Behind the Social Survey." Penguin Film Review 2 (1948, no. 7): 107-112.
Discussion of the British Social Survey; reports data on frequency of attendance as analyzed by age, income, and education.

694. Loye, David. "A Review of Research Bearing on the Impact of Television and Motion Pictures on Children and Adults." ERIC ED 121 294 (June 1974).
A literature review of television and movies as they affect values, attitudes, behaviors; discussion of research in need of attention.

695. Lozev, E. "Golemijat i Malkijat Ekran v Predpocitanijata na Zritelite." Kinoizkustvo 28 (March 1973): 9-15.

696. Lukic, Stoja. "Children, Youth and the Film." Society and Leisure 2 (1970): 87-92.
Data were gathered from 1,005 individuals ages 9 to 19 by means of interviews, diaries, and questionnaires; reports attendance unit, activities engaged in after seeing a movie, and film-related activities.

697. Lumsdaine, Arthur A. "Experimental vs. Survey Techniques for Determining the Effects of Motion Pictures." Paper presented at the Conference on Public Opinion Research, June 1951, Princeton, NJ. (Abstract in Public Opinion Quarterly 15 (Winter 1951-1952): 771-772.)
Benefits and disadvantages of the two methodologies are discussed.

698. Lundell, Torborg and Anthony Mulac. "Husbands and Wives in Bergman Films: A Close Analysis Based on Empirical Data." Journal of the University Film Association 33 (Winter 1981): 23-37.
Investigated questions concerning viewers perception of differences between Bergman's husband and wife characters and whether lay audiences verify critical evaluations of a particular character constellation in Bergman films.

699. Lunders, Leo. "Comment Evaluer l'Influence du Cinéma sur les Enfants?" (How to Evaluate the Influence of the Cinema on Children?). Revue Internationale du Cinéma 4 (1952): 50-55.
Critical review of quantitative and qualitative methodologies with suggestions for improvement.

700. Lundy, B. W. and Roy Johnston. "Movie Content and Behavioral Disturbance in Psychiatric and Neurological Patients." Paper presented at the American Psychological Association conference, August 1981, Los Angeles, CA.
Incidences of disturbance were gathered for a 12 month period to determine if patient behavior was related to film content.

701. Luther, Rodney. "Marketing Aspects of Drive-In Theatres." Journal of Marketing 15 (July 1950): 41-47.
Included is a report of a survey of drive-in audiences conducted in the Minneapolis-St. Paul area; data presented include frequency of attendance, attendance unit, and film-type preferences.

702. _____. "Television and the Future of Motion Picture Exhibition." Hollywood Quarterly 5 (1951): 164-177.
Analysis of competition between these media, including audience considerations, with an optimistic forecast.

703. Lydgate, William A. "Audience Pre-testing Heads Off Flops, Forecasts Hits, for Movie Producers." Sales Management, March 15, 1944, pp. 90, 94-98.
Discussion of the methods used by Gallup's Audience Research, Inc.

704. Lynch, Francis Dennis. "Clozentropy: A Technique for Studying Audience Response to Films." Unpublished Ph.D. dissertation, University of Iowa, 1972.
An instrument was developed for analyzing the ability of viewers to

predict what will occur next in different kinds of films; instrument was tested with a sample of 93 undergraduates.

705. _____. "Clozentropy: A New Technique for Analyzing Audience Response to Film." Speech Monographs 41 (August 1974): 245-252.
A summary of the author's dissertation.

706. Lyness, Paul I. "Patterns in the Mass Communications Tastes of the Young Audience." Unpublished Ph.D. dissertation, State University of Iowa, 1950.
Analysis of the tendency for certain subject matter to cluster in the content preferences of age-sex groups and the tendency for these preferences to carry over from medium to medium; fifth, seventh, ninth, and eleventh grade students comprised the sample; media examined include movies, newspapers, radio, magazines, and books.

707. _____. "Patterns in the Mass Communications Tastes of the Young Audience." Journal of Educational Psychology 42 (December 1951): 449-467.
A summary of the author's dissertation.

708. _____. "The Place of the Mass Media in the Lives of Boys and Girls." Journalism Quarterly 29 (Spring 1952): 43-54.
Childrens' use of pre-TV media, including movies, was determined by a questionnaire; leisure activities, attention paid to various media, and news sources are reported; a summary of the author's dissertation.

709. McClintock, Robert. "Finland Still Goes to Movies." Foreign Commerce Weekly, March 18, 1944, pp. 8-9, 11.
Mostly a review of industry-related issues; brief mention of audience attendance data.

710. McCoy, Edward P. "Influence of Color on Audiences' Rated Perception of Reality in Film." Audiovisual Communication Review 10 (January-February 1962): 70-72.
Undergraduates tended to evaluate scenes shot in black and white as being records of actuality more so than those shot in color.

711. McGuinnes, Anne L. "Can Youth Select Good Movies?" High Points 25 (May 1943): 63-66.
Survey of 13 seventh and eighth grade classes (n=455); inquired as to favorite actor and actress, five best movies seen, favorite theater, and frequency of attendance.

712. McGinnies, Elliott, Robert Lana, and Clagett Smith. "The Effects of Sound Films on Opinions About Mental Illness in Community Discussion Groups." Journal of Applied Psychology 42 (February 1958): 40-46.
Results of two experiments involving adult community groups; findings indicate that a single film did not produce significant changes in opinion regardless of whether or not the films were followed by discussion; a series of three films did induce significant shifts in opinion in the direction intended by the film.

713. McIntosh, Douglas M. "Attendance of School Children at the Cinema." Glasgow: Scottish Educational Film Association, Research Publications no. 1, 1945.
Questionnaires completed by 36,149 pupils in infant, primary, and secondary schools; reports frequency of attendance as sorted by education level, age, geographic location, and physical and mental handicaps.

714. McIntyre, Charles J. "Sex, Age and Iconicity as Factors Influencing Projection Onto Motion Picture Protagonists." Unpublished Ph.D. dissertation, Pennsylvania State College, 1953.
Undergraduates (n=425) in an experimental study responded to the MMPI and TAT; concludes that the TAT may not be as useful as the literature had suggested when used in conjunction with a film.

715. McKeever, William A. "The Moving Picture: A Primary School for Criminals." Good Housekeeping, August 19, 1910, pp. 184-186.
Anecdotal reports of the negative effect of movies; suggestion that movies possess the potential for moral or spiritual uplifting.

716. McLoone, M. "Report of BFI Summer School 1978: 'Film: Audience.'" Screen Education no. 28 (Autumn 1978): 86-88.

717. McManus, John T. and Louis Kronenberger. "Motion Pictures, the Theater, and Race Relations." Annals of the American Academy of Political and Social Science 244 (March 1946): 152-158.
Asserts that movies "should be one of the Nation's most effective means of dispelling group prejudice" and presents descriptions of films discussing such topics as anti-Semitism, anti-Negro, labor, and foreign countries; the influence of these films is discussed nonempirically.

718. McNelly, John T. and Eugenio Fonseca. "Media Use and Political Interest at the University of Costa Rica." Journalism Quarterly 41 (Spring 1964): 225-231.
Movie attendance was found to be nearly equal among three Latin American groups: university students, high status heads of households, and professionals.

719. McPherson, Clinton Marsud. "The Effect of Sound Motion Pictures as Measured by Differential Achievement on the Motivation of College Freshman Chemistry Students." Unpublished Ed.D. dissertation, Texas Technological College, 1959.
Science films did not affect motivation or degree of learning.

720. McWilliams, James. "A Description of Fear Induced in Children Attending a Film as Indexed by the Number of Trips to the Restroom." Unpublished M.S. thesis, Temple University, 1972.

721. Mabie, E.C. "The Responses of Theatre Audiences, Experimental Studies." Speech Monographs 19 (November 1952): 235-243.
Review of four studies which used the Meier Recorder tape device to report responses to live drama; relationship of the data gathered to the cinema situation is noted.

722. MacCann, Richard Dyer. "Film Scholarship: Dead or Alive?" Journal of the University Film Association 28 (Winter 1976): 3-10.
A review of the state of film scholarship with brief mention of audience research.

Film Audience   78

723.   Maccoby, Eleanor E., Harry Levin, and Bruce M. Selya. "The Effect of Emotional Arousal on the Retention of Aggressive and Nonaggressive Movie Content." American Psychologist 10 (1955): 359.
Tested the hypothesis that the content viewers retain after exposure to a movie will be a function of their emotional state at the time of viewing; 127 fifth and sixth graders comprised the sample; an abstract of a paper presented at the American Psychological Association conference, September 1955, San Francisco, CA.

724.   Maccoby, Eleanor E., Harry Levin, and Bruce M. Selya. "The Effect of Emotional Arousal on the Retention of Film Content: A Failure to Replicate." Journal of Abnormal and Social Psychology 53 (November 1956): 373-374.
Subjects were 190 fifth and sixth graders.

725.   Maccoby, Eleanor E. and William Cody Wilson. "Identification and Observational Learning from Films." Journal of Abnormal and Social Psychology 55 (July 1957): 76-87.
Results of two studies involving seventh-graders; identification occurred with like-sexed leading characters; viewers were more likely to identify with characters whose social class corresponded with their aspired social class; viewers tended to remember somewhat better the actions and words of the character with whom they identified.

726.   Maccoby, Eleanor, William C. Wilson, and Roger V. Burton. "Differential Movie-Viewing Behavior of Male and Female Viewers." Journal of Personality 26 (June 1958): 259-267.
Observation of the eye movements of 48 undergraduates as they viewed two films; results showed that males spent more time than females watching the male lead in the movie.

727.   MacDonald, Scott. "The Cinema Audience: Some New Perspectives." Film Criticism 3 (1979): 32-40.
Nonempirical analysis of audience response to, especially, political films.

728.   Mackie, J. "The Edinburgh Cinema Enquiry: Being an Investigation Conducted into the Influence of Films on School Children and Adolescents in the City." Edinburgh: Edinburgh Enquiry Committee, 1933.
Survey of 2,580 9 to 18 year old pupils; boys were found to attend more often than girls and poorer children more frequently than the more affluent.

729.   Maddison, John. "Le Cinéma et l'Information Mentale des Peuples Primitifs" (The Cinema and Mental Information of Primitive People). Revue Internationale de Filmologie 1 (October 1948): 305-310.
Review of literature on movies and Africans.

730.   Maddison, John and Flora Meaden. "Réactions Sociales du Cinéma en Angleterre" (Social Aspects of the Cinema in England). Revue Internationale de Filmologie 1 (September-October 1947): 211-216.
Review of British research.

731.   _____. "Les Ciné-Clubs d'Enfants en Angleterre" (Children's Cinema Clubs in England). Revue International de Filmologie 1 (September-October 1947): 217-225.
Descriptive information on club activities and membership.

732. Mahler, F. "De ce Merg Tinerii la Cinema?" Cinema 10 (May 1972): 12-13.
Rumanian inquiry on the film tastes of adolescents.

733. Majchrak, J. "K Aktualnym Problemom Vyuzitia Kratkeho Filmu." Panorama 2 (Spring 1980): 22-26.
Presents research results on the appeal of various kinds of short films.

734. _____. "Zanrove a Tematicke Preferencie Slovenskeho Filmoveho Obecenstva." Panorama 1 (Winter 1980): 22-30.
Synopsis of research on film-type preferences among Slovak moviegoers.

735. Makhdum, M. M. "Some Effects of the Cinema Situation on Character." Indian Journal of Psychology 13 (1938): 176-177.
Asserts that films depicting erotic themes influence viewers through the processes of identification, social facilitation, and excitation.

736. Mann, Jay, Jack Sidman, and Sheldon Starr. "Effects of Erotic Films on the Sexual Behaviors of Married Couples." Technical Reports of the U. S. Commission on Obscenity and Pornography, vol. 8, pp. 170-254. Washington, D. C.: U. S. Government Printing Office, 1970.
An experimental study.

737. Mann, Jay, Leonard Berkowitz, Jack Sidman, Sheldon Starr, and Stephen West. "Satiation of the Transient Stimulating Effect of Erotic Films." Journal of Personality and Social Psychology 30 (December 1974): 729-735.
No evidence was found to indicate that erotic films tend to produce a disinhibition effect or new learning; films apparently activated previously acquired sexual habits; sex movies tended to become less effective elicitors of sexual reactions upon successive viewing.

738. Mann, Jay, Jack Sidman, and Sheldon Starr. "Evaluating Social Consequences of Erotic Films: An Experimental Approach." Journal of Social Issues 29 (1973): 113-131.
Couples who viewed erotic films reported more sexual activity on viewing nights and more tolerance for exhibition of erotic films; results support social learning theory and fail to support the hypothesis that viewing erotic films has deleterious consequences.

739. Mann, Paul B. "The Development and Use of Educational Motion Pictures in New York City." School and Society 41 (February 23, 1935): 241-247.
A historical account with a brief review of some research on the effectiveness of films as an educational tool.

740. Marcus, Robert D. "Moviegoing and American Culture." Journal of Popular Culture 3 (Spring 1970): 755-766.
A nonempirical analysis.

741. Marcussen, Elsa B., Elsa Germeten, and Einar Ness. "Rapport am Forsoket med Filmundervisn pa Ruselokke Skole, 1956" (Report on an Experiment with Film Teaching in Ruselokke School, 1956). Oslo: Norges Almenvitenskapelige Forskningsrad (Norweigian Popular Science Research Council), 1957.

Reports results of an experiment in film teaching in an Oslo elementary school; two questionnaires, in addition, provide data on frequency of attendance and film preferences among the 300 12 to 13 year old students.

742. Margolis, Herbert F. "An Experiment at Biarritz." Hollywood Quarterly 2 (1946-1947): 273-279.
Discussion of the results of the U.S. Army's studies on the possibility of raising artistic taste among audiences through film education; reactions to non-U.S. films, film-type preferences, and objections to Hollywood's methods of film production and distribution are reported.

743. _____. "The American Scene and the Problems of Film Education." Penguin Film Review 2 (1947): 54-63.
Results of a before-after survey of students who had taken an eight-week film course; reports their evaluation of films, attitudes toward various industry practices, double features, the star system, and censorship.

744. "Market Research for Film Sell; Parables for Believers, Skeptics." Variety, May 12, 1976, pp. 162, 168, 172.
Discussion of the advantages and disadvantages of market research, various research techniques, and contemporary applications.

745. Marlin, Vanden Bosch. "The Effect of Self-Selected Movies, Popular Songs, and Books on Selected High School Students." Unpublished Ph.D. dissertation, University of Iowa, 1973.
Juniors and seniors were interviewed and their responses evaluated according to seven developmental tasks (e.g., "achieving a masculine and feminine role") and Erikson's stage one in the identity crisis.

746. Marsa, Linda. "CinemaScore: Poll Created Out of Frustration." Boxoffice 116 (December 1980): 12-13.
Describes the origin and methodology used by Ed Mintz's CinemaScore, a movie evaluation-feedback technique.

747. Martin, Chorsie E. and Frank W. Oglesbee. "Television Viewing Habits of College Students." Feedback 23 (Winter 1982): 21-24.
Responses to a questionnaire by 223 undergraduate and graduate students; finds movies, of seven media measured, the third "most-liked."

748. Martin, Richard R., John T. McNelly, and Fausto Izcaray. "Is Media Exposure Unidimensional? A Socioeconomic Approach." Journalism Quarterly 53 (Winter 1976): 619-625.
Study examined patterns of media exposure and the relationships among levels of exposure to different media; results of correlational analysis are presented by socio-economic (high and low) group; media examined include newspapers, magazines, books, radio, TV, and film.

749. Martindale, C.C. "The Cinema and the Adult." Studies: An Irish Quarterly Review 18 (September 1929): 443-448.
An anecdotal report asserting that the influence of the cinema "is bad, and that it so acts upon human minds as to render improvement difficult."

750. Marzi, Alberto. "Cinema e Minorati Psichici" (Cinema and the Psychologically Underdeveloped). Corso di Filmologia, February 1949.

751. _____. "Il Fanciullo Davanti al Cinema Spettacolare" (The Child and Entertainment Films). Cinedidattica 3 (February 1952): 5-6.
The article suggests positive and negative psychological aspects of films.

752. _____ and Renzo Canestrari. "Recherches sur les Problèmes du Cinéma" (Research on Cinema Problems). Revue Internationale de Filmologie 3 (July-December 1952): 179-192.
Review of research focusing on Italian studies and the problem of cinema and children.

753. Massey, Morris E. "A Market Analysis of Sex-Oriented Materials in Denver, Colorado, August, 1969--A Pilot Study." Technical Reports of the U.S. Commission on Obscenity and Pornography, vol. 4, pp. 3-98. Washington, D.C.: U.S. Government Printing Office, 1970.
Adult theater patrons' demographic characteristics were observed and reported.

754. Mata, L. "La Acción de Cinematógrafo en la Afectividad Infantil" (The Influence of the Cinematograph on Childhood Affectivity). Archivos Argentinos di Psicología Normal y Patología 1 (1933-1934): 90-91.
A brief case study of one child who imitated a crime portrayed in a film; author asserts the need for control or elimination of asocial content in movies.

755. Mathur, Ajit K. "Movies and the Students." Journal of Social Research 1 (July 1959): 29-37.
Results of an open-ended survey to 100 under- and post-graduates concerning their perceptions of the significance of movies.

756. Mauerhofer, Hugo. "Psychology of Film Experience." Penguin Film Review 2 (1949, no. 8): 103-109.
A descriptive analysis.

757. Mead, Corinne. "Motion Pictures a Stimulant to Reading Interest." Educational Screen 22 (September 1943): 241-242.
Reports an informal study conducted at the Winchester, MA library.

758. Meadows, Arthur. "Audience Research and the Marketing of Australian Films." Australian Journal of Screen Theory (nos. 1 and 2, 1978): 14-16.
Brief note on the application of social science theory and methods to consumer research.

759. Melles, G. "Het Publiek van de Nederlandse Speelfilm: Gelegenheidspubliek." Skoop 9 (March 1974): 4-9.
Results of a study concerning movie-going in the Netherlands.

760. Melnick, Daniel. "Intensive Politicization Episodes: Movies, Melas, and Political Attitudes in a North Indian District." American Behavioral Scientist 17 (January 1975): 439-476.
A survey of 1,132 Indian men; reports patterns of cinema attendance and differences between rural and urban residents as compared to mela (a social celebration often religiously oriented) attendance; re-

Film Audience 82

lationships between cinema and mela attendance were compared to political attitudes.

761. Mercey, Arch A. "Social Uses of the Motion Picture." Annals of the American Academy of Political and Social Science 250 (March 1947): 98-104.
A nonempirical discussion and analysis of movies as a means for education, information, and community action.

762. Merrill, W. E. "The Motion Picture Habits of Pupils in the Four Upper Elementary Grades in the Mesa Schools." University of Arizona Record 36 (1943): 47 pages.

763. Mersand, Joseph. "Facts and Fiction about the Educational Values of the Cinema." Educational Screen 17 (December 1938): 319-321, 324.
Discussion of the educational values in theatrical films; advocates that more research in this area is needed.

764. Mertens, Marjorie S. "The Effects of Mental Hygiene Motion Pictures on the Self-Regarding Attitudes and Self Perceptions of College Girls." Unpublished Ph.D. dissertation, Pennsylvania State College, 1951.
A pretest-posttest experiment using questionnaires and interviews and involving 254 freshmen; films were shown to successfully affect attitudes in the predicted direction.

765. Messaris, Paul. "The Film Audience's Awareness of the Production Process." Journal of the University Film Association 33 (Fall 1981): 53-56.
An experiment involving college students shows that "awareness of the filmmaker was the exception, rather than the rule."

766. Metfessel, Milton. "Personal Factors in Motion Picture Writing: I. Interests and Attitudes." Journal of Abnormal and Social Psychology 30 (1935): 333-347.
Responses to a questionnaire concerning the emotional and writing habits of 59 screenwriters.

767. Metzger, Wolfgang. "Kind und Film" (Child and Film). Psychologische Praxis 11 (1952): 18-32.
An advocacy piece discussing movies in general, choice of newsreels and previews in relation to children's tendencies to show lack of restraint, criminal behavior, and cruelty.

768. Meyersohn, Rolf. "Television and the Rest of Leisure." Public Opinion Quarterly 32 (Spring 1968): 102-112.
Comparative data on movie-going, newspaper and book reading, and leisure activities are presented.

769. Mialaret, G. and M. G. Melies. "Expériences sur la Comprehension du Langage Cinematographique par l'Enfant" (Experiments on the Understanding of Film Language by the Child). Revue Internationale de Filmologie 5 (July-December 1954): 221-228.
Experiments using children aged 4 to 12 and analyzing specific techniques (e.g., close-up) which cause difficulty in understanding.

770. Michael, Donald N. and Nathan Maccoby. "Factors Influencing Verbal Learning From Films Under Varying Conditions of Audience Partici-

pation." Journal of Experimental Psychology 46 (December 1953): 411-418.
An experiment assessing the relative contributions of the practice and motivation factors involved in learning from motion pictures; results suggest that increases in learning were largely a function of practice and not the effects of increases in motivation to learn.

771. Middlesborough Head Teachers Association. "Children and the Cinema: Report of an Investigation Carried Out in June 1946." Middlesborough: M. H. T. A., 1946.

772. Middleton, Russell. "Ethnic Prejudice and Susceptibility to Persuasion." American Sociological Review 25 (October 1960): 679-686.
Experimental subjects who viewed Gentleman's Agreement were more likely to show reductions in expression of anti-Semitic statements than control subjects; a reduced but considerable carry-over effect was observed with regard to anti-Negro prejudice.

773. Millard, John William. "A Study in the Sociology of Communications: Determinants and Consequences of Exposure to American Motion Picture Films in the Near and Middle East." Unpublished Ph. D. dissertation, Columbia University, 1955.
Use of a semi-structured questionnaire in Greece, Turkey, Lebanon, and Jordan; descriptive characteristics of movie-goers, reasons for their attendance, and the effects which movies have had on these individuals' attitudes toward the United States.

774. Miller, C. R. and L. Minsky. "Movies and Propagandizing." Survey Graphic 5 (November 1939): 716-718.

775. Miller, Emanuel. "What Children Like." Sight and Sound 5 (Winter 1936-37): 131-132.
Anecdotal report of film-type and content preferences; brief discussion of the effects of nature and crime films.

776. Miller, William Charles, III. "An Experimental Study of the Relationship of Film Movement and Emotional Involvement Response, and its Effect on Learning and Attitude Formation." Unpublished Ph. D. dissertation, University of Southern California, 1967.
Responses of 80 individuals to film motion was measured by galvanic skin response, an information retention test, and two attitude scales.

777. _____. "Film Movement and Affective Response and the Effect on Learning and Attitude Formation." AV Communication Review 17 (Summer 1969): 172-181.
A summary of the author's dissertation.

778. Minkowska, F. "Le Test de Rorschach, les Dessins d'Enfants et le Cinéma" (The Rorschach Test, Children's Drawings and the Cinema). Revue Internationale de Filmologie 1 (October 1948): 281-287.
Reviews literature and discusses applications of the Rorschach to the study of film.

779. Mitchell, Alice Miller. "Movies Children Like." Survey 63 (November 15, 1929): 213-215.
Survey of 10,052 children to ascertain film-type preferences; re-

spondents and their responses were sorted into one of three groups: public school pupils, Boy or Girl Scouts, or juvenile delinquents.

780. Mitnick, Leonard and Elliott McGinnies. "Influencing Ethnocentrism in Small Discussion Groups Through a Film Communication." Journal of Abnormal and Social Psychology 56 (January 1958): 82-90.
Significant reductions in ethonocentrism were produced in both the film with discussion group and the film-alone (no discussion) group; participants were high school pupils.

781. Mock, A. A. "The Relative Values of the Use of Motion Pictures with Bright and Dull Children." Unpublished M. A. thesis University of Southern California, 1929.

782. Mohaupt, W. "Film und Jugend" (Film and Youth). Unsere Schule 5 (1950): 358-362.

783. Mohrhof, Siegfried. "Bewertung von Jugendfilmen Unter der Lupe" (A Criticism of the Choices of Films for Children). Film-Bild-Ton 6 (April 1956): 28-30, 47-48.
Discussion of the results of a survey of 2,000 12 to 15 year olds; compared the schoolchildren's preferences for film subjects and censors' labeling of films suitable for children.

784. Montani, Angelo and Giulio Pietranera. "First Contribution to the Psycho-Analysis and Aesthetics of Motion Pictures." Psychoanalytic Review 33 (1946): 177-196.
Discussion of the psychoanalytic basis of movies and the relationship between films, the psychology of masses, and the psychoanalytic basis of the plot of the typical film; notes that movies "constitute the hieroglyphics of the Twentieth Century."

785. "Montclair Children and the Movies. A Survey in 1933." Educational Screen 13 (May 1934): 130.
Brief report of a survey administered to some 5,000 school children by Dorothea Marston and Winifred Crawford; frequency of attendance reported.

786. Montmollin, G. De. "La Mémoire des Films" (The Memory of Films). Revue Internationale de Filmologie 3 (1952): 220-221.
Brief note on an experiment involving 100 students and their recollection of films.

787. Moore, Douglas Cameron. "A Study of the Influence of the Film, The Birth of a Nation, on the Attitudes of Selected High School White Students Toward Negroes." Unpublished Ph. D. dissertation, University of Illinois at Urbana-Champaign, 1971.
A replication, using updated procedures, of Peterson and Thurstone's Payne Fund study; author's findings indicate that The Birth of a Nation "produced no measurable attitude change of hostility toward Negroes."

788. Moore, Floride. "Children's Concepts of Family Relationships as Revealed by Their Responses to Certain Motion Pictures." Unpublished Ph. D. dissertation, New York University, 1953.

789. "Morals and Movies." Nation 129 (September 18, 1929): 291-292.

An advocacy piece, employing the results of selected studies, concluding that "The movie producers ... have surrendered moral sophistication (on the screen, not personally) in behalf of box-office receipts."

790. Moreno, J. L. "Psychodrama and Therapeutic Motion Pictures." Sociometry 7 (1944): 230-244. Reprinted in Psychodrama Monographs, no. 11 (1945).
A discussion of the therapeutic benefits, especially catharsis, of using films in psychodrama sessions.

791. Morgan, Cammie K. "Despite Video, X-hibition is Stronger than Ever." Boxoffice 118 (July 15, 1982): 14-18.
Brief note on a survey of X-rated film patrons; reports average age and patrons' comparative experiences of general and adult theaters.

792. Morienval, Jean. "Les Enfants au Cinéma" (Children at the Cinema). Cineopse, October 1929, pp. 753-754.
A nonempirical discussion.

793. _____. "L'Enfant Devant le Cinéma" (The Child and the Cinema). Educateurs no. 26 (March-April 1950).

794. Morin, Edgar. "Le Problème des Effets Dangereux du Cinéma" (The Problem of the Dangerous Effects of the Cinema). Revue Internationale de Filmologie 4 (July-December 1953): 217-231.
Critical review of the literature on children's imitation of antisocial behavior such as criminal activity; suggests that the effect of films cannot be validly studied without accounting for the social context in which the film is viewed as well as the child's predispositions.

795. _____. "Préliminaires à une Sociologie du Cinéma" (Preliminaries to a Sociology of Cinema). Cahiers Internationaux de Sociologie 17 (1954): 101-111.
An advocacy piece by the president of the Motion Picture Association of America suggesting that movies illuminate aspects of society and society illuminates aspects of the movies; calls for use of social science research to examine the interaction between cinema and society.

796. Mosher, Donald L. "Psychological Reactions to Pornographic Films." Technical Reports of the U. S. Commission on Obscenity and Pornography, vol. 8, pp. 255-312. Washington, D. C.: U. S. Government Printing Office, 1970.
Undergraduates responses to a questionnaire.

797. _____. "Sex Differences, Sex Experience, Sex Guilt, and Explicitly Sexual Films." Journal of Social Issues 29 (1973): 95-112.
Males were aroused more than females by the film displaying oral-genital sex; females, high sex-guilt subjects, and less sexually experienced subjects all rated the films as more disgusting, offensive, and pornographic.

798. Motion Picture Association of America. "Juvenile Delinquency and Dramatized Entertainment." New York, March 1950.
An 18 page booklet presenting various authorities' views and concluding that the influence of film cannot be studied in isolation.

Film Audience

799. "Motivational Research in Promotion: Why Folks Go To, Stay From Pics." Variety, June 26, 1974, p. 7.
Results from a preliminary questionnaire distributed in Ohio and New Jersey are reported; among the patrons' complaints are: seats are too small, prices too high, uncomfortable theater temperature, and noisy audiences.

800. "Movie Attendance Levelling Out in Finland." Facts About Film Finland 2 (1976): 3-5.
Data from the Finnish Film Foundation including number of tickets purchased and total attendance in 1975.

801. "Moviegoers Favor at Home Viewing, Claims Gallup Study." Independent Film Journal, June 10, 1977, p. 8.

802. "Moviegoers Tell What Pleases Them ... What Turns Them Off." Film Bulletin 46 (April-May 1977): 2-4, 30.
Results of a national survey with data broken down by geographic area of the U.S.

803. "Movies' Effect Depends on Mood of Audience." Science News Letter 68 (September 17, 1955): 191.
Brief report of a study investigating the relationship between children's affective state prior to exposure to a film and their subsequent behavior.

804. "Moving Pictures as a Factor in Municipal Life." Municipal Review, October 14, 1914, pp. 708-712.

805. "The Moving Picture Habits of High-School Students." School and Society 39 (March 17, 1934): 338-339.
Reports on the results of a survey and experiment involving 1,851 students; data include reasons for the students' choice for film attendance; experiment involved the effect of instruction in film appreciation on subsequent evaluation of films.

806. "The Moving Picture and the National Character." American Review of Reviews, September 1910, pp. 315-320.
Anecdotal discussion of the positive and dysfunctional effects of movies on audiences; discussion of censorship issues.

807. "MPAA Survey Seeks Answer to Biz Decline; TV Still Chief Villain." Variety, January 11, 1958, p. 10.
Results of an Opinion Research Corp. survey inquiring as to the reasons for decreased film attendance; other data reported include reasons for most recent attendance and respondents' means for obtaining awareness of films.

808. Mravcova, M. "Vycteno z Anket." Film a Doba 22 (September 1976): 528.
Discusses results of audience research on 14-30 year old Bulgarian film-goers.

809. ———. "Polska Mladez a Film." Film a Doba 23 (February 1977): 111-112.
Reports recent audience research activity conducted in Poland among young movie-goers.

810. Mueller, Charles W. and Edward Donnerstein. "Film-Facilitated Arousal and Prosocial Behavior." Journal of Experimental Social Psychology 17 (January 1981): 31-41.
Two experiments involving male undergraduates; tests the applicability of the excitation transfer model which predicts that arousal transferred from an unrelated source will facilitate behavioral predispositions.

811. Muller, H. "Die Jugendlichen und das Filmtheater" (Young People and Cinema). Der Neue Film 1 (1947, no. 11).

812. Murphy, A. D. "Audience Demographics, Film Future." Variety, August 20, 1975, pp. 3, 74.
Using data from the U. S. Department of Labor, Murphy finds that the prime movie market cohort, 25 to 34 year olds, "will soar 51 percent" to about 2. 7 million.

813. _____. "Demographics Favoring Films Future." Variety, October 8, 1975, p. 3.

814. _____. "The American Non-Filmgoer." Variety, October 8, 1975, pp. 3, 34.
Details of an Opinion Research Corporation study, commissioned by the MPAA are presented.

815. _____. "B. O. Data a Reliable Attendance Gauge." Variety, February 4, 1981, pp. 3, 40.
Data on seasonal fluctuations in attendance are presented.

816. Murphy, William Charles. "The Relationship Between Mental Age and the Types of Motion Pictures Liked by Children in Grades 4 to 9, Inclusive." Unpublished M. A. thesis, Ohio State University, 1935.
Film-type preferences of 400 children; mental age was determined by use of the Illinois General Intelligence Scale.

817. Murray, James P. "Black Movies/Black Theatre." Drama Review 116 (December 1972): 56-61.
Anecdotal report in which it is suggested that blacks may now represent half of the movie-going audience in the U. S.

818. Musatti, Cesare L. "Le Cinéma et la Psychanalyse" (Cinema and Psychoanalysis). Revue Internationale de Filmologie 2 (1950, no. 6): 185-194.
Discussion of the use of movies and psychoanalysis.

819. Musun, Chris. "The Marketing of Motion Pictures." D. B. A. dissertation, University of Southern California, 1969 (published as The Marketing of Motion Pictures: Both Sides of the Coin: Art-Business, Los Angeles, Musun, 1969).
Historical, descriptive, anecdotal treatment.

820. Muth, Heinrich. "Land-Jugend und Kino" (The Cinema and Rural Youth). In Ulrich Planck, Die Lebenslage der Westdeutschen Landjugend (Munich: Juventa-Verlag, 1956).
Review of methodology and research results concerning the influence of films on children; suggests that sociological inquiries have been scarce; results of a study on the movie attendance habits, and various social correlates, among youths from rural areas.

821. Nagaki, Teiichi. Jido Eiga to Jido Geki (Films for Children and Dramas for Children). Tokyo: Senshin-Sha, 1931. (Study of Children, series B).
The film section (pp. 165-214) discusses reasons for film-type preferences, educational aspects of cinema, and censorship.

822. National Research Center of the Arts. Americans and the Arts: A Survey of Public Opinion. New York: National Research Center of the Arts, 1975.
Personal interviews with 3,005 persons; reports preferences in the arts, participation in artistic activities, attendance at cultural events, and obstacles to attendance.

823. Nawy, Harold. "The San Francisco Erotic Marketplace." Technical Reports of the U.S. Commission on Obscenity and Pornography, vol. 4, pp. 155-224, Washington, D.C.: U.S. Government Printing Office, 1970.
Through observation of 2,791 customers at three adult movie theaters, demographic characteristics are presented; questionnaire data from 251 of these patrons provides validation for external observation.

824. ———. "In the Pursuit of Happiness? Consumers of Erotica in San Francisco." Journal of Social Issues 29 (1973): 147-161.
Observation and questionnaire data from adult movie customers regarding demographic characteristics are reported; 97 percent were males; 70 percent white; 39 percent wore a suit and tie, 49 percent wore neat casual clothing, 31 percent wore a wedding band, 85 percent entered the theater alone.

825. Neblette, C.B. "The Place of the Motion-Picture in Modern Life." Photo-Era 57 (October 1926): 175-180.
An anecdotal examination of the positive and negative social influences of the cinema.

826. Neergaard, Ebbe. "Feature Films Preferred by Danish Youth." Quarterly of Film, Radio and Television 7 (1952-1953): 279-290.
Results of a 1946 survey of 9,000 youths.

827. Nelson, Jeffrey A. "Research in Radio, Television, and Film by Graduate Students in Speech." Central States Speech Journal 19 (Summer 1968): 105-112.
Reports the frequency of theses and dissertations on these three media from 1929 to 1967; reports methodologies used.

828. Neumeyer, Murray Walter. "A Study of the Effect of Film Upon the Religious Attitudes of High School Students." Unpublished Ed.D. dissertation, Syracuse University, 1973.
An attitude scale and questionnaire were administered to 91 high school students; results showed that a film significantly increased the effectiveness of gaining acceptance of a religious curriculum point of view.

829. "New Survey: Metropolitan New Yorkers Better Film-goers than Suburbanites." Variety, May 10, 1967, p. 11.
Frequency of film attendance was higher in the five boroughs of New York City than in surrounding counties; the finding could be explained in terms of Schramm's principle of least effort in the selection of mass communications media.

830. Newspaper Advertising Bureau. "Movie Going in the Metropolis." New York: Newspaper Advertising Bureau, n. d.
A 40 page report of a study conducted in June 1978; evaluations of movies, movie-going decision making, movie opinion leaders, likes and dislikes about movies are reported.

831. _____. "Movie-Going in the United States and Canada." New York: Newspaper Advertising Bureau, October 1981.
A 52 page report of a telephone survey; changes in movie-going from 1973 to 1981, demographic correlates to movie attendance, movie decision making, and likes and dislikes about movies and theaters.

832. "1981 Set New Boxoffice Records, MPAA Reports." Boxoffice, January 1982, p. 23.
Attendance data and the usefulness of the movie rating system are reported; data gathered by the Opinion Research Corp.

833. Noelle-Neumann, Elisabeth. "Mass Communication Media and Public Opinion." Journalism Quarterly 36 (Fall 1959): 401-409.
Cites the usefulness of empirical studies to demonstrate that they are more enlightening than conventional sources of information; "the rule that the more the content of the communication has reference to practical everyday life, or the greater the sociological or psychological significance of a communication, the greater will be its influence on the thought and conduct of the people."

834. Nora, F. F. "The Effect of a Liberal Persuasive Film in Shifting Attitudes of a Group of Journalism Students." In Studies in Higher Education, Biennial Report of the Committee on Educational Research for 1938-1940. Minneapolis: University of Minnesota, 1941, pp. 96-97.

835. Norberg, K. "Perception Research and Audio-Visual Education." Audio-Visual Communication Review 1 (1953): 18-29.

836. North, C. J. and N. D. Golden. "The Latin American Audience Viewpoint on American Films." Journal of the Society of Motion Picture Engineers 17 (July 1931): 18-25.
Reviews literature concerning film-type preferences and the use of dubbing and subtitles.

837. North, Magdalena June. "Films in Changing Ethnic Attitudes and Behavior in the Elementary Grades." Unpublished Ed. D. dissertation, Yeshiva University, 1977.
An experiment involving 224 Chinese and Puerto Rican third and fourth graders; measured attitudes toward themselves, Negroes, and Italians; results showed positive changes in racial/ethnic attitudes.

838. Norwood, Don J. "An Experimental Study of the Comparative Effects of Aggressive Film and Television Content on Physiological Arousal and Psychological Mood." Unpublished Ph. D. dissertation, Southern Illinois University, 1976.
"It was subjectively concluded that substantial agreement existed between" skin conductance response (physiological arousal) and responses to a mood adjective check list (psychological mood).

839. Nowlis, V. "Some Studies of the Influence of Films on Mood and Attitude." Technical Report to the Office of Naval Research, 1960.

840. Nozet, Hughes. "L'Influence du Cinéma sur la Jeunesse: Etudes Expérimentales" (The Influence of the Cinema on Young People: Experimental Studies). Bianco e Nero 11 (1951): 79-83.
Discussion of methodological problems involved in the study of reactions to films.

841. Nudelman, N. M. "Sootnoshenie Obrazov, Aktualiziruemykh Slovesnym Opisaniem i Kinofilmom" (The Relationship Between Images Actualized by Verbal Description and Motion Pictures). Voprosy Psikhologii 4 (July-August 1975): 118-123.
A study of the extent of empathy and identification with a literary image of a hero as compared to a filmic image of a hero; findings suggest the image of the literary hero is more generalized than that of the filmic hero.

842. Oberlander, Keith John. "An Experimental Determination of the Effects of a Film About Moral Behavior and of Peer Group Discussion Regarding Moral Dilemmas Upon the Moral Development of College Students." Unpublished Ph. D. dissertation, University of Southern California, 1980.
Analysis of the ability to teach moral behavior through instructional strategies; use of Kohlberg's six stage development scheme as measured by Rest's Defining Issues Test.

843. O'Brien, James McGeoghegan. "Experiencing the Popular Film: An Audience Gratifications Study." Unpublished Ph. D. dissertation, Northwestern University, 1977.
Compared with other mass media, films were found to be selected rather than habitual, a creative and self-fulfilling activity, and effortful to consume.

844. O'Dell, Sylvia Lynn. "A Study of Parents' Attitudes Towards the Motion Picture Association of America Rating System." Unpublished M. S. thesis, Oklahoma State University, 1973.
Parents did not feel that the rating system could be relied upon to prevent children from seeing unsuitable material in films.

845. Odeon Theatres. "Children's Matinees." Sight and Sound 11 (Summer 1942): 18-20.
A nonquantitative, informal study of children's preferences for film-types and their reactions to films.

846. Oehler, Kurt T. (Attitudinal Change Depending on the Emotional Significance of Given Information). Psychologische Beitrage 19 (1977): 600-614.
A before-after experiment using questionnaires to study attitudes toward war; GSR and pulse rate also measured; the more excited the subjects became during the film, the less frequently they showed a change in attitude.

847. O'Guinn, Thomas. "The Audience's Choice: Movie Selection and Word of Mouth." Paper presented at the International Communication Association conference, May 1981, Minneapolis, MN.

An exploratory study examining the role of word of mouth in the context of other variables as it affects audience first run movie selection; respondents to the survey were undergraduates.

848. Oldfield, R. C. "La Perception Visuelle des Images du Cinéma de la Télévision et du Radar" (Visual Perception of Cinema, Television and Radar Images). Revue Internationale de Filmologie 1 (October 1948): 263-279.
A nonempirical analysis and comparison between media.

849. Olsen, Marvin E. "Motion Picture Attendance and Social Isolation." Sociological Quarterly 1 (April 1960): 107-116.
Support for the hypothesis that people, to a large extent, go to the movies because they cannot find other, more personal forms of recreation (i. e., movies are used as a social substitute).

850. _____. "Correction of 'Motion Picture Attendance and Social Isolation.'" Sociological Quarterly 6 (Spring 1965): 179.
Methodological error invalidates the major finding of the original study.

851. Olusoga, Sikiru. "An Analysis of Black Motion Picture Patrons to Determine the Demand for Black Oriented Movies." Unpublished M. A. thesis, San Francisco State University, 1973.

852. Omohundro, John Thomas. "Los Españoles y el Cine" (The Spaniards and the Cinema). Revista Española de la Opinion Pública 45 (July-September 1976): 231-265.
Personal interviews with 2,432 Spaniards over fifteen years old indicated that the Spanish cinema was generally perceived to be in a state of permanent crisis with most of the evils perceived attributed to censorship; a number of other censorship-related topics were examined and associations between personality type and demographic variables computed.

853. "ORC Poll: Non-Urban Attendance Up, Teenage Market Share Down." Independent Film Journal, October 15, 1975, p. 15.

854. Orr, Donald. "The Impact of In-Flight Entertainment Upon Passengers on Selected Flights of a Recognized Commercial Airline." Unpublished M. A. thesis, Temple University, 1966.

855. Orton, William A. "Motion Pictures. Social Implications." Encyclopaedia of the Social Sciences 11 (1933): 65-68.
Overview of censorship, regulation, economics, and the social significance of films.

856. Osaka Prefecture Association of Juvenile Correction. "Chuto-gakusei no Kogyoeiga Kanran ni Kansuru Chosa" (Survey on Film-viewing by Secondary School Pupils). Osaka, 1935. (Juvenile Correction Pamphlet, series 51).
Report of a survey conducted in May 1935; details the policy of schools regarding students' movie-viewing and the use of films at school.

857. Otis, Laura. "Selective Exposure to the Film Close Encounters." Journal of Psychology 101 (March 1979): 293-295.
Results of a field study in which support for the selective exposure

hypothesis was found: persons attending Close Encounters were significantly more likely to report believing in flying saucers than persons attending The Gauntlet or Saturday Night Fever.

858. Palets, David L., Judith Koon, Elizabeth Whitehead, and Richard B. Hagens. "Selective Exposure: The Potential Boomerang Effect." Journal of Communication 22 (1972): 48-53.
Tested the influence of an English film (Tell Me Lies) that opposed American policy in the Vietnam War on American respondents; based on their findings the authors concluded that a foreign film with an emotional appeal annoyed or frustrated the respondents even though most of the respondents were opposed to the U.S. policy prior to seeing the film.

859. Palmer, C. A. "Commercial Practices in Audience Analysis." Journal of the University Film Association 6 (Spring 1954): 9-10.
Discussion of various audience research methods.

860. Panda, K. C., J. K. Das, and R. N. Kanungo. "A Cross-Cultural Study of Film Preferences on an Indian Student Population." Journal of Social Psychology 57 (1962): 93-104.
Films were categorized by type (e.g., "family," "war," etc.) and students reported their preferences for each type; in general, "social" films were the most preferred; differences in preference are reported by age, sex, and education level.

861. Panda, K. C. and R. N. Kanungo. "A Study of Indian Students' Attitude Towards the Motion Picture." Journal of Social Psychology 57 (1962): 23-31.
Students generally showed a favorable attitude toward movies; males had significantly more favorable attitudes than females; college students' attitudes were significantly more favorable than secondary students; significant differences by age were also reported.

862. Panzarella, Marion A. "A Study to Develop a Cognitive Preference Test Based on Motion Picture Stimuli." Unpublished Ed. D. dissertation, State University of New York at Buffalo, 1970.
Differences in cognitive preferences, as measured by a title test, among three school grades were found to be significant.

863. Parrot, Philippe, P. Spinat, R. Guitton, and F. Corbal. "Une Identification Héroique de l'Adolescent Délinquant: Eddie Constantine" (A Heroic Personification of Juvenile Delinquency: Eddie Constantine). Reeducation 2 (January-February 1957): 23-33.
Analysis of essays on favorite actor by 24 to 18 year old boys; reasons for their preferences are presented with an analysis of unconscious motives for their preferences.

864. Pasquariello, Vincent J. "An Inquiry Into the Influence of Motion Pictures on Children." Unpublished M. A. thesis, University of Southern California, 1950.

865. Patel, A. S. "Attitudes of Adolescent Pupils Toward Cinema Films." Journal of Education and Psychology 9 (1952): 225-230.
Boys held a more favorable attitude toward motion pictures than girls.

866. Paterson, Andrew W. "An Experiment in Pupil Appraisal." Sight and Sound 12 (October 1943): 70-72.
Descriptive discussion of a study designed to "awaken in pupils their powers of observation and criticism" for films.

867. Paulsen, Kathe. "Was Bleibt? Kinder besinnen sich auf einen Film" (What Remains? Children Recall a Film). Film-Bild-Ton 7 (October 1957): 8-13.
Investigation of memory; 22 months after 23 eleven-year-olds had seen a film they were asked to write compositions on what they recalled from the picture; comparative data on adults also collected.

868. Peck, Jeff. "The Child Audience for Theatrical Films in Australia." Media Information Australia no. 17 (August 1980): 43-46.
Results of a 23-item questionnaire focusing on sources of information about films, attendance habits, and film-type preferences.

869. Penn, Roger. "An Experimental Study of the Meaning of Cutting-Rate Variables in Motion Pictures." Unpublished Ph.D. dissertation, University of Iowa, 1967.
Inquiry on the influence of cutting-rate on perception of meaning; 450 respondents evaluated films using semantic differential and word association instruments.

870. _____. "Effect of Motion and Cutting Rate in Motion Pictures." AV Communication Review 19 (1971): 29-50.
A summary of the author's dissertation.

871. Pennacchi, Fabio. "The Cinema and Adolescence with Special Reference to Nervous and Mental Diseases." International Review of Educational Cinematography 2 (September 1930): 1043-1070.
An advocacy piece using clinical cases as evidence for the influence movies have on children.

872. Perentesis, John L. "Effectiveness of a Motion Picture Trailer as Election Propaganda." Public Opinion Quarterly 12 (Fall 1948): 465-469.
Analysis of election returns for a municipal election in Detroit indicated that one candidate benefited appreciably over his opponent through the showing of special motion picture trailers supporting his candidacy.

873. Peri, Joseph. "The Effects of Film Repetition, Programmed Discussion and Audience-Set on the Changing of Verbally Professed Attitudes Towards Due Process of Law." Unpublished Ed.D. dissertation, University of California, Los Angeles, 1968.
Investigated the extent of attitudinal change toward due process of law among junior high school students from two different socioeconomic backgrounds; evaluated the effectiveness of five procedures for enhancing the influence of films designated to affect attitudes.

874. Perron, Roger. "Essai de Mise en Relation de Certain Types de Contenus Filmiques et des Réactions des Spectateurs Enfants" (A Study of the Relationship Between Certain Kinds of Film Sequences and the Reactions of Juvenile Spectators). Paper presented at the 2nd International Congress of Filmology, 1955, Paris.
Verbal and nonverbal responses of 7 to 11 year old boys and girls were recorded during the screening of nine different film sequences;

consistency of the children's reactions was measured and three types of audience participation were identified.

875. Perry, Charles A. "Frequency of Attendance of High-School Students at the Movies." School Review 31 (October 1923): 573-587.
Analysis of 37,505 questionnaires; data analyzed by sex, geographic area, and attendance companion.

876. Perry, Paul K. "Marketing and Attitude Research Applied to Motion Pictures." Paper presented at the International Gallup Conference, March 1968, New Delhi.
Review of Gallup's Audience Research, Inc.'s activities; discusses title tests, subject matter tests, the Audit of Marquee Values, and measuring audience enjoyment.

877. Peters, Charles C. "The Relation of Motion Pictures to Standards of Morality." Journal of Educational Sociology 6 (December 1932): 251-255.
Description of the procedures, sample, and reliability scores for the instrument; results are not presented.

878. _____. "The Relation of Motion Pictures to Standards of Morality." School and Society 39 (March 31, 1934): 414-415.
A summary of the author's book, which was part of the Payne Fund series.

879. Peterson, Jack Arno. "The Effectiveness of Selected Motion Pictures in Changing the Beliefs of Nebraska Secondary School Students Relative to the United Nations and its Activities." Unpublished Ph.D. dissertation, University of Nebraska, 1949.
A pretest-posttest questionnaire was administered to high school students and personal interviews were conducted; results suggest the utility of movies in effecting more positive beliefs about the U.N.

880. Peterson, Ruth C. and L. L. Thurstone. "The Effect of a Motion Picture Film on Children's Attitudes Toward Germans." Journal of Educational Psychology 23 (April 1932): 241-246.
Four Sons was shown to 133 high school students; pretest-posttest questionnaires were used to assess attitudes toward war, German people, and nationality preferences; results showed that the film made the students more friendly toward the Germans.

881. Phelps, Edna Shumaker. "A Critical Summary of Studies of the Effect of Motion Pictures Upon the Habits, Ideals, and Attitudes of Children." Unpublished M.A. thesis, University of Southern California, 1935.

882. Philippon, Odette. "L'Influence du Cinéma sur l'Enfance et l'Adolescence, l'Enquête Nationale Française" (The Influence of the Cinema on Childhood and Adolescence, French National Investigation). Nouvelle Revue Pedagogique 7 (1952): 526-530.
Results of a study by the Catholic Committee for Childhood of France; major conclusion is that children who go to the movies more than once a week need psychiatric attention.

883. Pierson, A. "La Jeunesse Devant les Images" (Youth and Pictures). Pedogogie, Education et Culture, November 1949, pp. 532.

884. Pitta, A. and E. Capriolo. "I Ragazzi votano per 'Domani e Troppo Tarde'" (Children's Poll on "Domani e Troppo Tarde"). Cinema 5 (April 15, 1951): 198-202.
Survey of 1,214 10 to 15 year olds.

885. Pivniceru, C. "Notiunea de 'Public' nu Spune Nimic, Daca nu Stim din Cine e Format Acest Public." Cinema 14 (March 1976): 11.
Analysis of the Rumanian film audience.

886. Poffenberger, A. T. "Motion Pictures and Crime." Scientific Monthly, April 1921, pp. 336-339.
Asserts that "wrongly used and not carefully guarded, (movies) might easily become a training school for anti-Americanism, immorality and disregard for law"--especially among the mentally deficient.

887. Poffenberger, Thomas M. "A Technique for Evaluating Family Life and Mental Health Films." Unpublished Ed. D. dissertation, Michigan State College, 1954.
Presents the results of a questionnaire administered to 442 individuals which attempted to develop a method for film evaluation.

888. _____. "A Technique for Evaluating Family Life and Mental Health Films." Marriage and Family Living 18 (August 1956): 219-223.
A summary of the author's dissertation.

889. Ponzo, Ezio. "Testimonianze di Adolescenti su un Episodio Filmico" (Statements by Young People About a Film). Scuola Positiva 4 (1952): 514-525.
Accuracy of recall among 115 11 to 19 year old boys was tested by means of showing them a film followed by questioning.

890. _____. "Temoignages d'Adolescents sur un Episode Filme" (Statements by Young People About a Film). Revue Internationale de Filmologie 5 (April-June 1954): 147-159.
Reprint of the Scuola Positiva article.

891. Ponzo, Mario. "Di Alcune Osservazioni Psicologiche fatte Durante Rappresentazioni Cinematografiche" (About Some Psychological Observations Made During Cinematographic Presentations). Atti della Regia Academia della Science de Torino 47 (1911): 943-948.

892. _____. "Ricerche e Considerazioni Intorno all'Influenza dell'Esercizio sulle Rappresentazioni Spaziali Eutanee" (Research and Considerations on the Influence of Eutaneous Spatial Representations). Atti della Regia Academia delle Science de Torino 47 (1911): 1037-1061.

893. _____. (The Film and Child Delinquency.) L'Infanzia Anormale 12 (1919).

894. _____. "Cinéma et Psychologie" (Cinema and Psychology). Revue Internationale de Filmologie 1 (October 1948): 295-297.
Speech to the International Congress of Psychology conference in which avenues for research are suggested.

895. _____. "Il Cinema e la Creazione Fantastica del Tipo" (Cinema and the Imaginative Creation of Types). Bianco e Nero 8 (1948).

896. _____. "Il Cinema e le Imagini Collettive" (The Cinema and Collective Images). Archivo de Psicologia, Neurologia e Psichiatria 10 (1949): 389-405.
Results of experiments on collective stereotypes; concludes that films can create favorable conditions for the development of collective images and, consequently, can be used as a means for modifying social behavior.

897. _____. "Le Cinéma et les Images Collectives" (The Cinema and Collective Images). Revue Internationale de Filmologie 2 (1950, no. 6): 141-151.
A review of literature.

898. Porter, Elfa McWilliam. "The Curve of Retention in Moving Pictures for Young Children." Unpublished M. A. thesis, State University of Iowa, 1930.
Respondents in four age levels, ranging from second-graders to graduate students and adults, were tested over time; data are reported by film-type.

899. Post, Gene Leroy. "A Study of the Effect of a Subliminal Stimulus Upon Attitudes Developed Toward a Character Portrayed in a Motion Picture Film." Unpublished Ed. D. dissertation, Oklahoma State University, 1965.
A subliminal message had no significant effect on subjects' attitudes.

900. Poyer, Georges. "Psychologie Differentielle et Filmologie" (Differential Psychology and Filmology). Revue Internationale de Filmologie 1 (September-October 1947): 111-116.
Discussion of avenues for research.

901. Prados, M. "The Use of Films in Psychotherapy." American Journal of Orthopsychiatry 21 (1951): 36-46.

902. Pratt, John. "Notes on Commercial Movie Technique." International Journal of Psycho-Analysis 24 (1943): 185-188.
A nonempirical discussion of audience reaction to and interaction with movies from a psychological perspective.

903. Preston, Mary I. "Children's Reactions to Movie Horrors and Radio Crime." Journal of Pediatrics 19 (August 1941): 147-168.
Responses to an emotional inventory by 200 children; data reported include filmic effects on nervousness, eating, nail biting, callousness, dreams, and daydreaming.

904. Price, Frank Turner. "Some Effects of Film-Mediated Professional Models on the Self-Perceptions of Black School Children." Unpublished Ph. D. dissertation, Wayne State University, 1970.
Elementary school children's physical and intellectual self-esteem, feelings of personal worth and internal control were measured before and after exposure to films presenting black and white models.

905. "Les Problèmes Sociaux du Cinéma: Cinéma et Criminalité Précoce" (Social Problems of the Cinema: Cinema and Early Criminality). Revue Internationale du Cinéma Educateur 4 (January 1932): 73-75.

906. "Profile of Typical German Filmgoer." Variety, May 12, 1976, p. 13.
Frequency of attendance by age and sex.

907. "Public Reaction: The Lion has Wings." Documentary NewsLetter, February 1940, p. 5.
Results of interviews with 200 people reporting reasons for attendance and affective response to the film.

908. "The Quarter's Poll: Moving Pictures." Public Opinion Quarterly 13 (Summer 1949): 359-360.
Comparison of the quality of movies over time, reasons for less frequent attendance, reasons for not enjoying a film, and the types of films people would rather not see.

909. Quigley, Martin. "Public Opinion and the Motion Picture." Public Opinion Quarterly 1 (April 1937): 129-133.
A historical accounting of the public's attitude toward movies.

910. _____. "Who Goes to the Movies." Motion Picture Herald, August 10, 1957, pp. 21-22.
Frequency of attendance reported by age, sex, and education.

911. Rachty, Gehan and Khalil Sabat. "Importation of Films for Cinema and Television in Egypt." Paris: UNESCO, n. d. (approximately 1980).
Includes a brief discussion of the social effects of imported films.

912. Raethgen, Marialuise. "Jugend und Film" (Youth and Film). Unpublished B. A. thesis, Frankfurt, 1952.

913. Raines, I. I. "Preferences of a Small Town Motion Picture Audience." Current Economic Comment, May 1951, pp. 51-59.
Results of a questionnaire sent to adults; reports frequency of attendance, film-type preferences, and attitudes toward advertising films; data are analyzed by age, sex, education, and marital status of the 279 respondents.

914. Ramseyer, Lloyd Louis. "A Study of the Influence of Documentary Films." Unpublished Ph. D. dissertation, Ohio State University, 1938.
Use of an attitude scale and information test administered to 7th through 12th graders and adults.

915. _____. "Factors Influencing Attitudes and Attitude Change." Educational Research Bulletin (Ohio State University) 18 (January 1939): 9-14, 30.
A review of literature discussing the effect of two WPA films (The Plow That Broke the Plains and The River) on people's attitudes; differences by respondent sex and occupation are noted.

916. _____. "Measuring 'Intangible' Effects of Motion Pictures." Educational Screen 18 (September 1939): 236-237, 261.
Discussion of attitudinal literature in general and the author's work in particular.

917. Randall, Richard. "Classification by the Motion Picture Industry." Technical Reports of the U. S. Commission on Obscenity and Pornography, vol. 5, pp. 219-292. Washington, D. C.: U. S. Government Printing Office, 1970.

Reported that underage teenagers unaccompanied by adults were frequently able to gain admittance to R and X rated films in New York City; a high level of "self-enforcement" of the age restriction on admission to R and X films by teenagers themselves was found.

918. Randolph, David K. "An Experimental Study of the Effect on an Audience of Two Showings of a Sound Film Utilizing Two Narrations from Opposite Points of View." Unpublished M.A. thesis, San Francisco State College, 1964.
Inquiry into the influence of narration on the attitudes and interpretations of viewers; 131 undergraduates participated.

919. Rasmus, Mildred H. "Degeneration of Emotional Response Upon Reshowing of Motion Picture Situations." Unpublished M.A. thesis, State University of Iowa, 1933.
Use of galvanic skin response in an experimental setting with 15 undergraduates who viewed love, personal danger, impersonal danger, and comedy scenes; degeneration of response was greatest in comedy and impersonal danger scenes.

920. Raths, Louis E. and Frank N. Trager. "Public Opinion and Crossfire." Journal of Educational Sociology 21 (February 1948): 345-368.
A before-after questionnaire showed that the film "does not change anyone's basic attitudes; but it is one more instrument ... which can help in that learning process which ultimately will make of America a richer and fuller democratic society."

921. Raven, S. "Home from Home." Spectator 207 (November 24, 1961): 736-738.

922. Real, Michael R. and Christopher A. Hassett. "Audience Perceptions of the Academy Award Telecast." Paper presented at the International Communication Association conference, May 1981, Minneapolis, MN.
Telephone survey of 141 adults; measured motives for viewing and the influence of mass media and interpersonal channels on movie selection.

923. Reardon, John P. "The Cinema and the Child." Studies: An Irish Quarterly Review 18 (September 1929): 431-442.
Review of literature focusing mostly on movies as they relate to education and child development.

924. Rebeillard, Monique. "Etat Actuel de la Recherche Filmologique en Neuropsychiatrie Infantile" (Present State of Filmological Research in Infantile Neuro-psychiatry). Unpublished Ph.D. dissertation, La Productrice (Paris), 1955.
Self-report and physiological methods were used to determine frequency of attendance, comprehension and recall of films, and affective responses to movies among "normal and maladjusted" children.

925. Redclay, Lillian Bilkey. "Adolescent Reactions to a Film Regarding Pre-Marital Sex Experiences." Unpublished Ed.D. dissertation, Pennsylvania State University, 1964.
A questionnaire was constructed to ascertain evaluation of the film and information related to various behavior depicted in the film.

926. Redslob, E. and A. Brini. "Les Méfaits de la 'Symphonie Pastorale'" (The Dangers of "La Symphonie Pastorale"). Annales d'Occulistique 106 (1947): 104-106.
Case study of a 14 year old girl in which hysterical blindness occurred as a consequence of her viewing the film La Symphonie Pastorale.

927. Reighard, Patton Breon. "Retention of Sequential Events in Dramatic Narrative Film." Unpublished Ph. D. dissertation, University of Texas at Austin, 1977.
An experimental study in which subjects were undergraduates; data were analyzed by sex, birth order, left and righthandedness, and field dependency; results discussed in terms of the functional lateralization of the brain and its relationship to performance on the Closure Flexibility test and a retention test.

928. Reilly, Sandra. "Children's Emotional Reactions to Frightening Media." Unpublished M. A. thesis, University of Wisconsin, 1980.
Sixth and tenth grade children's fright experiences from television shows and movies were measured by a survey; the children's mothers also reported on their child's experience.

929. Reitze, Arnold W. "The Relationship of Acquired Information or Knowledge Obtained from Certain Educational Motion-Picture Films to the Intelligence, Grade, Age, Sex, and Type of Educational Training of Pupils." Unpublished Ph. D. dissertation, New York University, 1937.
A study involving public school students demonstrated that "most pupils gain considerable information through mere exposure to educational motion-picture films."

930. _____. "The Relationship of Acquired Information or Knowledge Obtained from Certain Educational Motion Picture Films to the Intelligence, Grade, Age, Sex, and Type of Educational Training of Pupils." Journal of Educational Sociology 12 (1938): 177-181.
A summary of the author's dissertation.

931. Renshaw, Samuel. "Sleep Mobility as an Index of Motion-Picture Influence." Journal of Educational Sociology 6 (December 1932): 226-230.
Description of the procedures, sample, and setting for the study; results are not presented.

932. "Replies to a Questionnaire." Sight and Sound 23 (October-December, 1953): 99-104, 112.
Survey of seven film directors and ten film critics.

933. "Report on Pre-Release Preferences of Moviegoers for December 1976." Film Bulletin 45 (November/December 1976): 5-8.
Based on a survey by Audienscope, audience predispositions for twelve movies are reported; Network was the number one choice and Rocky the last choice.

934. Respress, James R. "The New Motion Picture Rating Code and its Effect on Teenage Audiences." Unpublished M. A. thesis, Michigan State University, 1973.
Findings indicated that teenagers were aware of the code and its meaning, they had no trouble gaining access to restricted films,

theater owners were not pleased with the rating system, and many theater owners feared local and state prosecution for exhibition of restricted films.

935. Reymaker, J. de. "Methodes voor het Onderzoek van de Invloed van de Film op de Jeugd" (Research Methods used in Examining the Influence of Films on Young People). Unpublished thesis, University of Louvain, 1950.
A critical review of the empirical literature on film preferences, the influence of film on mental life, and attitudinal factors.

936. Reynolds, James Conrad. "The Effect of Viewer Distance on Film Induced Anxiety." Unpublished Ed. D. dissertation, Indiana University, 1968.
The problem addressed was whether viewer anxiety could be induced by a film and, if so, whether the level of induced anxiety was a function of the type of film and/or a function of the viewer distance from the film; a pretest-posttest design was used.

937. Riesman, David and Evelyn Riesman. "Movies and Audiences." American Quarterly 4 (1952): 195-202.
Review of research and discussion of the difficulties encountered in doing film audience research.

938. Riley, Matilda White and John W. Riley, Jr. "A Sociological Approach to Communications Research." Public Opinion Quarterly 15 (Fall 1951): 445-460.
Discussion of Mannheim's concept of sociology of knowledge: "A description and structural analysis of the ways in which social relationships, in fact, influence thought."

939. Rimberg, John David. "The Motion Picture in the Soviet Union, 1918-1952: A Sociological Analysis." Unpublished Ph. D. dissertation, Columbia University, 1959.
An opinion survey suggests that entertainment is the primary concern of the movie-goers and that they are prepared to accept only a limited amount of propaganda; concludes that most Soviet-released films reflect compromises concerning film content.

940. Rinehart, Stanley R. "Factors Affecting the Decline of the Motion Picture Audience in the United States Since World War II." Unpublished M. B. A. thesis, Ohio State University, 1959.

941. Ritze, Frederick Henry. "Responses of Pakistani College Students to a Selected American Film." Unpublished Ed. D. dissertation, Columbia University, 1967.
Written responses by 403 undergraduates to film character, color, music, main idea of the film, and specific aspects liked or disliked.

942. Rivkin, Allen. "The Hollywood Letter." Free World 12 (October 1946): 66-67.
Informal discussion of Gallup's Audience Research, Inc.

943. Road, Sinclair. "The Influence of the Film." Penguin Film Review 1 (1946): 57-66.
Suggests that movies exercise "in contemporary society an influence which is enormous, though still largely unmeasured"; points out the

difficulty involved in trying to assess the influence of cinema and the positive effects that may be caused by the films.

944. Robertus, Patricia and Rita James Simon. "The Movie Code: A View from Parents and Teenagers." Journalism Quarterly 47 (Autumn 1970): 568-569, 629.
Teenagers were more likely to use the rating system than parents when making their film selection.

945. Robinson, Deanna Campbell. "An Exploration of Elite Audience Attitudes Toward Television and Theater Movies." Unpublished M. A. thesis, University of Oregon, 1972.
Through factor analysis eight elite viewer types were identified; the most positive viewers were most emphatic in their belief in the use of TV and film for self-enhancement, planned their viewing in advance, made the most careful selection decisions, and were more analytical than less enthusiastic viewers.

946. _____. "Film Analyticity: Variations in Viewer Orientation." Unpublished Ph. D. dissertation, University of Oregon, 1974.
Four studies which investigated use of film for self-enhancement, selection of films, critical viewing behavior, and behavioral reactions to films.

947. _____. "Television/Film Attitudes of Upper-Middle Class Professionals." Journal of Broadcasting 19 (Spring 1975): 195-209.
A summary of the author's M. A. thesis.

948. Robinson, J. A. and A. Barnett. " 'Jaws' Neurosis." New England Journal of Medicine 193 (November 27, 1975): 1154-1155.
Report of a case study of cinematic neurosis.

949. Roessler, E. and W. Roessler. "Sittlich Filmbeurteilung Zehn- bis Vierzehnjähriger: Eine Psychologische-Pädagogische Studie zu dem Film 'Teufelskerle' " (Moral Evaluation of Films by 10-14 Year Olds: A Psychological-Pedagogic Study Concerning the Film "Teufelskerle" (Boys' Town)). Film, Jugend, Schule 44 (September 1955): 1-8.
Thirty boys responded to a questionnaire and wrote essays about the film.

950. Roessler, Robert and Forrest Collins. "Personality Correlates of Physiological Responses to Motion Pictures." Psychophysiology 6 (May 1970): 732-739.
High ego strength subjects were found to be more responsive on two physiological measures, as well as for self-report data, than low ego strength subjects for both a stressor and a bland movie.

951. Roessler, W. E. "Miterzieher Film: Eine Pädagogische Studie im Anschluss an den Film 'Das Gorsse Abenteuer' " (The Film as an Aid to Education: A Pedagogic Study Carried Out with the Aid of the Film "The Great Adventure"). Film, Jugend, Schule 43 (April 1956).
406 10- to 14-year-olds responded to questions posed about a film they saw.

952. Rose, Ernest D. "Motion Picture Research and the Art of the Film Maker." Journal of University Film Producers Association 15 (1963, no. 2): 8-11, 23.

Presents results of studies dealing with audience reactions to various film techniques.

953. ———. "Attitude as a Function of Discrepancy Resolution in Multiple Channel Communication." Unpublished Ph. D. dissertation, Stanford University, 1964.
An experiment involving 165 male undergraduates; Osgood and Tannenbaum's congruity principle is used in explaining the results.

954. Rose, Nicholas. "A Psychological Study of Motion Picture Audience Behavior." Unpublished Ph. D. dissertation, University of California, Los Angeles, 1951.
Use of infra-red photography to record smiling and laughing behavior of an audience watching a comedy film.

955. ———. "Some Comments on Motion Picture Research." Journal of the University Film Producers Association 6 (Spring 1954): 3-8.
A discussion of audience research techniques especially the use of infra-red photography.

956. Rosen, Irwin C. "The Effect of the Motion Picture 'Gentleman's Agreement' on Attitudes Toward Jews." Journal of Psychology 26 (October 1948): 525-536.
Results of college students' responses to an attitude scale and essay-type questions; results indicate that after viewing the film the experimental group changed in direction of increased tolerance toward Jews.

957. Rosenman, Martin F. "Dogmatism and the Movie 'Dr. Strangelove.'" Psychological Reports 20 (1967, Part I): 942.
Using Rokeach's Dogmatism Scale, the hypothesis that open-minded subjects would rate Dr. Strangelove as better than would close-minded subjects was supported.

958. Rosenthal, N. H. "Films and Australian--Asian Relations." Revue Internationale de Filmologie 11 (July-September 1961): 28-36.
Pilot study investigating the impact of Indian films on Australians; questionnaire distributed to 46 (mostly female) adults.

959. Rosenthal, Solomon P. "Change of Socio-Economic Attitudes Under Radical Motion Picture Propaganda." Unpublished Ph. D. dissertation, Columbia University, 1934.
200 undergraduates participated in a before-after experiment which found that a selected film was effective in changing attitudes on a wide range of socio-economic problems in the direction intended.

960. ———. "Change of Socio-Economic Attitudes Under Radical Motion Picture Propaganda." Archives of Psychology no. 166 (April 1934): 5-46.
A summary of the author's dissertation.

961. Rosten, Leo C. "A 'Middletown' Study of Hollywood." Public Opinion Quarterly 5 (April 1939): 314-320.
Review of literature with a suggestion for a research study.

962. ———. "Movies and Propaganda." Annals of the American Academy of Political and Social Science 254 (November 1947): 116-124.
A nonempirical analysis of the nature of propaganda and its relationship to motion pictures.

963. Rowson, Simon. "The Social and Political Aspects of Films." Journal of the British Kinematography Society 2 (April 1939): 75-86.
Largely advocacy in tone with some attendance and other statistical data.

964. Rubin, Herbert E. and Elias Katz. "Motion Picture Psychotherapy of Psychotic Depressions in an Army General Hospital." Sociometry 9 (1946): 86-89.
Preliminary report on the use of films as a therapeutic agent in the treatment of soldiers with psychotic depressions; data were gathered by observation of patients' responses to the film; beneficial outcomes are discussed.

965. Ruch, Floyd L. "Predicting the Box Office Returns of Motion Pictures." American Psychologist 1 (October 1946): 454.
A two-stage questionnaire procedure was employed to detect what the public wanted to know about a picture before deciding to see it.

966. Ruckmick, Christian A. "How Do Motion Pictures Affect the Attitudes and Emotions of Children? The Galvanic Technique Applied to the Motion-Picture Situation." Journal of Educational Sociology 6 (December 1932): 210-216.
Description of the study, sample, and procedures; results are not presented.

967. _____. "Affective Responses to the Motion-Picture Situation by Means of the Galvanic Technique." Psychological Bulletin 30 (1933): 712-713.
Respondents were 150 normal individuals ranging in age from six to fifty years whose responses were compared to fifty psychopathic hospital patients.

968. Ruette, Victor de. "The Cinema--An Educational or Demoralizing Agent?" International Review of Educational Cinematography 5 (April 1933): 270-282.
A two part study of the demoralizing influence movies may have on the nerves; the second part suggests constructive uses of films in education.

969. _____. "The Cinema and Child Psychology." International Review of Educational Cinematography 6 (January 1934): 38-49.
A review of literature with a special focus on the educational uses of film.

970. Rufsvold, Margaret I. "Audio-visual Materials and Libraries for Children and Young People." In Frances Henne, Alice Brooks, and Ruth Ersted (eds.), Youth, Communication and Libraries (Chicago: American Library Association, 1949), pp. 78-92 (papers presented before the Library Institute at the University of Chicago, August 11-16, 1947).
Discussion of the use of films and other materials.

971. Rusted, Brian. "Evaluation in Context: A Comparative Study in Film Evaluation." Paper presented at the 4th International Conference on Culture and Communication, April 1981, Philadelphia, PA.
Purpose was to determine if there are cultural differences in the evaluation of films; compared two groups of newspaper reviews by English speaking reviewers from Ontario and French speaking reviewers from Quebec.

972. Ryan, Steve S. "An Adjective Rating Scale for Film Previews." Paper presented at the University Film Association conference, College Park, MD, August 1977. Available in ERIC ED 144 157.
Factor analysis of college students' responses finds six dimensions of meaning that occur in the rating of film previews.

973. Salomon, Gavriel. "Internalization of Filmic Schematic Operations in Interaction with Learners' Aptitudes." Journal of Educational Psychology 66 (August 1974): 499-511.
Three experiments involving eighth and ninth grade pupils; results supported the hypothesis that filmic modeling is internalized by observers and can be used by them.

974. Santelli, Cesar. "Children and War Films." Living Age 338 (August 1, 1930): 664-670.
The film Verdon, Visions d'Histoire impressed primary school children with the discomforts of war but did not worry them greatly.

975. Sarett, Carla Joan. "Socialization Patterns and Preschool Children's Television and Film-Related Play Behavior." Unpublished Ph. D. dissertation, University of Pennsylvania, 1981.
Naturalistic observation of free-play periods in preschools catering to children of either professional or working class parents; analysis focused on the structuring of social relationships and the purposiveness of the activity in play as related to mediated themes.

976. Sava, V. "Nova Filme Dintr-un An." Cinema 10 (November 1972): 4-7, 46.
Workers from a Bucharest factory respond to a questionnaire concerning nine Rumanian films released in 1972.

977. Sbrana, G. "Esplosione Delinquenziale in un Ragazzo per un Moto d' Animo Indotto del Cinema" (Outbreak of Delinquency in a Child due to Emotions Aroused at the Cinema). Atti Convegno Criminologia, 1952.

978. Scannell, Joan S. "Affecting Children's Attitudes Toward Stereotyped Vocational Roles with Educational Films." Unpublished M. A. thesis, University of Kansas, 1975.
An experiment involving 645 fourth, fifth, and sixth graders' responses to a questionnaire; the female-image film affected the children's attitudes, especially among the boys and 4th and 6th graders.

979. Schechter, Mrs. Jacob. "How the United Parents Associations Regards Radio and Motion Pictures as These Affect Children." High Points 23 (September 1941): 5-11.
Advocacy piece urging education of "our young people to become properly receptive, discriminating in their judgments and develop for themselves criteria and higher standards for determining their choice"; brief review of some empirical literature.

980. Schifirnet, Constantin. "Optiunea Pentru a Adolescentilor Scolari" (Choice of the Film by Adolescent Students). Sociologia in Actiune 2 (1973): 361-365.
Investigated motives for attendance and preference for the cinema and theater; analysis of motives for cinema choice suggests that

going to the movies acts in a formative way in establishing the cultural horizon of secondary education students.

981. Schiller, Patricia. "Effects of Mass Media on the Sexual Behavior of Adolescent Females." Technical Reports of the U. S. Commission on Obscenity and Pornography, vol. 1, pp. 191-195. Washington, D. C.: U. S. Government Printing Office, 1970.
Movies were cited as being more provocative or sexually stimulating to a greater extent among college than high school respondents.

982. Schlanger, Benjamin and William A. Hoffberg. "Effects of Television on the Motion Picture Theater." Journal of the Society of Motion Picture and Television Engineers 56 (January 1951): 39-43.
Analysis of the need for refinements and improvements in theaters to draw audiences back to the movies.

983. _____. "New Approaches Developed by Relating Film Production Techniques to Theater Exhibition." Journal of the Society of Motion Picture and Television Engineers 57 (September 1951): 231-237.
Technical discussion with mention of audience factors.

984. Schmid, F. "Der Jugendfilm" (The Film for Young People). Film, Bild, Funk 3 (1950).

985. Schmidt, G. and V. Sigusch. "Sex Differences in Response to Psychosexual Stimulation by Films and Slides." Journal of Sex Research 6 (1970): 268-283.

986. Schneider, R. "Erzieht der Film zu Oberflächlichen Sehen? Ein Theoretischer Beitrag fur die Praxis" (Does the Film Bring About Superficial Observation? Theoretical Contribution for Practical Application). Welt der Schule 4 (1951).

987. "School Children and Moving Pictures in England." School and Society 6 (July 21, 1917): 78-79.
Reports on the results of a study in Manchester; children's frequency of attendance and number of film programs for children are reported.

988. Schubert, Helga. "Zur Verwendung von Filmreproduktionen für die Neurosendiagnostik" (Use of Film in the Diagnosis of Neuroses). Zeitschrift für Psychologie 172 (1966): 182-202.
Neurotic and normal subjects were shown a silent film portraying 24 realistic life situations; the neurotic group reported a larger number of unusual responses than the normal group.

989. Schwartz, Stanley. "Film Music and Attitude Change: A Study to Determine the Effect of Manipulating a Musical Soundtrack Upon Changes in Attitude Toward Militarism--Pacifism Held by Tenth Grade Social Studies Students." Unpublished Ph. D. dissertation, Syracuse University, 1970.
An experiment involving 159 pupils who responded to two forms of the Droba Scale of Militarism and Pacifism.

990. Schweitzer, Harold Clayton, Jr. "Comparison of Color and Black and White Films in the Modification of Attitudes." Unpublished Ph. D. dissertation, Fordham University, 1963.

Four films and four separate attitude questionnaires were used in this study with seventh and eighth graders; results showed that color films had a slight but nonsignificant advantage over black and white films in modifying attitudes and in the retention of attitude change.

991. Scollon, Robert W., Jr. "A Study of Some Communicator Variables Related to Attitude Restructuring Through Motion Picture Films." Unpublished Ph.D. dissertation, Pennsylvania State University, 1956.
An experiment using a questionnaire and Army basic trainees.

992. "Scot Filmgoing Up, Statistics Reveal." Variety, April 14, 1976, p. 40.
Brief report from the Scottish Abstract of Statistics.

993. Scott, Edward M. "Personality and Movie Preference." Psychological Reports 3 (March 1957): 17-18.
The Minnesota Multiphasic Personality Inventory was administered to 154 undergraduates and rank order correlations were computed between the MMPI and the students' movie preference choices; seven personality variables and six film-types resulted.

994. Scott, Paul T. "The Mass Media in Los Angeles Since the Rise of Television." Journalism Quarterly 31 (Spring 1954): 161-166, 192.
Examination of newspapers, radio, and film and concludes that "the worst is probably over for the motion picture industry."

995. "The Screen Answers Back: A Films and Filming Survey." Films and Filming 8 (May 1962): 11-18, 45.
Survey of film critics, directors, producers, screenwriters and actors inquiring as to the critic's role, influence of the critics on filmmaking, and an assessment of the critical state of the art.

996. Seagoe, May V. "The Child's Reaction to the Movies." Journal of Juvenile Research 15 (July 1931): 169-180.
Responses to a questionnaire by 800 first through eighth graders; data reported include: the social situation of movie attendance, film-type preferences, educational values, and preferences for actors.

997. _____. "Children's Television Habits and Preferences." Quarterly of Film, Radio and Television 6 (1951-1952): 143-153.
Questionnaires distributed to 323 kindergarteners through seventh graders; presents frequency of film attendance data and compares TV ownership with frequency of attendance.

998. Seelmann-Eggebert, U. "Jugend und Film" (Youth and Film). Der Neue Film 1 (1947).

999. Segers, Frank. "Gallup Check Re Likes: Theatre, and/or, Homes." Variety, May 25, 1977, pp. 13, 38.
Little dissatisfaction with films found in this U.S. survey but a majority of the respondents preferred viewing films on TV rather than at theaters.

1000. Seve, Lucien. "Cinéma et Méthode. I" (Cinema and Method). Revue Internationale de Filmologie 1 (July-August 1947): 42-46.
Discussion of methodological issues.

1001. _____. "Cinéma et Méthode. II" (Cinema and Method). Revue Internationale de Filmologie 1 (September-October 1947): 171-174.

1002. _____. "Cinéma et Méthode. III" (Cinema and Method). Revue Internationale de Filmologie 1 (October 1948): 351-356.

1003. Shaw, Robert. "Package Deal in Film Opinions." The Screen Writer, March 1947, pp. 28-37.
A profile of Gallup's Audience Research, Inc. operation including discussion of the Profile Preview System.

1004. Sheffield Juvenile Organization Committee. "Survey of Children's Cinema Matinees in Sheffield." S. J. O. C., September 1931.

1005. Sherif, Muzafer and S. Stansfeld Sargent. "Ego-Involvement and the Mass Media." Journal of Social Issues 3 (Summer 1947): 8-16.
States that while it is easy to establish that ego-involvement in the movies occurs, it is difficult to evaluate its effect on behavior; radio and the press are compared to film.

1006. Shippy, Lena W. "The Photoplay and Character Development." Unpublished M. A. thesis, University of Kansas, 1935.

1007. Shook, Mollie Stell Wiggins. "Changing the Racial Attitudes of White Students Toward Blacks Using Commerically Produced Films." Unpublished Ed. D. dissertation, Duke University, 1972.
A quasi-experiment involving high school students using a 90-item attitude scale; subjects viewed three commercial films and it was found that racial attitudes were changed in the direction predicted.

1008. Short, Ray LeRoy. "A Social Study of the Motion Picture." Unpublished M. A. thesis, State University of Iowa, 1916.
Includes the results of a questionnaire distributed to public school children; reports frequency of attendance and film-type preferences.

1009. Short, William H. "The Effect of Motion Pictures on the Social Attitudes of High-School Children." Journal of Educational Sociology 6 (December 1932): 220-226.
A summary of Peterson and Thurstone's Payne Fund report; construction of the attitude scale is described but the results are not presented.

1010. Shull, Claude Archer. "The Suitability of the Commercial Entertainment Motion Picture to the Age of the Child." Unpublished Ed. D. dissertation, Stanford University, 1939.
Results of a questionnaire distributed to 28,123 fourth to eighth graders; frequency of attendance, day of the week with most frequent attendance, and film-type preferences reported; suggests policy recommendations for children's film-viewing.

1011. _____. "A Study in Suitability of Motion-Picture-Theater Programs to the Needs of the Child." Journal of Educational Sociology 13 (January 1940): 274-279.
A summary of the author's dissertation.

1012. Shuttleworth, Frank K. "Measuring the Influence of Motion-Picture Attendance on Conduct and Attitudes." Journal of Educational Sociology 6 (December 1932): 216-219.

Questionnaire study of over 1,000 children; findings indicate that frequent movie-goers achieved lower scores on the conduct test and displayed less desirable attitudes than non-movie-goers.

1013. Sicker, Albert. "Kind und Film. Der Einfluss des Filmes auf das Seelenleben des Kindes. Eine Experimentelle Studie unter Verwendung des Pigem-und des Tuanima-Tests" (Children and Film. The Influence of Films on the Child's Mental Life. An Experimental Study Using the Pigem and Tuanima Tests). Beihefte zur Schweizerischen Zeitschrift für Psychologie und ihre Anwendungen, no. 28, 1956.
Influence of movies was explored qualitatively and quantitatively; includes frequency of attendance and film preferences at different ages.

1014. Siebenand, Paul Alcuin. "The Beginnings of Gay Cinema in Los Angeles: The Industry and the Audience." Unpublished Ph.D. dissertation, University of Southern California, 1975.
The study examined the audience for gay films; the author interviewed writers, directors, producers, critics, exhibitors; 62 patrons attending one Los Angeles theater completed and returned a survey of audience characteristics left at this theater.

1015. Siegel, Alberta Engvall. "The Effect of Film-Mediated Fantasy Aggression on Strength of Aggressive Drive in Young Children." Unpublished Ph.D. dissertation, Stanford University, 1955.
An experiment testing the catharsis hypothesis in which 24 three to five year olds participated.

1016. _____. "Film-Mediated Fantasy Aggression and Strength of Aggressive Drive." Child Development 27 (September 1956): 365-378.
A summary of the author's dissertation.

1017. Sierra y Amezquita, Maria. "Moral Influence of the Movies on Children and Adolescents." World Education 5 (1940): 375-376.
Summary of research with the author advocating either prohibiting attendance among children or the provision for age-suitable film programs.

1018. Siersted, Ellen and H. Lund Hansen. "Réactions des Petits Enfants au Cinema: Résumé d'une Série d'Observations Faites au Danemark" (Reactions of Small Children in the Cinema: Summary of a Series of Observations Made in Denmark). Revue Internationale de Filmologie 2 (1950, nos. 7-8): 241-245.
Infra-red photographs recorded the reactions of primary school children to several films; follow-up questioning was also used to determine behavioral and affective responses.

1019. Silvey, Robert and Judy Kenyon. "Why You Go to the Cinema." Films and Filming 11 (June 1965): 4-5.
Statistical analysis of the attendance habits of Britons including reasons for attendance, film-type preferences, and use of other media.

1020. Simon, Armando. "A Quantitative Nonreactive Study of Mass Behavior with Emphasis on the Cinema as Behavioral Catalyst." Psychological Reports 48 (June 1981): 775-785.

Discussion of quantification of fads in the mass media through unobtrusive means; conceptual distinctions between a fad, panic, and fashion are drawn.

1021. Simon, Daniel. "The Influence of the Denver Film Critics Upon the Movie Selection Habits of the General Audience." Unpublished M. A. thesis, University of Denver, 1974.

1022. Simon, Dorothy Kavinoky. "The Effect of Movies on Children." Unpublished M. A. thesis, University of Buffalo, 1931.

1023. Simonet, Thomas Solon. "Regression Analysis of Prior Experiences of Key Production Personnel as Predictors of Revenues from High-Grossing Motion Pictures in American Release." Ph. D. dissertation, Temple University, 1977 (reprinted by Arno Press, 1980).
Statistical analysis of the experience records of the producer, director, original author, screenwriter, and three leading performers.

1024. Simonet, Thomas. "Industry." Film Comment 14 (January-February 1978): 72-73.
Discussion of early attempts at film audience research.

1025. Simonet, Thomas. "Performers' Marquee Values in Relation to Top-Grossing Films." Paper presented at the Society for Cinema Studies conference, March 1978, Philadelphia, PA.
Statistical analysis using Gallup's data as reported in the "Continuing Audit of Marquee Values" during the 1944-1948 period.

1026. _____. "Market Research: Beyond the Fanny of the Cohn." Film Comment 16 (January-February 1980): 66-69.
Discussion of contemporary efforts by Hollywood at film audience research.

1027. _____ and Kenneth Harwood. "Identified Auteurs Among Top-Grossing American Film Directors, 1945-1969." Paper presented at the Society for Cinema Studies conference, April 1976, Burlington, VT.
Statistical analysis comparing top-grossing film directors with the top directors identified by Andrew Sarris.

1028. _____. "Popular Favorites and Critics' Darlings Among Film Directors in American Release, 1930-1971." Paper presented at the Society for Cinema Studies conference, March 1977, Evanston, IL.
Statistical analysis comparing critical attention paid to film directors with public response as measured by film rentals.

1029. Simson, W. A. "The Social and Emotional Effects of the Cinema." Proceedings of the British Association, September 1948.

1030. Sinha, Durganand. "Sociological Aspects of Film." Science and Culture 20 (December 1954): 281-283.
Reviews literature on the effects of movies on audiences and suggests reasons for the special susceptibility of movie audiences.

1031. Sinoir, Guy. "A Propos de l'Influence du Cinéma sur la Délinquance Juvenile. Quelques Idées sur une Enquête" (The Influence of the Cinema on Juvenile Delinquency. A Few Ideas About an Inquiry). Educateurs 26 (1950).

1032. Sinoir, Guy M. "Les Correlations Entre le Cinéma et la Délinquance Juvenile" (Correlation Between the Cinema and Juvenile Delinquency). Actes du Congrès Internationale sur la Presse Périodique, Cinématographie et Radio pour Enfants, March 1952, pp. 195-203.
Results of three French surveys; comparison of movie-going habits of delinquents and nondelinquents.

1033. Sisson, Edward O. "Immoral Education." Educational Review 73 (January 1927): 54-58.
An advocacy piece in which it is asserted that movies affect the subconscious by suggesting that "wealth comes by a sort of magic ... a sense that money can be made easily and fast, if only one can catch the trick!"

1034. Siudzinski, Edward S. "A Study of Television Interests and Viewing Habits, and a Comparison of These with the Interests and Habits in Radio, Motion Pictures, and Reading, as Shown by Students in Selected Senior High Schools in Metropolitan New York." Unpublished Ph. D. dissertation, Fordham University, 1958.
Responses to a questionnaire by 1,175 high school seniors; data analyzed by sex, age, intelligence, socio-economic status, and length of time for television ownership.

1035. "60% of People Polled by Hong Kong Survey Attend Pix Year Round." Variety, February 4, 1976, p. 26.
Survey reports frequency of attendance by season of the year, popularity of film-types, and recall of advertisements seen in cinemas.

1036. Skilbeck, Oswald. "Some Psychological Problems in the Film Industry." Human Factor 11 (1937): 174-177.
Nonempirical discussion of problems associated with members of the film-making community.

1037. Skoleinspektoren I Hamar (The Inspector of Schools, Hamar). "Barn og Film-Resultater av en Film-Undersokelse Blant Barn i Hamar" (Children and Film--Results of a Film Survey Among Children in Hamar). Skoleinspektoren in Hamar, Stubstad, Brede, 1958 (stencilled).
Movie habits and preferences of children from a medium-sized Norweigian town; data were gathered by questionnaire in 1955 from 421 8-15 year olds.

1038. Smeltzer, Dennis Keith. "The Psychophysiological Reactions of Male and Female Subjects with Varying Film Viewing Experience While Viewing Selected Cinemagraphic Elements." Unpublished Ed. D. dissertation, Northern Illinois University, 1976.
Reactions to varying camera distances, panning shots, tracking shots, and zooming shots were measured by semantic differential among 29 undergraduates.

1039. Smith, Brian. "Rest--and Unrest." Sight and Sound 17 (Winter 1948-49): 179-180.
Discussion of methodological concerns for film audience research, especially patrons' reactions to films.

1040. Smith, Sandra Hamiltine. "Attraction to and Memory for Filmed Characters Stimulated by Racial Similarity and Social Desirability of Characters." Unpublished Ph. D. dissertation, University of California at Berkeley, 1976.

1041. Smythe, Dallas W., Parker B. Lusk, and Charles A. Lewis. "Portrait of an Art-Theater Audience." Quarterly of Film, Radio and Television 8 (Fall 1953): 28-50.
Results of a field study using a prepared questionnaire; data reported include social characteristics, frequency of attendance, reasons for art theater attendance, film-type preferences, and attitudes toward foreign films.

1042. Smythe, Dallas W., John R. Gregory, Alvin Ostrin, Oliver P. Colvin, and William Moroney. "Portrait of a First-Run Audience." Quarterly of Film, Radio and Television 9 (Summer 1955): 390-409.
Results of a field study using a prepared questionnaire; data reported include social characteristics, frequency of attendance, reasons for first-run attendance, and film-type preferences.

1043. Snejder, M. Hudozestvennoe Kino vospitalel'noj Rabote Skoly (The Film and Education at School). Moscow: Academy of Pedagogic Sciences of the R.S.F.S.R., 1950.
Longitudinal study of children's comprehension of films shows that understanding becomes more complete with age.

1044. Sobel, Dava. "Cinematic Neurosis: Scary Movies Can Drive You Crazy." Science Digest 80 (December 1976): 28-33.
A popular treatment and discussion of Bozzuto's and Robinson and Barnett's research.

1045. Sohn, Mark Fohs. "Change in Factual Knowledge and Reported Use of Illicit Drugs Resulting from the Viewing of a Motion Picture." Unpublished Ph.D. dissertation, University of Maryland, 1975.
An experiment involving 166 community college students; results showed that a single viewing of a film did not result in an increase or decrease of factual knowledge.

1046. Sola, J. "Els Catolics i el Cinema" (Catholics and the Cinema). Criterion 5 (1929): 86-87.

1047. Solecka-Fijalkowska, B. "Kino Studyjne w Zielonej Gorze." Kino 7 (May 1972): 18-21.
Results of a study investigating the audience for an art-theater in Zielona Gora.

1048. Somers, Dale A. "The Leisure Revolution: Recreation in the American City, 1820-1920." Journal of Popular Culture 5 (Summer 1971): 125-147.
Historical discussion of the factors which stimulated the rise of leisure-time activities including movies, theater, and spectator sports.

1049. Soriano, Marc. "Problèmes de Méthode Posés par le Cinéma Considéré comme Experimentation Psychologique Nouvelle" (Problems of Method in the Cinema Considered as New Psychological Experimentation). Revue Internationale de Filmologie 1 (September-October 1947): 117-125.
Discusses the study of perception, interest in the film content, and applications for psychology.

1050. Sorokina, V.N. "K Voprosu o Vosprijatii Ocenke Kinoiskusstva Zritelem" (On the Question of Judging Film Art by Audiences). Filosofskie Nauki, 1965, no. 3, pp. 71-79.

1051. Sorokina, V. N. "O Nekotorych Rezul'tatach Sociologiceskogo Issledovanija Vosprijatija i Ocenke Kinoiskusstva Zritelem" (On Some Results of Sociological Research on Acceptance and Judgment of Film Art by Audiences). Filosofija, 1965, no. 6, pp. 148-155.

1052. "The Spectrum Report on Australian Film Audiences." Cinema Papers no. 15 (January 1978): 236-237.
Results of a questionnaire distributed to 1,000 12 to 70 year old Australians; reports selectivity of movie choices, film-type preferences, and factors affecting attendance and nonattendance.

1053. Speyer, Esther. "Movies and Children: A Challenge to Parents." Journal of Educational Sociology 20 (March 1947): 422-424.
Brief review of research in progress.

1054. Spiegelman, Joseph Marvin. "Ambiguity and Personality in the Perception of a Motion Picture." Unpublished Ph.D. dissertation, University of California, Los Angeles 1952.
Tested the hypothesis that individual differences in the perception of a movie are a function of global aspects of personality as elicited by the Rorschach; 24 graduate students answered open-ended questions about a film.

1055. Spiegelman, Marvin. "Effect of Personality on the Perception of a Motion Picture." Journal of Projective Techniques 19 (1958): 461-464.
A summary of the author's dissertation.

1056. Spigle, Irving Samuel. "The Cumulative Effect of Selected Educational Motion Pictures on the Attitudes of High School Boys and the Relationship of Attitude Changes to Selected Personality and Intelligence Factors." Unpublished Ed.D. dissertation, Indiana University, 1955.
An experiment involving 79 high school seniors; the use of films to effect attitudes was found to have opposite effects depending on the subjects' attitudinal predisposition prior to film exposure.

1057. Sprager, Harva Kaaren. "Hollywood's Foreign Correspondents." Quarterly of Film, Radio and Television 6 (1952): 274-282.
Results of a survey distributed to foreign correspondents in Hollywood who report industry news for their home media; concludes that "on the whole, the foreign readers are getting the same stardusted image of the Hollywood scene as does the American public."

1058. Stebbins, Robert A. "Estudio sobre Cine" (A Survey of the Cinema). Revista Española de la Opinion Publica 11 (January-March 1968): 189-320.
Survey of 1,185 Spanish film distributors, 142 film directors, 168 actors and actresses, and a study of film violence and its effect on 46 persons; thoughts on the state of the Spanish cinema and film legislation are reported.

1059. Steele, Daniel Gene. "Female Responsiveness to Erotic Films and its Relation to Attitudes, Sexual Knowledge and Selected Demographic Variables." Unpublished Ph.D. dissertation, Baylor University, 1973.

Female undergraduates found films depicting heterosexual behavior most sexually stimulating; homosexual behavior was found to be least sexually stimulating; correlations between ratings of stimulation and demographic variables were also made.

1060. Stefanov, I. "Sociologiceska Harakteristika na Kinopublikata" Kinoizkustvo 28 (October 1973): 1-13.
Descriptive statistics of the Bulgarian movie audience.

1061. Steinmetz, Robert Alan. "Factors Which Appear to Influence the Subjective Evaluation of a Motion Picture." Unpublished Ph. D. dissertation, University of Southern California, 1979.
Subjective analysis by the author of 235 film reviews and 14 film books resulted in identification of 35 factors which seem to influence evaluations of movies.

1062. Stephens, Harmon B. "The Relation of the Motion Picture to Changing Moral Standards." Annals of the American Academy of Political and Social Science 128 (November 1926): 151-157.
Using anecdotal reports as evidence it is concluded that movies have had a negative effect on the moral conduct of the young in particular.

1063. Stephenson, William. "Applications of Communication Theory: IV. Immediate Experience of Movies." Operant Subjectivity 1 (1978): 96-116.
"The immediate experiences of movie-goers may be evaluated from the perspective of a communication theory that regards these experiences as a field from which natural operant factors may be derived."

1064. Sterner, Alice P. Radio, Motion Picture, and Reading Interests: A Study of High School Pupils. New York: Teachers College, Columbia University, 1947 (Contributions to Education, no. 932).
Investigated the habits of students for seven media, the relationships between these media, and the relationship of sex, school grade, intelligence, and socio-economic status to the pupils' choice of media.

1065. _____. "Radio, Motion Picture, and Reading Interests: A Study of High School Pupils." Unpublished Ph. D. dissertation, Columbia University, 1948.
Check lists and diaries of 372 pupils.

1066. Stillwell, Robert R. "A Study of the Effects of Motion Pictures on the Attitudes of Seventh Graders." Unpublished M. S. thesis, Ohio State University, 1939.
Six films were shown and attitudes toward economic security, imperialism, militarism, and nationalism were measured using a questionnaire administered to 110 pupils; results showed that movies "bore an influence on the students' attitudes."

1067. Stoddard, George D. "Measuring the Effect of Motion Pictures on the Intellectual Content of Children." Journal of Educational Sociology 6 (December 1932): 204-209.
Description of the study and procedures but results are not presented.

1068. _____. "What Motion Pictures Mean to the Child." Bulletin of

the State University of Iowa, no. 713 (1933), pp. 3-8.
Review of the research on movies' effect on learning, health and sleep, and behavior; discussion of how parents and teachers can help children as they engage in the movie experience.

1069. Stuart, Frederic. "The Effects of Television on the Motion Picture and Radio Industries." Ph. D. dissertation, Columbia University, 1960 (reprinted by Arno Press, 1976).
Analysis of the impact of TV on the consumer and the two media.

1070. Stuckrath, Fritz. "Wie Kinder Filme Sehen" (How Children See Films). Film, Bild, Ton 1 (1952, no. 10).

1071. _____. "Die Wirkung des Spielfilms auf die Jugend" (The Influence of the Entertainment Film on Youth). Bildung and Erziehung 4 (1951).

1072. _____. "Das Kino Fabriziert das Weltbild" (The Cinema Makes the World Picture). Westermaens Padagogische Beitrage 7 (1951): 327-329.

1073. _____. Der Film als Erziehungsmacht (The Film as an Educational Force). Hamburg: Verlag der Gesellschaft der Freunde des Vaterländischen Schul- und Erziehungswesens (Zur Hamburger Schulreform Series 10), 1953.
A collection of twelve previously published articles which discuss emotional effects of the cinema on children; movie-going habits of children are compared to their museum, library, and theater habits.

1074. _____. "Seelenlage und Filmerleben beim Kind" (The Mental State and Cinematographic Experience of the Child). Film-Bild-Ton 8 (February 1959): 3-7.
Case study of a 10 year old girl in which a film was used to invoke identification and reduce her psychological problems.

1075. _____. "Das Sohn-Problem als Schlüssel zum Filmerleben" (Cinematographic Experience and the Personal Problems of the Child). Film-Bild-Ton 9 (June 1959): 29-32, 49-50.
A sequel to the author's February article; case study of a 12 year old boy.

1076. "Study Blames TV for Theatre Drop." Broadcasting, February 3, 1958, p. 58.
Results of a Sindlinger and Co. survey.

1077. Stupp, Vicki O'Donnell. "Analysis of Film as Communication." Paper presented at the Speech Communication Association Summer Conference on Mass Communication in Education and Society, Austin, TX, July 1975. Available in ERIC ED 157 129.
Review of literature on the attitudinal and behavioral effects of film on audiences.

1078. Sturmthal, Adolph F. and Alberta Curtis. "A Study of Audience Reactions to Two Educational Films." Educational Screen 22 (October 1943): 306, 314-315.
Use of questionnaires and the program analyzer by high school and college students.

1079. Sullenger, T. Earl. "Modern Youth and the Movies." School and Society 32 (October 4, 1930): 459-461.
Survey of 3,295 high school pupils; film-type preferences, frequency of attendance, attendance unit, favorite pictures, and theaters preferred are reported; data are analyzed by year in school and sex.

1080. Svoboda, J. "Veda-Film-Divak." Film a Doba 23 (March 1977): 169-170.
Discussion of audience research in the USSR.

1081. Swanson, Charles E. and Robert L. Jones. "Television Owning and Its Correlates." Journal of Applied Psychology 35 (1951): 352-357.
Examination of the relationship between TV ownership and use of other media and educational and income levels; sample was composed of adults who responded to questions posed by personal interviewers.

1082. Sward, Keith. "Boy and Girl Meet Neurosis." The Screen Writer 4 (September 1948): 8-10, 24-26.
Nonempirical discussion of "psychiatric films."

1083. Symonds, P.M. "Criteria for the Selection of Pictures for the Investigation of Adolescent Fantasies." Journal of Abnormal and Social Psychology 34 (1939): 271-274.

1084. Szekfu, A. "A Mozilatogatas Gyakorisagarol. Nehany Tarsadalmi-Demografiai Tenyezo Szerepe, Valamint Osszefuggesek mas Kulturalis Tevekenysegekkel a Felnott Lakossag Koreben" (On the Frequency of Cinema Attendance. Role of Some Socio-Demographic Factors as Well as Relations Connected with Other Cultural Activities Among Adult Inhabitants). Radio es TV Szle 2 (1976): 147-154.

1085. Takase, Yasusada. "A Study on the Cultural Effect of Moving Pictures." Japanese Journal of Experimental Psychology 2 (1935): 251-262.
A cultural effect of movies was ascertained to some extent but their effectiveness was inversely related to age; a relationship to frequency of crime was not noticed.

1086. Takenaka, T. "Jogakusei no Goraku Chosa. II. Jogakusei no Goraku Toshiteno Eiga" (An Investigation of the Amusements of School Girls. II. The Cinema as an Amusement of School Girls). Kyoiku Shinri Kenkyu 15 (1940): 106-129.
Older girls found movies the most attractive amusement.

1087. Talarico, E. "The Film as Mental Reaction." Bianco e Nero 9 (1948).

1088. Tankard, James W. and Yorgo Pasadeos. "Correlation Between Media Variables and Birth Rate." Journalism Quarterly 58 (Winter 1981): 633-634.
Examined the effect of media growth on birth rates in developing countries; newspapers, TV, radio, and cinema were examined.

1089. Tannenbaum, P.H. and Eleanor P. Gaer. "Mood Change as a Func-

tion of Stress of Protagonist and Degree of Identification in a Film-Viewing Situation." Journal of Personality and Social Psychology 2 (1965): 612-616.
Manipulation of the sequence of events in the final section of The Ox-Bow Incident to establish a sad, happy, or ambiguous ending resulted in increased stress among students to the sad ending, a marked decline with the happy ending, and a small decrease with the ambiguous one and when no ending was shown.

1090. Tarroni, Evelina. "I Bambini Guardano" (Children Watch). Almanacco del Cinema Italiano (1952): 30-33.
Analysis of some 2,000 compositions written by 10 to 16 year olds concerning their impressions and judgments of a film which affected them.

1091. _____. "L'Apporto dell'Esperienza Filmica alla Vita Psichica del Fanciullo" (The Influence of Cinematographic Experience on the Mental Life of Children). Ragazzi d'Oggi 1 (January 1953): 17-20.
Suggests the need to evaluate children's reactions to movies after their screening, as opposed to during their presentation; brief examples of preliminary results of this technique are presented.

1092. _____. "Personaggio ed Attore nei Film per Ragazzi" (Character and Actor in Films for Children). Ragazzi d'Oggi 4 (April 1953): 17-19.
Observation of reactions to screen characters with an emphasis on identification.

1093. _____. "La Memoria del Film" (Recollections of a Film). Cine-Gioventù 2 (May 1954).
Children's drawings made after viewing a film were analyzed for reactions.

1094. _____ and Sandro Paderni. "Enquête sur les Raisons d'Intérêt pour les Genres des Films en Rélation avec l'Âge, le Sexe, le Type de Comportement et le Milieu Social et Familier" (Study of the Reasons for Interest in Different Kinds of Films as Related to Age, Sex, Behavior, Social and Family Milieu). CIDALC, 1950.

1095. _____. "Film per Ragazzi e Pericoli del Semplicismo" (Films for Adolescents and Dangers of Over-Simplicity). Cinema 5 (March 1951): 99-101.
Discussion of methodological issues with a focus on questionnaires.

1096. _____. "Cinema e Gioventù: Studio degli Aspetti Sociali e dei Motivi di Interesse" (Cinema and Youth: A Study of the Social Aspects and Causes of Interest). Istituto di Pedagogia dell'Università di Rome, 1952.
Frequency of attendance, interest in the cinema as compared to other activities, and film-type preferences were examined in relation to age and sex.

1097. Taviani, P. and V. Taviani. "Cinema e Società" (Cinema and Society). Critica Sociologica 31 (1974): 108-113.

1098. Tavistock Clinic. "A Psychological Study of Film Production for Child Audiences." London: Petroleum Films Bureau, 1952, 36 pages.
Investigated the effect of three films emphasizing safety.

1099. Taylor, Ryland A. "The Repeat Audience for Movies on TV." Journal of Broadcasting 17 (Winter 1972-1973): 95-100.
Older movies recovered audiences less quickly than more recent films; films with a large first-time viewing audience recovered less quickly when rerun; a lack of systematic influence by movie type and recovery rate was found.

1100. _____. "Television Movie Audiences and Movie Awards: A Statistical Study." Journal of Broadcasting 18 (Spring 1974): 181-186.
Academy Awards, New York Film Critics' Awards, and Film Daily's Awards were found to be significantly related to television audience size for motion pictures on TV; National Board of Review Awards were not significantly related to Nielsen ratings.

1101. _____. "Televised Movies: Directors Win Audience." Journal of Broadcasting 20 (Fall 1976): 495-500.
Statistical analysis indicates that a film director's "track record" plays a significant role in building or diminishing the audience size for televised movies.

1102. Teahan, John E. and Edward C. Podany. "Some Effects of Films of Successful Blacks on Racial Self-Concept." International Journal of Social Psychology 20 (Autumn/Winter 1974): 247-280.
Attitudes toward blacks were not altered after subjects viewed twelve short films; more favorable attitudes toward whites were observed by subjects of higher socio-economic class.

1103. "10 Years of Attendance Fall in U.K." Variety, May 12, 1982, p. 294.
Tabular report covering the 1972-1981 period; number of cinemas, seating capacity, admissions, and box office presented.

1104. Tenenbaumowna, E. "Rola Kina W Zainteresowaniach Dzieciecych" (Role of the Cinema in Children's Interests). Polskie Archinum Psychologji 6 (1933-34): 163-168.
Analysis of film type preferences among boys and girls.

1105. Teutsch, Barbara. "Film und Jugendkriminalität" (Film and Juvenile Criminality). Der Neue Film 6 (1952).

1106. _____. "Warum Gehen sie ins Kino? Eine Untersuchung über die Würzeln Kindlicher Filmbegeisterung" (Why Do They Go to the Cinema? A Study of the Reasons for Juvenile Enthusiasm for the Cinema). Korrespondenz für Filmkunst 3 (1952): 10.

1107. Thayer, David Lewis. "A Study of the Influence of Conventional Film Lighting on Audience Response." Unpublished Ph.D. dissertation, State University of Iowa, 1960.
An experiment involving 297 undergraduates; data on subjects' attitudes toward different styles of lighting, their enjoyment, believability and mood, etc.; findings include that films lighted according to convention were rated as technically better productions than those in which convention was violated.

1108. Therien, Gilles. "Le Cinéma Québeçois: Une Recherche sur la Voie de l'Ecriture" (The Québec Cinema: An Investigation on the Medium of Writing). Revue des Sciences Humaines 45 (January-March 1979): 105-114.

1109. Thomas, Coronal. "A Comparison of Interests of Delinquent and Non-Delinquent Boys." Journal of Juvenile Research 16 (1932): 310-318.
Responses to a questionnaire given to 154 public school boys and 101 boys in a detention home; inquired as to newspaper, book, and magazine reading, movie attendance, and radio listening; delinquents attended movies more often than public school boys; filmtype preferences are reported.

1110. Thomas, Dana L. "Flicker of Hope? Things May be Looking Up for the Movie Theatres." Barron's 38 (June 23, 1958): 3, 17-19.
Discussion of strategies being used to draw audiences back to the movies.

1111. Thorun, W. "Die Wirkung des Films auf Jugendliche" (The Effect of Film on Young People). Bildung und Erziehung 3 (1950): 609.

1112. Thrasher, Frederic M. "The Sociological Approach to Motion Pictures in Relation to Education." Education 5 (April 1938): 467-473.
Asserts that informal education "plays a very great part in molding and developing the child" and hence the need to understand the effect of movies on children; reviews some Payne Fund research and criticizes Mortimer Adler's Art and Prudence.

1113. Thurstone, L. L. "A Scale for Measuring Attitude Toward the Movies." Journal of Educational Research 22 (September 1930): 80-94.
Description of the construction and use of a 40-item attitude scale.

1114. _____. "The Measurement of Change in Social Attitude." Journal of Social Psychology 2 (May 1931): 230-235.
The effect of a film on 182 school children's attitude toward Chinese; results indicated an attitude shift in the expected direction (more favorable).

1115. _____. "Influence of Motion Pictures on Children's Attitudes." Journal of Social Psychology 2 (August 1931): 291-305.
The effect of a film on 240 ninth to twelfth grade students' attitude toward crime and the effect of a film on 254 ninth to twelfth grade students' attitude toward Prohibition; the latter film had no effect while the former did produce a significant effect.

1116. Timmons, William Milton. "An Experimental Inquiry into the Effects of Pictorial Fidelity on Audiovisual Communication." Unpublished Ph.D. dissertation, University of Southern California, 1975.
Tested McLuhan's hypothesis that TV has more psychological impact than film due to the lower image fidelity of TV; subjects were 713 high school students; results were inconclusive.

1117. Tinacci-Mannelli, Gilberto. "Cinema e Sociologia. In Margine a un Convegno" (The Movies and Sociology. Marginal Notes on a Congress). Rassegna Italiana di Sociologia 3 (April-June 1962): 313-320.
Report of a meeting in Frascati; discussion of the relationship of movies to sociology; the degree of social reality, literature, and exposure to experiences of different cultures as presented by motion pictures.

1118. Tinacci-Mannelli, Gilberto. "Influenza dell' Appartenenza Socio-Culturale Degli Spettatori sull' Accettazione e Interpretazione di un Film Africano" (The Influence of the Social-Cultural Standing of the Spectators on Acceptance and Interpretation of an African Film). Rassegna Italiana di Sociologia 4 (January-March 1963): 91-126.
Reactions to the African documentary film Demain à Nanguila; questionnaire focused on the respondents' interests in the film, affective responses, and identification with characters in the picture; results are presented by socio-economic level of the respondents.

1119. _____. "Reazioni di Tre Gruppi Sociali Diversi a un Film-Inchiesta sulla Gioventù" (Reactions of Three Different Social Groups to a Film Inquiry on Youth). Rassegna Italiana di Sociologia 5 (January-March 1964): 133-149.
Acceptance and interpretations of a film (I Nuovi Angeli) by three socio-cultural groups of respondents.

1120. Tonn, G. "Untersuchung über die Einstellung 13-15-jahriger Schüler und Schülerinnen zum Spielfilm unter Anwendung der Fragebogenmethode" (Study of Attitudes Concerning the Entertainment Film of Pupils of Both Sexes Ages 13-15, Using the Questionnaire Method). Hamburg, 1951, 88 pp.

1121. Tonnessen, Hans Olav. Ungdom og Kino-En Undersoking over Kinovaner of Film-interesser hos Oslo Ungdem i Alderen 12 til 18 Ar (Youth and the Cinema - An Investigation into the Cinema Habits and Film Preferences of Young People in Oslo Between 12 and 18 Years). Pedagogical Research Institute, University of Oslo, 1952.
Results of a survey of 744 school children reporting frequency of attendance, attendance unit, film preferences, and differences on these dimensions by age and social background.

1122. Toulouse, M. M. and R. Mourgue. "Des Réactions Respiratoires au Cours de Projections Cinématographiques" (Respiratory Reactions During Cinema Projections). Revue Internationale de Filmologie 2 (1949, no. 5): 77-83.
Reports results of an experiment.

1123. Townshend, The Marchioness of Raynham. "The Cinema and the Child." Revue Internationale de l'Enfant 8 (1929): 698-703.
A second-hand report of a study inquiring as to children's responses to and preferences for movies.

1124. Trapp, Peter. "Schund, Film und Jugendkriminalität" (Literary Trash, Movies, and Juvenile Delinquency). Psychologe: Berater für Gesunde und Praktische Lebensgestaltung 4 (1952): 460-467.
Advocacy piece maintaining that movies are not primary causes of delinquency.

1125. Traversa, Carlo. "Psicologia del Cinema" (Psychology of the Cinema). Stampa, Cinema, Radio per Ragazzi (1952): 69-75.
An analysis of children's reactions to movies and their consequences.

1126. "Trib-Star Checks Out Film Fans, and Where They Get Info (Not TV)." Variety, December 15, 1976, p. 34.
Survey shows that "film going tops other forms of entertainment in both adult interest and attendance"; 92 percent of the respondents reported they obtained information about films from newspapers (only 6 percent for both TV and word-of-mouth).

1127. Trier, R. "Children's Reactions to Films." Danish Foreign Office Journal (1952, no. 6): 18-21.

1128. Troger, Walter. "Methoden der Jugendfilmforschung: Ein Überblick" (A Summary of Methods Suitable for Young Persons). Jugend, Film, Fernsehen 3 (1959): 1-13.
Discussion of methodological concerns regarding spectator reactions to movies; the "wiggle test," photographic records, and electroencephalography are included.

1129. Troland, Leonard Thompson. "Psychology of Natural Color Motion Pictures." American Journal of Physiological Optics 7 (1926): 375-385.
A review and discussion of the literature.

1130. Troth, Marilyn Mumma. "The Relative Effectiveness of the Motion Picture and the Single Still Picture Presentation Modes in Facilitating the Perception of Dynamic Action Concepts." Unpublished Ph.D. dissertation, East Texas State University, 1971.
Experimental study in which the relative capability of two types of pictorial representation were compared for transmission of intended meanings of isolated, dramatized, action concepts; subjects were fourth and sixth graders (n=210); findings indicate that motion pictures were highly superior to still pictures in facilitating the perception of intended meaning.

1131. Tudor, Andrew. "Film and the Measurement of its Effects." Screen 10 (July-October 1969): 148-159.
Review of research including discussion of selective perception, the two-step flow hypothesis, attitudinal research, and the star identification syndrome.

1132. Turovskaja, M. "Kinematograf kak Predmet Massovogo Potreblenija. Kino i Massovye Zurnaly" (Cinema as an Object of Mass Consumption. Cinema and Mass Magazines). Kino i Vremja 1 (1977): 198-218.

1133. Tusher, Will. "Older Audience Needs a Fresh Sell on Film." Variety, September 30, 1981, pp. 1, 128.
Results of a Newspaper Advertising Bureau study which showed that "today's young audience, strong moviegoers, would hold to that habit as they move into middle age"; newspapers were found to be "the foremost media source used by the public to decide which movie to see."

1134. Twomey, John E. "Some Considerations on the Rise of the Art-Film Theater." Quarterly of Film, Radio and Television 10 (1955-1956): 239-247.
A nonempirical discussion of the development, growth, and future of the art theater and its patrons.

1135. Tyrrell, Charles W. "Experimental Appraisal of Films and Verbal Incited Discussion in Church Youth Groups." Unpublished Ph.D. dissertation, Indiana University, 1952.

1136. United Kingdom. "Audience Reaction to the Film 'The Undefeated.'" Social Survey, report no. 164, 1950, 11 pp.

1137. Urbano, Salustiano del Campo. "El Público Cinematográfico" (The Cinema Audience). Revista Española de la Opinion Pública 8 (April-June 1967): 209-278.
Results of a survey conducted in Spain reports on movie attendance, ticket prices, preferences for various types of films, themes, directors and actors; opinions on the quality of the Spanish cinema were solicited.

1138. "Urges Close Study of MPAA Report." Variety, January 22, 1958, pp. 10, 22.
MPAA executive vice president Ralph D. Hetzel comments on the Opinion Research Corp. survey, "The Public Appraises the Movies."

1139. Uruno, Fuijo. "Audience of Motion Pictures--An Analysis." Japanese Journalism Review 9 (1959): 108-134.

1140. Utz, Walter Julius. "The Comparative Effect of Color and Black and White Film Clips Upon Rated Perception of Reality." Unpublished Ph.D. dissertation, University of Illinois, 1968.
An experiment involving 1,015 undergraduates' responses on three semantic differential scales; no significant differences were found between the black and white and the color test groups.

1141. Vahemesta, Aigar. "Filmivaataga Tupoloogiast" (A Typology of the Recipients of Artistic Films). Society and Leisure 2 (1970): 87-101.
The audience for artistic films in Estonia was broken down into ten aggregates based on their value orientation toward motion pictures; socio-demographic indices as they relate to the typology are presented.

1142. Valenti, Jack. "Rating the Movies." Journal of Communication 26 (Summer 1976): 62-63.
Reports the results of a national poll which indicated that as of 1974, 91 percent of the total public was aware of the MPAA rating system.

1143. Valenti, Jack. "The Challenge of Change." Boxoffice 117 (March 1981): 22, 46.
MPAA president reports on the 9 percent drop in admissions during 1980; discussion of the demographic composition of the film audience.

1144. Vanden Bosch, Marlin. "The Effect of Self-Selected Movies, Popular Songs, and Books on Selected High School Students." Unpublished Ph.D. dissertation, University of Iowa, 1973.
Results of interviews with 12 high school juniors or seniors on the effects of three self-selected media; responses are evaluated according to Havighurst's developmental tasks framework and stage one in Erikson's identity crisis concept.

1145. Vargas, A.L. "British Films and Their Audience." Penguin Film Review 2 (1949, no. 8): 71-76.
A nonempirical assessment of British production in which the author concludes that filmmakers have "badly underestimated the intelligence of British film-goers."

1146. Veeder, Gerry Elizabeth Kleindinst. "The Influence of Subliminal Suggestion on the Response to Two Films." Unpublished Ph.D. dissertation, Wayne State University, 1975.
Subliminal pictures seemed to reinforce feelings about clearly defined characters; subliminal words seemed to clarify or shape feelings about vague or neutral characters.

1147. Vincenzo, Joe, Clyde Hendrich, and Edward J. Murray. "The Relationship Between Religious Beliefs and Attending the Fear-Provoking Religiously Oriented Movie: 'The Exorcist.'" Omega: Journal of Death and Dying 7 (1976): 137-143.
Subjects who did not attend The Exorcist believed more in prayer and less in exorcism and attended church more frequently than subjects who had attended the movie.

1148. Vinovich, George Starr. "The Communicative Significance of Musical Affect in Eliciting Differential Perception, Cognition, and Emotion in Sound-Motion Media Messages." Unpublished Ph.D. dissertation, University of Southern California, 1975.
An experimental study the findings of which suggest that human response to sound movies is, "in many instances, a conditioned response to a few key musical characteristics."

1149. Volpicelli, Luigi. (The Social Value of the Film.) Bianco e Nero 9 (1948, no. 5).

1150. Volpicelli, Luigi. "Bambini e Bambine al Cinema" (Young Children at the Cinema). Cinedidattica, November-December 1952; January-July-August 1953.
Study of the role played by movies in children's recreation.

1151. Wagner, E. "Wie Urteilen die Schüler über den Film?" (How do Students form an Opinion About the Cinema?). Padagogisher Wegweiser (1951, no. 4): 25.

1152. Wagner, Geoffrey. "The Lost Audience." Quarterly of Film, Radio and Television 6 (1952): 338-350.
An examination of the reasons for declining attendance at movies.

1153. Wagner, Ryszard. "Film Fabularny Jako Zrolo Historyczne" (Feature Films as Historical Data). Kulturai Spoleczenstwo 18 (April-June 1974): 181-194.
Argues that movies may offer the best source of information concerning the details of everyday life and social consciousness.

1154. Walker, Virginia Dickenson. "The Effect of Cognitive Complexity, Interaction Style and Liking on Adolescents' Impression Complexity of Characters in a Film." Unpublished Ph.D. dissertation, Northwestern University, 1976.
High school students viewed a 16mm version of a Star Trek TV episode with their teachers who observed the pupils' reactions.

1155. Wall, W.D. "The Adolescent and the Cinema. I." Educational Review 1 (October 1948): 34-46.

1156. _____. "The Adolescent and the Cinema. II." Educational Review 1 (February 1949): 119-130.

1157. _____ and E. M. Smith. "The Film Choices of Adolescents." British Journal of Educational Psychology 19 (June 1949): 121-136.
Two methods for ascertaining film-type preferences among 13 to 16 year olds were used; data are cross-tabulated by sex and education.

1158. _____ and E. M. Smith. "Les Adolescents et le Cinéma" (Adolescents and the Cinema). Revue Internationale de Filmologie 2 (1950, no. 6): 153-158.
A summary of results of studies conducted by the authors in Birmingham; film-type preferences, frequency of attendance, and the perceived effects of movies on children's peers are reported.

1159. _____ and W. A. Simson. "The Effects of Cinema Attendance on the Behavior of Adolescents as Seen by Their Contemporaries." British Journal of Educational Psychology 19 (February 1949): 53-56.
Responses to a questionnaire by some 2,000 13 to 16 year olds; respondents were asked to report on other adolescents' imitation of behavior seen in films.

1160. _____. "The Emotional Responses of Adolescent Groups to Certain Films. Part I." British Journal of Educational Psychology 20 (November 1950): 153-163.
Analysis of the affective responses of 476 boys and 379 girls aged 13-17 to twelve films; data are also examined in terms of identification with film stars and comparison of the respondents' answers by sex.

1161. _____. "The Responses of Adolescent Groups to Certain Films. Part II." British Journal of Educational Psychology 21 (1951): 81-88.

1162. Wallace, Webster Lively. "Attitudes of Black College Freshmen Toward Contemporary 'Controversial' Black Films." Unpublished Ph.D. dissertation, Georgia State University, 1975.
Questionnaires and essays were completed by 111 students; results are presented by sex, family income, and frequency of attendance.

1163. Wallon, Henri. "De Quelques Problemes Psycho-Physiologiques que pose le Cinéma" (Psycho-Physiological Problems of the Cinema). Revue Internationalde de Filmologie 1 (July-August 1947): 15-18.
Points for research and problems encountered in the conduct of research are discussed.

1164. Wallon, Henri. "L'Enfant et le Film" (The Child and the Film). Revue Internationale de Filmologie 2 (1949, no. 5): 21-28.
Nonempirical analysis of the child's reactions to movies.

1165. Wallon, H. "L'Espace et le Temps Filmiques" (Space and Time in the Film). Revue Internationale de Filmologie 3 (1952): 213-214.
Possibilities for research in this area are suggested.

1166. Walsh, George Ethelbert. "Moving Picture Drama for the Multitude." The Independent, February 6, 1908, pp. 306-310.
An anecdotal report on the medium and its audience.

1167. Wanderer, Jules J. "In Defense of Popular Taste: Film Ratings Among Professional and Lay Audiences." American Journal of Sociology 76 (September 1970): 262-272.

Positive correlations were found between upper-middle-class individuals and film critics' tastes in evaluating films.

1168. Wanger, Walter. "The Role of Movies in Morale." American Journal of Sociology 47 (November 1941): 378-383.
Advocates that movies can be used to clarify, inspire, and entertain and that the primary role of movies in building national morale has been to provide recreation and entertainment for the public.

1169. Ward, Joyce C. "Children Out of School." London: Central Office of Information, Social Survey New Series no. 110, 1948, 90 pp.

1170. _____. "Children and the Cinema." London: Central Office of Information, Social Survey New Series no. 131. 1949, 100 pp.
Reports frequency of attendance, attendance unit, film-type preferences, and membership in film clubs.

1171. Warner, Harry P. "Television and the Motion Picture Industry." Hollywood Quarterly 2 (1946): 11-18.
Brief mention of audience considerations.

1172. Wasem, Erich. "Der 'Wiggle Test' als Anhaltspunkt für die Jugendeignung eines Films" (The "Wiggle Test" as an Indication of the Suitability of a Film for Young Audiences). Jugend und Film, December 1955, pp. 9-12.
Detailed analysis of an application of the Wiggle Test.

1173. "WBBM in Live-Lens Survey." Variety, May 9, 1979, p. 31.
Report of a television station's survey which found that underage children were admitted to R-rated movies 75 percent of the time.

1174. Weber, Alan Melchior. "The Responses of College Students to Film." Unpublished Ph.D. dissertation, University of Illinois at Urbana-Champaign, 1973.
A five-category classification system was developed for verbal responses to films; participants were 80 undergraduates.

1175. Weigall, Arthur. "The Influence of the Kinematograph Upon National Life." Nineteenth Century 89 (April 1921): 661-672.
An advocacy piece in which it is concluded that "we must rely on the censorship to save us from the influences ... which are at work throughout the land, insidiously upsetting our ideas of conduct and slowly but surely altering the standards which at present govern our national life."

1176. Weimer, Jerry William. "The Effect of Film Treatments on Attitudes that Correlate with Drug-Behavior." Unpublished Ed.D. dissertation, University of South Dakota, 1976.
Sixth grade students were shown one of two films in an experiment; results showed that one film had counter productive effects for male students.

1177. Weisgerber, Robert Arthur. "The Effect of Science Motivational Films on the Attitudes of Secondary School Pupils Toward the Field of Science." Unpublished Ed.D. dissertation, Indiana University, 1960.
Findings suggest that films were able to influence the attitudes and interests of the subjects only in certain limited ways.

1178. Wells, Carl D. "The Motion Picture Versus the Church." Sociology and Social Research 16 (1932): 540-546.
Largely subjective comparison between the church, "with an immediate rural heritage," and the cinema, "which originated in the city, appeals to city people, and is adjusted to city life."

1179. Wensch, G. "Wie Denkt das Kind über den Film?" (What Does the Child Think of the Film?). Die Schule 28 (1952).

1180. Westfall, Leon H. A Study of Verbal Accompaniments to Educational Motion Pictures. New York: Teachers College, Columbia University, 1934 (Contributions to Education, no. 617).
Results of an experiment to determine the relative merits of several forms of verbal accompaniment to movies; study involved about 5,000 fifth graders; a five to one preference for talking pictures over any other form of verbal accompaniment was found.

1181. "What Says Poll About Film Fans." Variety, November 21, 1973, pp. 37, 38.
Results of a Gallup survey of Canadians describing attendance habits, demographics, and attitudes toward movies.

1182. "What Students Think of Movies." Photo-Era 62 (January 1929): 49 and 62 (February 1929): 102-103.
Presentation of selected results from the National Board of Review's survey of 200 high school students; data reported include frequency of attendance, attendance unit, preferences for actors, favorite films, and film-type preferences.

1183. Whitmyre, John W. "Psychiatric Patient Audience Reactions to Types of Motion Pictures." Journal of Clinical Psychology 14 (July 1958): 259-264.
Two groups of hospitalized male patients' overt disturbed behavior was observed while viewing two series of five movies; data on movie-type and patient group are analyzed.

1184. Wickline, Lee Edwin. "The Effect of Motivational Film on the Attitudes and Understanding of High School Students Concerning Science and Scientists." Unpublished Ed. D. dissertation, Pennsylvania State University, 1964.
No significant differences in changes of attitude between the experimental and control groups after exposure to ten motivational films.

1185. Wiedemann, D. "Jugendliche vor der Leinwand" (Adolescents on the Screen). Film und Fernsehen 4 (November 1976): 28-32.
Problems involved with and results of audience research on young patrons in the German Democratic Republic.

1186. Wiese, Mildred J. and Stewart G. Cole. "A Study of Children's Attitudes and the Influence of a Commercial Motion Picture." Journal of Psychology 21 (January 1946): 151-171.
A pretest-posttest study of approximately 1,500 high school students' responses to a questionnaire inquiring as to the American and Nazi way of life; the film used was Tomorrow the World.

1187. Williams, Dwight A., Jr. "Mass Media Preference Patterns: A Cross Media Study." Paper presented at the International Communication Association conference, April 1971, Phoenix, AR. Available in ERIC ED 049 611.

1188. Williams, J. Harold. "Attitudes of College Students Toward Motion Pictures." School and Society 38 (August 12, 1933): 222-224.
Using Thurstone's 40-item attitude scale and a sample of 104 teachers college students it was found that the sample held a highly favorable attitude toward movies.

1189. Williams, Robert C. "Film Shots and Expressed Interest Levels." Speech Mongraphs 35 (June 1968): 166-169.
An experiment involving 180 twelfth graders investigating their interest in close-up, medium, and long-shots in a film.

1190. Wilner, Daniel M. "Attitude as a Determinant of Perception in the Mass Media of Communication: Reactions to the Motion Picture, 'Home of the Brave.'" Unpublished Ph. D. dissertation, University of California, Los Angeles, 1951.
Five groups of undergraduates using an experimental design; measured attitudes towards blacks.

1191. Wilner, Nancy and Mardi J. Horowitz. "Intrusive and Repetitive Thought After a Depressing Film: A Pilot Study." Psychological Reports 37 (August 1975): 135-138.
The study tested a hypothesis concerning increased intrusive and repetitive thoughts after any undischarged negative emotional-ideational state; no significant differences were found between the experimental and control groups.

1192. Winick, Charles. "Tendency Systems and the Effects of a Movie Dealing with a Social Problem." Journal of General Psychology 68 (April 1963): 289-305.
Six hypotheses were raised concerning the impact of The Man With The Golden Arm; identification with the film's hero was greater for middle-class and female viewers than for lower-class and male viewers; shifts in attitude on the topic of drug addiction are reported.

1193. _____. "Some Observations of Patrons of Adult Theaters and Bookstores." Technical Reports of the U.S. Commission on Obscenity and Pornography, vol. 4, pp. 225-243. Washington, D.C.: U.S. Government Printing Office, 1970.
Interviews with 100 patrons provides validation for demographic classifications based on external observation.

1194. _____. "A Study of Consumers of Explicitly Sexual Materials: Some Functions Served by Adult Movies." Technical Reports of the U.S. Commission on Obscenity and Pornography, vol. 4. pp. 245-262. Washington, D.C.: U.S. Government Printing Office, 1970.
Demographic characteristics of adult movie patrons in nine different communities are presented; a discussion of the uses served by adult movies is offered.

1195. Witty, Paul. "Children's Interest in Comics, Radio, Motion Pictures and TV." Educational Administration and Supervision 38 (1952): 138-147.
Brief review of literature on these media; reports results of ques-

tionnaires distributed to high school pupils in which it was found that 44 percent said they attended movies less often since the advent of TV.

1196. _____ and Harry Bricker. "Your Child and Radio, TV, Comics and Movies." Chicago: Science Research Associates, 1952.
A 49-page pamphlet designed as a guide for parents; some literature is reviewed.

1197. _____ and Anne Coomer. "Activities and Preferences of a Secondary-School Group." Journal of Educational Psychology 34 (February 1943): 65-76.
Data on number of magazines read, books read, newspaper reading, movie attendance, and amount of time spent listening to the radio are presented by sex for ninth through twelfth graders.

1198. _____, Sol Garfield, and William Brink. "Interests of High-School Students in Motion Pictures and the Radio." Journal of Educational Psychology 32 (March 1941): 176-184.
Comparison of black and white students' responses to a questionnaire; frequency of attendance and film-type preference data presented according to race, sex, and grade level.

1199. Wolff, Harold. "Pre-Testing Movies." Science Illustrated 2 (February 1947): 44-45, 115.
Discussion of the methods used by Gallup's Audience Research, Inc.; case study of research on The Jolson Story.

1200. Wolfson, Kim. "The Effect of Advertising and Other Factors on a Consumer's Decision to Attend a Movie." Unpublished paper, University of Massachusetts, December 1981.
Results of a questionnaire completed by 23 undergraduates; film genre, social reasons, and film actors were the highest rated items affecting attendance decisions.

1201. Woodard, A. F. "Motion Pictures for Children." Social Service Review 6 (September 1917): 10-12.

1202. Woodbury, Dorothy Jean. "A Hierarchy of Empathy Applied to Child and Adolescent Response to Filmed Literature." ERIC ED 136 299 (1976).
Using an instrument derived from "A Hierarchy of Empathy" the empathetic responses of preschool children, fifth and sixth graders, and adults were observed by three judges; results support the developmental and hierarchical hypotheses.

1203. Woodbury, Roy F. "Children and Movies." Survey 62 (May 15, 1929): 253-254.
Discussion and evaluation of the enforcement of an attendance restriction law which prohibits attendance among under 16-year-olds in New York and New Jersey.

1204. Worchel, Stephen. "The Effect of Films on the Importance of Behavioral Freedom." Journal of Personality 40 (September 1972): 417-433.
Findings indicate that "movies may serve to motivate a viewer to perform acts related to those he has seen in the movie and further, the movie may increase for him the importance of the freedom to do so."

1205. "Worldwide Cinemagoing." Screen Digest, July 1979, pp. 127-129.
Tabular data on the pattern of worldwide movie-going during the 1960-1976 timespan.

1206. Worthington, Janet Kay Evans. "A Comparison of Responses of Selected Eleventh-Graders to Written and Filmed Versions of Selected Short Stories." Unpublished Ph.D. dissertation, Florida State University, 1977.
Students' (n=14) oral responses to film and literary experiences were tape recorded and categorized according to a modified version of Purves' system for classifying responses to literature; a preference for filmed versions over written versions of the same story was found.

1207. Wozniacki, Janusz. "Kino i Teatr a Uczestnictwo w Kulturze" (Cinema and Theater Participation in Culture). Kultura i Spoleczenstwo 21 (1977): 163-173.
Examined the motivations for movie and theater attendance among 40 college-educated adults; findings included need for entertainment and relaxation, need to learn and gain new experiences, wish to admire art, expectations of family and friends.

1208. Wyeth, Ezra R. "Children and the Cinema: A Summary of A Survey." Visual Aids Review 1 (August 1950): 22-23.
Primary and secondary school children (n=1,401) responded to a questionnaire concerning film-type preferences.

1209. X, A. "El Cine i els Somis" (The Cinema and Dreams). Criterion 15 (1928): 442-443.

1210. Yauger, Ruth Jane. "The Value of Movies and Film Strips as Devices to Motivate Ninth Grade Home Economics Students to Improve Their Food Habits." Unpublished M.S. thesis, Ohio State University, 1948.
An experiment involving 60 pupils' responses to a pretest-posttest questionnaire.

1211. Yeager, Suzanne White. "G-GP-R-X: A Q-Study of the Movie Industry's Latest Attempt at Self-Regulation." Unpublished M.A. thesis, University of Missouri, 1971.
Parents had skeptical reactions to the rating system and tended to use the ratings solely as reinforcement for opinions derived from reading reviews or from interpersonal contacts.

1212. Young, Iona. "Preliminary Survey of Interests and Preferences of Primary Children in Motion Pictures, Comic Strips, and Radio Programs as Related to Grade, Sex, and Intelligence Differences." Unpublished M.A. thesis, Kansas State College, 1942.
Personal interviews with 117 first through third graders.

1213. Young, Iona. "A Preliminary Survey of Interests and Preferences of Primary Children in Motion Pictures, Comic Strips, and Radio Programs as Related to Grade, Sex, and Intelligence Differences." Kansas State Teacher's College Emporia Bulletin Information 22 (1942, no. 9), 40 pp.

1214. Young, Kimball. "Review of the Payne Fund Studies." American Journal of Sociology, September 1935, pp. 250-255.
A critical review with a focus on methodology.

1215. "Youngsters and Film Patronage." Variety, January 22, 1958, p. 10.
Results of an Opinion Research Corp. survey reporting frequency of attendance by age, factors influencing film attendance decisions, and the public's reactions to film advertisements.

1216. Zaborny, Piotr. "Wykorzystanie Podazy Seansow Filmowych w Kinach Polskich" (Film Supply in Polish Cinemas). Kultura i Spoleczenstwo 22 (1978): 1-2, 233-244.
Analysis of the effect of the introduction of television on cinema attendance.

1217. Zagona, Salvatore and Marynell Kelly. "The Resistance of the Closed Mind to a Novel and Complex Audio-Visual Experience." Journal of Social Psychology 70 (1966): 123-131.
Use of the Dogmatism Scale with 515 undergraduates as a correlate with acceptance of a film.

1218. Zane, Thomas Lee. "The Effects of Different Litter Control Procedures on Movie Audiences." Unpublished M.A. thesis, Western Michigan University, 1974.
Four experimental conditions were used in two different movie screenings; the normal theater practice produced the least effective results while the offer of a reward produced the most effective results.

1219. Zanker, R.R. "Children's Likes and Dislikes." Sight and Sound 13 (October 1944): 73-75.
Results of a questionnaire responded to by 97 boys and 47 girls regarding a film program presented by the Chester Film Society.

1220. Zazzo, Bianka. "Analyse des Difficultés d'une Sequence Cinématographique par la Conduite du Recit Chez l'Enfant" (An Analysis of the Difficulties of a Cinematographic Sequence Based on the Child's Narration). Revue Internationale de Filmologie 3 (January-March 1952): 25-36.
Fifty-three 6- to 12-year-old children were asked to recount what they had been shown in a film and to place in the correct order stills from the film; results were sorted by age and discussed in terms of accuracy of comprehension.

1221. _____. "Le Cinéma à l'École Maternelle" (Cinema at the Nursery School). Revue Internationale de Filmologie 3 (January-March 1952): 81-88.
Results of a questionnaire sent to the supervisors of nursery schools (n=110); the supervisors reported on the childrens' reactions to films.

1222. _____. "Effets de la Grosseur et de la Mobilité des Plans sur les Réactions des Spectateurs-Enfants" (Effects of Size and Movement of Shots on the Reactions of Juvenile Spectators). Paper presented at the 2nd International Congress of Filmology, Paris, 1955.
Seven to 11 year old boys' and girls' reactions to various film tech-

niques were observed; shots with camera movement and long shots were more likely to provoke reactions than shots without camera movement or close-ups.

1223. _____. "Une Enquête sur le Cinéma et la Lecture chez les Adolescents" (An Inquiry on Movies and Reading Among Adolescents). Enfance (1957), Supplement, pp. 389-411.
Results of a questionnaire regarding 20 films adapted from books; respondents (n=3,927) were aged 14-18; "We have established very clearly ... that movies are for many youth an introduction to literary culture and especially in the families of the less favored."

1224. _____ and Rene Zazzo. "Une Experience sur la Compréhension du Film" (An Experiment in Film Understanding). Revue Internationale de Filmologie 2 (1950, no. 6): 159-170.
Individuals aged 6 to 25 years who were under treatment in a psychiatric hospital were asked to recount their comprehension of action, chronology of events, roles played by actors and understanding of reverse angle photography.

1225. _____ and Rene Zazzo. "Le Concours International du Film Récréatif pour Enfants" (The International Competition for a Recreational Film for Children). International Children's Centre 4 (May 1954): 235-258.
Infra-red photography was used to record children's reactions to 50 films.

1226. _____ and Rene Zazzo. "La Jeunesse et le Cinéma: Etude Experimentale du Centre Internationale de l'Enfance Effectuée au Laboratoire de Psychobiologie de l'Enfant" (Youth and the Cinema: An Experimental Study Carried out by the Centre Internationale de l'Enfance at the Laboratory for Child Psycho-Biology). Centre Internationale de l'Enfance 8 (April 1958): 185-197.
Summary of studies; reports reasons for film choice, film-type preferences, attitudes toward censorship.

1227. Zazzo, Rene. "Niveau Mental et Comprehension du Cinéma" (Mental Level and Understanding of the Cinema). Revue Internationale de Filmologie 2 (1952, no. 5): 29-36.
Report of several experiments.

1228. Zeisel, Hans. "A Note on the Effect of a Motion Picture on Public Opinion." American Sociological Review 14 (August 1949): 550-551.
Recomputation of Hulett's data leads the author to assert that the film's effectiveness was greater than Hulett concluded.

1229. Zillmann, Dolf and Joanne R. Cantor. "Affective Responses to the Emotions of a Protagonist." Journal of Experimental Social Psychology 13 (March 1977): 155-165.
When a film protagonist behaved benevolently or neutrally the affective response of viewers was similar to the protagonist; when the protagonist behaved malevolently, viewers' affective response was discordant with the film character; the latter finding conflicts with predictions based solely on empathy.

1230. _____, Bella Mody, and Joanne R. Cantor. "Empathetic Perception of Emotional Displays in Films as a Function of Hedonic Excitatory State to Prior Exposure." Journal of Research in Personality 8 (December 1974): 335-349.

1231. Zochbauer, Franz. "Kontrolluntersuchungen über den Erfolg Filmischer Erziehung" (Control Investigation of the Success of Film Education). Jugend und Film, December 1956, pp. 1-8.
Questionnaire distributed to 3,000 primary school boys investigated the effect of film education on frequency of attendance and critical response to films.

1232. Zochbauer, Franz. "Von Neuen Götter. Zur Problematik des Starkultes" (New Gods. Problems of Film-Star Worship). Jugend und Film (1958): 1-12.
Responses to a questionnaire by 4,000 children; discusses the influence of movie stars on the children's manners, morals, and social attitudes.

1233. Zygulski, Kazimierz. "Film i Kultura Masowa" (The Film and Mass Culture). Kultura i Spoleczenstwo 3 (July-September 1959): 81-108.
Survey of Polish movie-going habits involving 1,115 persons; data analyzed by age, sex, and education; frequency of attendance, attendance unit, sources of information for movies, preference for movies as a leisure-time activity as compared to other activities.

SUBJECT INDEX

Academic Achievement see Educational Aspects and Scholastic Achievement
Actors and Actresses see Stars
Adult Discount 131, 366
Advertising 185, 295, 354, 467, 547, 574, 913, 1035, 1200, 1215
Affective Responses see Emotional Effects
Age Restrictions & Suitability (see also MPAA Ratings) 9, 48, 168, 423, 436, 504, 598, 661, 783, 856, 1010, 1011, 1017, 1172, 1203
Aggression 14, 143, 144, 252, 288, 289, 432, 566, 723, 838, 1015, 1016
Appreciation 99, 634, 692, 742, 743, 805, 866
Art Film Patrons 8, 210, 1041, 1047, 1134, 1141
Attendance Habits 108, 246, 247, 251, 301, 425, 449, 499, 506, 508, 592, 687, 868, 1037
Attendance: Seasonal Fluctuations 38, 815, 1035
Attendance Unit 75, 247, 251, 569, 660, 682, 696, 875, 1079, 1121, 1170, 1182, 1233
Attitude Change 21, 48, 101, 104, 120, 122, 169, 204, 256, 275, 296, 304, 318, 320, 321, 322, 351, 352, 393, 414, 428, 429, 461, 464, 479, 483, 493, 521, 522, 581, 585, 610, 617, 625, 632, 690, 764, 776, 777, 787, 828, 834, 837, 839, 846, 873, 879, 880, 881, 914, 915, 916, 918, 920, 953, 956, 959, 960, 978, 990, 991, 1007, 1009, 1012, 1056, 1066, 1077, 1102, 1114, 1115, 1176, 1177, 1184, 1186, 1190, 1228
Attitude Toward Movies 34, 52, 53, 66, 222, 277, 656, 861, 865, 945, 1041, 1113, 1120, 1162, 1181, 1188
Audience Research, Inc. see Gallup Organization
Audienscope 36, 389, 933

Behavioral Effects 26, 63, 64, 85, 133, 143, 144, 213, 214, 215, 217, 218, 318, 320, 322, 330, 337, 345, 364, 492, 536, 603, 607, 700, 794, 810, 874, 903, 926, 928, 954, 955, 973, 975, 1012, 1015, 1016, 1045, 1077, 1158, 1159, 1183, 1218
Blacks 95, 101, 267, 451, 539, 787, 817, 851, 904, 1007, 1102, 1162, 1190, 1198

Catharsis 26, 121, 1015, 1016
Censorship 182, 201, 305, 538, 571, 806, 821, 852, 855, 1175, 1226
Cinema Clubs 19, 731, 1170
Cinematic Neurosis 117, 472, 948, 1044
Cognitive Effects 63, 64, 142, 671, 862, 1013, 1087, 1091, 1154
Comprehension 199, 424, 513, 559, 663, 769, 924, 1043, 1224, 1227

Film Audience

Critics 15, 152, 167, 174, 314, 932, 971, 995, 1021, 1028, 1167
Cultural Aspects 95, 190, 213, 214, 215, 218, 311, 502, 1085

Documentary Films 146, 914, 915, 1118
Dreams see Sleep
Drive-In Theater Audiences 129, 271, 349, 416, 547, 701

Economic & Financial Aspects (see also Marketing) 240, 371, 530, 576, 615, 673, 677, 678, 940, 1023, 1025, 1103, 1152
Educational Aspects 121, 132, 163, 190, 202, 203, 245, 274, 286, 287, 312, 344, 363, 439, 441, 453, 468, 481, 482, 491, 525, 544, 567, 570, 620, 621, 622, 626, 632, 652, 739, 741, 763, 770, 821, 923, 968, 969, 978, 996, 1068, 1078, 1112, 1231
Emotional Response & Effects 9, 63, 64, 191, 235, 281, 316, 345, 387, 450, 466, 509, 511, 514, 544, 545, 546, 555, 583, 608, 649, 659, 723, 724, 776, 777, 858, 919, 966, 967, 1018, 1029, 1073, 1160, 1168, 1202
Erotic see Sexually Explicit
Evaluation of Movies 148, 160, 167, 184, 204, 222, 233, 273, 288, 345, 378, 379, 380, 682, 711, 746, 887, 888, 949, 951, 971, 1050, 1051, 1062, 1135, 1167, 1174, 1231
Exhibition & Distribution 92, 127, 129, 134, 197, 418, 435, 576, 615, 673, 702, 791, 983, 1014, 1041, 1042

Family 109, 247, 248, 249, 487, 659, 887, 888
Film-Type Preferences (Among Adults) 3, 30, 114, 115, 116, 159, 183, 253, 280, 325, 354, 391, 556, 583, 734, 836, 913, 993, 1019, 1041, 1042, 1052, 1137
Film-Type Preferences (Among Children) 2, 3, 4, 38, 75, 85, 108, 128, 202, 203, 209, 251, 255, 283, 305, 326, 376, 377, 417, 420, 438, 486, 541, 563, 569, 589, 592, 610, 635, 638, 639, 641, 646, 655, 656, 775, 779, 816, 821, 826, 845, 860, 996, 1008, 1013, 1079, 1096, 1104, 1109, 1121, 1157, 1158, 1170, 1182, 1198, 1208, 1226
Frustration 14, 26, 299

Gallup Organization 126, 394, 395, 396, 397, 703, 876, 942, 999, 1003, 1138, 1181, 1199, 1215

Identification 13, 14, 20, 111, 257, 267, 399, 415, 558, 610, 620, 621, 622, 648, 663, 725, 841, 1074, 1092, 1118, 1131, 1160, 1192, 1229
Intelligence 199, 200, 580, 816, 929, 930
Interpersonal Influence 148, 239, 662, 667, 670, 847, 922, 1131
Interpretation of Films 16, 17, 60, 65, 1070

Juvenile Delinquency 12, 18, 68, 113, 178, 188, 192, 207, 219, 244, 255, 265, 300, 350, 390, 419, 448, 449, 462, 500, 571, 610, 633, 656, 679, 715, 754, 767, 798, 863, 886, 893, 905, 977, 1031, 1032, 1085, 1105, 1109, 1124

Learning see Educational Aspects and Scholastic Achievement

Subject Index

Legislation see Censorship
Leisure 187, 194, 230, 237, 241, 260, 276, 277, 533, 534, 587, 588, 687, 768, 1048, 1150
Literature see Print Media
Literature Reviews 33, 69, 206, 216, 226, 243, 324, 336, 404, 406, 560, 961

Marketing 175, 198, 675, 701, 744, 758, 819, 876
Mass Media & Mass Media Use 37, 46, 47, 58, 70, 71, 81, 154, 165, 307, 358, 365, 368, 369, 420, 475, 495, 497, 520, 533, 586, 684, 686, 706, 707, 708, 745, 748, 994, 1019, 1034, 1064, 1065, 1088, 1109, 1144, 1187, 1195, 1196, 1197, 1212, 1213
Measurement Techniques (non-questionnaire)
  Content Analysis 229, 232, 346, 579, 631, 657
  Galvanic Skin Response 455, 456, 507, 590, 645, 776, 777, 838, 846, 966, 967
  Infrared Photography 591, 954, 955, 1018, 1225
  Miscellaneous 291, 376, 377, 380, 721, 859
  Program Analyzer 204, 304, 348, 395, 537, 1078
  Rorschach 778, 1054, 1055
  Thematic Apperception Test 299, 714
  Wiggle Test 1128, 1172
Memory 61, 62, 65, 106, 135, 146, 199, 208, 238, 295, 360, 480, 567, 582, 584, 658, 683, 786, 867, 889, 890, 898, 924, 927, 1040, 1093, 1220
Mood 193, 288, 465, 803, 838, 839, 1089, 1107
Morals & Effects on Morality 20, 102, 168, 266, 408, 585, 789, 842, 877, 878, 949, 1062
Motives for Attendance see Reasons for Movie Going; Selection Factors in Movie Attendance
Movie Stars see Stars
MPAA Ratings 1, 39, 41, 42, 43, 48, 49, 51, 54, 55, 56, 57, 624, 670, 791, 832, 844, 917, 934, 944, 1142, 1173, 1211

Negro see Blacks
Non-Attendance 107, 125, 198, 227, 339, 358, 418, 470, 496, 563, 687, 799, 802, 814, 908, 940, 1052, 1152

Opinion Research Corporation see Gallup Organization

Payne Fund Research 164, 216, 229, 231, 282, 318, 608, 612, 689, 877, 878, 880, 931, 966, 967, 1009, 1012, 1067, 1112, 1214
Perception of Film 16, 17, 384, 386, 835, 848, 1049
Personality & Personality Traits 22, 24, 25, 59, 131, 156, 290, 386, 503, 950, 993, 1054, 1055, 1056, 1144
Physiological Effects 76, 130, 149, 168, 302, 305, 310, 454, 455, 551, 552, 590, 618, 623, 664, 666, 685, 838, 1122
Political 10, 718, 727, 761, 872, 963
Pornography see Sexually Explicit
Preference for Movies (Compared to Other Media) 85, 112
Prejudice 617, 717, 772
Print Media (see also Mass Media & Mass Media Use) 27, 61, 62, 85, 228, 326, 358, 361, 365, 368, 420, 495, 496, 497, 520, 521, 619, 657,

663, 671, 684, 706, 707, 708, 745, 748, 757, 768, 1034, 1057, 1064, 1065, 1196, 1197, 1206, 1212, 1213, 1223
Production Elements & Response To   145, 146, 274, 430, 457, 522, 526, 527, 537, 683, 710, 765, 869, 870, 952, 989, 990, 1038, 1107, 1129, 1140, 1189, 1222, 1224
Propaganda   104, 142, 308, 309, 351, 632, 774, 872, 939, 962
Psychological Effects   78, 93, 98, 136, 137, 138, 139, 140, 157, 158, 242, 243, 267, 288, 298, 299, 312, 383, 384, 386, 403, 405, 432, 433, 451, 452, 465, 490, 510, 512, 524, 637, 653, 654, 655, 661, 666, 720, 751, 784, 871, 936, 957, 964, 1005, 1098, 1102, 1116, 1129, 1191, 1217
Psychological Reactance   39, 41, 42, 43, 48, 49, 51, 54, 1204
Public Opinion   234, 297, 542, 543, 665, 833, 909, 920, 1151, 1228

Radio (see also   Mass Media & Mass Media Use, Television)   88, 90, 154, 306, 318, 319, 358, 361, 365, 420, 475, 495, 496, 497, 520, 568, 582, 619, 643, 684, 903, 979, 1069, 1198, 1212, 1213
Ratings   see   MPAA Ratings
Reading   see   Print Media
Reasons for Movie-Going (Among Adults)   5, 11, 313, 332, 340, 557, 587, 682, 849, 850, 1207
Reasons for Movie-Going (Among Children)   75, 162, 541, 569, 600, 641, 650, 980, 1106
Recall   see   Memory
Regulation   see   Censorship
Rehabilitation   see   Therapy
Religious Aspects   90, 235, 715, 828, 882, 1046, 1135, 1147, 1178
Repeat Attendance   31, 32, 46, 47
Research
    Definition   7
    History   1024, 1026
    Methods & Methodology   100, 270, 291, 334, 346, 347, 348, 409, 410, 412, 413, 437, 473, 474, 478, 507, 604, 605, 644, 697, 699, 704, 705, 714, 721, 778, 840, 859, 935, 937, 1000, 1001, 1002, 1039, 1095, 1128, 1172
    Need For   78, 97, 105, 171, 205, 266, 317, 327, 427, 642, 722
    Topics For   431, 553, 900, 961, 1163, 1165
    Miscellaneous   212, 1185
Retention   see   Memory

Scholastic Achievement   96, 307, 667, 668, 719, 1067
Selection Factors in Movie Attendance   40, 44, 45, 50, 107, 162, 230, 251, 259, 277, 278, 314, 355, 391, 420, 557, 587, 682, 805, 830, 847, 1133, 1200, 1215, 1226
Selective Exposure, Perception & Retention   95, 122, 296, 857, 1131
Sexually Explicit   67, 82, 144, 166, 236, 289, 292, 345, 434, 609, 735, 736, 737, 738, 753, 796, 797, 823, 824, 981, 985, 1059, 1193, 1194
Sleep & Dreams   166, 193, 359, 494, 627, 931, 1209
Social Reality (Shaping and Perception of)   243, 586, 593, 606, 1140
Sociology & Sociological Research   28, 29, 72, 77, 141, 225, 226, 373, 374, 398, 489, 572, 630, 647, 691, 773, 795, 820, 938, 939, 943, 1030, 1051, 1112, 1117
Sources of Information About Films   32, 687, 868, 1126, 1233
Stars   85, 354, 356, 357, 477, 563, 616, 711, 996, 1025, 1182, 1232
Stress (see also   Psychological Effects)   399, 433, 573, 618, 645
Subliminal Stimuli   899, 1146

Television (see also Mass Media & Mass Media Use) 79, 80, 88, 123, 125, 194, 227, 250, 264, 294, 407, 532, 547, 676, 694, 695, 702, 747, 768, 807, 945, 947, 982, 997, 1034, 1069, 1076, 1081, 1099, 1100, 1101, 1116, 1154, 1171, 1195, 1196, 1216
Therapy   86, 595, 790, 901, 964
Titles of Films
   All the President's Men   296
   Avant le Deluge   555
   The Birth of a Nation   787
   Blitzkrieg im Westen   142
   Boys' Town   13, 949
   Chance of a Lifetime   340
   Un Chien Andalou   426
   Citizens Band   224
   Close Encounters of the Third Kind   857
   Confrontations of Death   304
   Crossfire   920
   Demain à Nanguila   1118
   Die Feuerspringer von Montana   524
   Dr. Strangelove   957
   Don't Be a Sucker   204
   The Exorcist   472, 498, 1147
   Four Sons   880
   The Gauntlet   857
   Gentleman's Agreement   772, 956
   Great Adventure   951
   Home of the Brave   1190
   I Nuovi Angeli   1119
   In Cold Blood   114, 115, 116
   It's Midnight, Dr. Schweitzer   460
   The Jolson Story   1199
   Keys of the Kingdom   621
   The Lion Has Wings   907
   The Lone Hand   299
   Lost Boundaries   101
   The Man with the Golden Arm   1192
   M*A*S*H   667
   Nanook of the North   16, 17, 191, 192
   Network   933
   The Ox-Bow Incident   1089
   Parable   235
   Plow that Broke the Plains   915
   The Quiet One   155
   The River   915
   Rocky   933
   The Rocky Horror Picture Show   46, 47
   Saturday Night Fever   31, 857
   Sister Kenny   542, 543, 1228
   Star Wars   31, 32
   La Symphonie Pastorale   926
   Tell Me Lies   858
   Tomorrow the World   212   1186
   A Tree Grows in Brooklyn   155
   The Undefeated   1136
   Verdun, Visions d'Histoire   974
   Wages of Fear   131, 433

Film Audience 138
Uses & Gratifications   252, 260, 596, 597, 619, 843, 946, 1194, 1207

Value   69, 176, 293
Violence   see   Aggression

War   308, 309, 974

TITLE INDEX

A Mozilatogatas Gyakorisagarol, Nehany Tarsadalmi-Demografiai Tenyezo Szerepe, Valamint Osszefuggesek mas Kulturalis Tevekenysegekkel a Felnott Lakossag Koreben 1084
A Propos de l'Influence du Cinéma sur la Délinquance Juvenile. Quelques Idées sur une Enquête 1031
Abhandlungen zur Jugend-Filmpsychologie 192
About Some Psychological Observations Made During Cinematographic Presentations 891
Acción de Cinematógrafo en la Afectividad Infantil 754
Action du Cinéma sur les Mineures Délinquantes 656
Activities and Preferences of a Secondary-School Group 1197
Adjective Rating Scale for Film Previews 972
Adolescent Homocide. The Influence of Motion Pictures and of Home and Social Environment 679
Adolescent Reactions to a Film Regarding Pre-Marital Sex Experiences 925
Adolescent and the Cinema 9, 91
Adolescent and the Cinema. I, 1155; II, 1156
Adolescent et le Cinéma 91
Adolescents and the Cinema 639, 1158
Adolescents et le Cinéma 639, 1158
Adolescents on the Screen 1185
Adolescents' Fright Reactions to Television and Films 158
Adolescents' Use of the Mass Media 58
Adult Discount: An Aspect of Children's Changing Taste 366
Advertised on Television 547
Affecting Children's Attitudes Toward Stereotyped Vocational Roles with Educational Films 978
Affective Feeling for a Film Character and Evaluation of an Anti-Social Act 536
Affective Response to the Film, "Parable," as a Function of Theological Belief 235
Affective Responses to the Emotions of a Protagonist 1229
Affective Responses to the Motion-Picture Situation by Means of the Galvanic Technique 967
Ambiguity and Personality in the Perception of a Motion Picture 1054
America, Mass Society, and Mass Media 69
American Attitudes of British School Children 493
American Films and Foreign Audiences 21
American Limited Audience Cinema as an Art Form 210
American Non-Filmgoer 814
American Scene and the Problems of Film Education 743
Americans and the Arts: A Survey of Public Opinion 822
Amusement Situation in the City of Boston 272

Analisi delle Preferenze di Films, Scrittori e Riviste con il Metodo delle
   Componenti Principali 159
Analisi delle Relazione Dinamiche tra Effetto Carartico ed Effetto Frustrante
   di uno Stimolo Cinematografico Emotivo 26
Analyse des Difficultés d'une Séquence Cinématographique par la Conduite du
   Recit Chez l'Enfant, 1220
Analysis of Black Motion Picture Patrons to Determine the Demand for Black
   Oriented Movies 851
Analysis of Film as Communication 1077
Analysis of Preferences of Films, Writers and Reviews by the Method of
   Principal Components 159
Analysis of Riesman's Historical Thesis Through American Film Titles 371
Analysis of the Academic Achievement and Mental Level of 257 Elementary
   School Pupils in Relation to Frequency at Motion Picture Theatres
   668
Analysis of the Difficulties of a Cinematographic Sequence Based on the
   Child's Narration 1220
Analysis of the Dynamic Relations Between Cathartic and Frustrating Effects
   from an Emotional Motion Picture 26
Analysis of the Film "Don't Be a Sucker": A Study in Communication 204
Analyzing the Movie Market 233
Anger Arousal by a Motion Picture: A Methodological Note 133
Ansatzpunkte 97
Appeal of the Moving Picture 469
Applications of Communication Theory: IV. Immediate Experience of Movies
   1063
Apport de la Psychiatrie à la Filmologie 510
Apporto dell'Esperienza Filmica alla Vita Psichica del Fanciullo 1091
Are the Movies a Menace? 442
Art Films and Eggheads 8
Artistic Education through Films. Children's Drawings Reveal the Cultural
   Possibilities of the Educational Cinema 190
Assessment of the Effectiveness of a Film Presentation in Changing Audience
   Attitudes Toward and Knowledge of Industrial Arts 690
Attacking Prejudice with Comic Satire and Serious Drama 617
Attempt to Determine the Influence of the Theater and Movies on School Chil-
   dren Between the Ages of 11 and 14: Summary 268
Attendance at Moving Pictures as Related to Intelligence and Scholarship 580
Attendance of School Children at the Cinema 713
Attendance of School Pupils and Adults at Moving Pictures 285
Attitude Changes Effected by an Industrially Produced Education Film 461
Attitude as a Determinant of Perception in the Mass Media of Communica-
   tion: Reactions to the Motion Picture, "Home of the Brave" 1190
Attitude as a Function of Discrepancy Resolution in Multiple Channel Com-
   munication 953
Attitude of High School Students Toward Motion Pictures 34
Attitudes Toward Motion Pictures Among College Students 53
Attitudes and Behavior on Viewing Sexual Activities in Public Places 625
Attitudes of Adolescent Pupils Toward Cinema Films 865
Attitudes of Black College Freshmen Toward Contemporary "Controversial"
   Black Films 1162
Attitudes of College Students Toward Motion Pictures 1188
Attitudinal Change Depending on the Emotional Significance of Given Informa-
   tion 846
Attraction to and Memory for Filmed Characters Stimulated by Racial Simi-
   larity and Social Desirability of Characters 1040
Audience and Its Taste: A Study of 79 Children 365
Audience Demographics, Film Future 812

Audience of Motion Pictures--An Analysis 1139
Audience Perceptions of the Academy Awards Telecast 922
Audience Pre-testing Heads Off Flops, Forecasts Hits, for Movie Producers 703
Audience Racial Composition and Interaction as Determinants of the Appeal of Black Films to Whites 539
Audience Reaction to Selected Film Techniques with Respect to Demographic Background 537
Audience Reaction to the Film "The Undefeated" 1136
Audience Reactions in Schools 35
Audience Research 692
Audience Research and the Marketing of Australian Films 758
Audience Research in the Movie Field 642
Audience Size and Likelihood and Intensity of Response During a Humorous Movie 667
Audience's Choice: Movie Selection and Word of Mouth 847
Audienscope Survey Technique 36
Audio-Visual Materials and Libraries for Children and Young People 970
Audio-Visual Psychotherapeutics: Portable Moving Pictures with Sound as a Rehabilitation Measure 86
Audio-Visual Viewing Habits of Selected Subgroups of Delinquents 68
Audiovisual Media Meet Their Public 250
Auditorium Versus Classroom Showing of Motion Pictures in History Teaching 626
Auditory and Visual Retention in Relation to Arousal 666

B. O. Data a Reliable Attendance Gauge 815
Bambini Guardano 1090
Bambini e Bambine al Cinema 1150
Barn og Film-Resultater av en Film-Undersokelse Blant Barn i Hamar 1037
Befolkningens Forbrug af Kommunikation 81
Beginnings of Gay Cinema in Los Angeles: The Industry and the Audience 1014
Berechtigung und Wirksamkeit des Jugendverbotes in der Sicht der Jugend 598
Berstein Children's Film Questionnaire 87
Bewertung von Jugendfilmen Unter der Lupe 783
Bid for Teens 92
Bilateral Effect of Film Context 353
Black Movies/Black Theatre 817
Books Which Children Like to See Pictured 228
Box Office 530
Boy and Girl Meet Neurosis 1082
Brief Survey of the Use of Motion Pictures for the Treatment of Neuropsychiatric Patients 595
Brit. Film Council Data Shows Deadly Effect on Cinema B. O. of Unrestricted Movies on TV 123
Brit. Filmgoing in 11 percent Decline 124
Brit. Study Undermines Belief that Movies Cut Exhib B. O. 125
British Cinema Audience 5, 6
British Cinema at the Gallup 126
British Film; Statistics of Production, Exhibition, Total Cinemas, Attendance and Rates 127
British Films and Their Audience 1145
British Youth Dislikes Love in the Movies 128

Film Audience 142

Campus Denizens Go-for-Pix, Disks, Radio, But Not TV 154
Can Youth Select Good Movies? 711
Can Youth's Appreciation of Motion Pictures Be Improved? 378
Capacity to Report Upon Moving Pictures as Conditioned by Sex and Age 106
Catholics and the Cinema 1046
Catolics i el Cinema 1046
Causes Psychologiques de l'Interêt des Projections Cinématographiques 410
Certain Aspects of the Motion Picture Problem: A Study in the Inventory of Interests 195
Certain Influences of Movies on Adolescent Youth 74
Challenge for Research 163
Challenge of Change 1143
Change in Factual Knowledge and Reported Use of Illicit Drugs Resulting from the Viewing of a Motion Picture 1045
Change of Socio-Economic Attitudes Under Radical Motion Picture Propaganda 959 & 960
Changing the Racial Attitudes of White Students Toward Blacks Using Commercially Produced Films 1007
Character Disturbances and the Cinema 514
Character and Actor in Films for Children 1092
Character of Reality in the Film Experience of Children and Adolescents 606
Characteristics of Elementary-School Children Who Read Comic Books, Attend the Movies, and Prefer Serial Radio Programs 495
Cheap Amusements 196
Check on Picture Attendance 179
Chi Va al Cinema e Perche 180
Child and Entertainment Films 751
Child and Film 767
Child and the Cinema of Today 661
Child and the Cinema 793
Child and the Film 446
Child and the Film 1164
Child at the Cinema 205
Child at the Cinema 241
Child at the Cinema: Spectator and Subject of Study 485
Child Audience for Theatrical Films in Australia 868
Child Welfare and the Cinema 231
Children Out of School 1169
Children Watch 1090
Children and Adolescents at the Cinema 450
Children and Crime in the Cinema 265
Children and Film--Results of a Film Survey Among Children in Hamar 1037
Children and Film. The Influence of Films on the Child's Mental Life. An Experimental Study Using the Pigem and Tuanima Tests 1013
Children and Movies 1203
Children and Movies: A Critical Summary of the Scientific Literature 610
Children and War Films 974
Children and the Cinema 19, 636, 1170
Children and the Cinema. A New Method of Observation 437
Children and the Cinema. The Golden Mean 499
Children and the Cinema: A Report of an Inquiry into Cinema-going Among Juveniles Undertaken by the Department of Social Welfare and Community Development in Accra and Kumasi 255
Children and the Cinema: A Summary of A Survey 1208
Children and the Cinema: Report of an Investigation Carried Out in June 1946 771
Children and the Cinema: The Effect in Juvenile Delinquency 113
Children and the Cinema: The Report of the Inter-Departmental Committee 112

Children and the Entertainment Film 338
Children and the Movies 611
Children at the Cinema 182, 792
Children at the Movies: How Motion Pictures Form Social Attitudes 581
Children in Cinema 337
Children's Choice in Pictures 417
Children's Cinema Clubs in England 731
Children's Concepts of Family Relationships as Revealed by Their Responses to Certain Motion Pictures 788
Children's Emotional Reactions to Frightening Media 928
Children's Entertainment Films: Good Company 335
Children's Interest in Comics, Radio, Motion Pictures and TV 1195
Children's Interests in Moving Pictures, Radio Programs, and Voluntary Book Reading 520
Children's Likes and Dislikes 1219
Children's Matinees 845
Children's Poll on "Domani e Troppo Tarde" 884
Children's Reactions to Films 1127
Children's Reactions to Movie Horrors and Radio Crime 903
Children's Taste in Films 336
Children's Television Habits and Preferences 997
Children's Comprehension of Movie Language 559
Children, Youth and the Film 696
Child's Leisure Hour--How it is Affected by the Motion Picture 588
Child's Reaction to the Movies 996
Chills and Thrills in Radio, Movies and Comics 361
Chinese Reactions to the Cinema 147
Choice of the Film by Adolescent Students 980
Chudozestvennyj vkus: Opyt Konkretno-Sociologiceskogo Issledovanija 628
Chuto-gakusei no Kogyoeiga Kanran ni Kansuru Chosa 856
Cine i els Somis 1209
Ciné-Clubs d'Enfants en Angleterre 731
Cinema à l'Ecole Maternelle 1221
Cinema--An Educational or Demoralizing Agent? 968
Cinema Ad Assn. Analysis of Film Fans in Britain 183
Cinema Advertising 574
Cinema and Adolescence with Special Reference to Nervous and Mental Diseases 871
Cinema and Child Psychology 969
Cinema and Children 393
Cinema and Children: Articles, Documents and Information 324
Cinema and Collective Images 896 & 897
Cinema and Delinquency 571
Cinema and Dreams 1209
Cinema and Emotion 513
Cinema and Identification 257
Cinema and Juvenile Delinquency 178
Cinema and Mental Information of Primitive People 729
Cinema and Method. I, 1000; II, 1001; III, 1002
Cinema and Psychoanalysis 818
Cinema and Psychology 387, 411, 894
Cinema and Rural Youth 820
Cinema and Society 1097
Cinema and Society: An Ambigous Relationship Elucidated 331
Cinema and Sociology 630
Cinema and Television Audiences in Italy 456
Cinema and Theater Participation in Culture 1207
Cinema and Transference 258

Cinema and Young People 177
Cinema and Youth: A Study of the Social Aspects and Causes on Interest
    1096
Cinema and the Adult 749
Cinema and the Child 305, 655, 923, 1123
Cinema and the Imaginative Creation of Types 895
Cinema and the Movie-Goers: A Comprehensive Sociological Study on Movie-
    Goers Conducted in Industrial Centers in the Ural 629
Cinema and the Physiology of the Sensations 392
Cinema and the Psychologically Underdeveloped 750
Cinema and the Public, Preliminary Results of an International Inquiry 554
Cinema and the Reactions of Children and Adolescents 603
Cinema and the Social Sciences 72
Cinema and the Study of Fatigue 685
Cinema and the Urban Spectator 303
Cinema as a Psycho-Traumatic Childhood Experience; Psychotherapy 137
Cinema as an Object of Mass Consumption. Cinema and Mass Magazines
    1132
Cinema at the Nursery School 1221
Cinema Attendance Habits in Canada 329
Cinema Attendance of Adolescents 269
Cinema Attendance of a Sub-Elite Latin American Group 294
Cinema Audience 1137
Cinema Audience: Some New Perspectives 727
Cinema Chronicle 155
Cinéma dans l'Enseignement Américain 132
Cinema e Gioventù: Studio degli Aspetti Sociali e dei Motivi di Interesse
    1096
Cinema e Minorati Psichici 750
Cinema e Psicologia 411
Cinema e Ragazzi 393
Cinema e Ricerca Sociale 406
Cinema e Società 1097
Cinema e Societa: Un Rapporto Ambiguo, da Approfondire 331
Cinema e Sociologia. In Margine a un Convegno 1117
Cinema e le Creazione Fantastica del Tipo 895
Cinema e le Imagini Collettive 896
Cinéma et Affectivité 513
Cinéma et Délinquance Juvenile 178
Cinéma et Délinquance 462
Cinéma et Methode. I, 1000; II, 1001; III, 1002
Cinéma et Physiologie des Sensations 392
Cinéma et Psychologie 387, 894
Cinéma et Societe au Maghreb 501
Cinéma et Sociologie 630
Cinéma et Transfert 258
Cinéma et l'Enfant 655
Cinéma et l'Identification 257
Cinéma et l'Information Mentale des Peuples Primitifs 729
Cinéma et la Psychanalyse 818
Cinéma et le Goût du Public, Elements d'Enquête Internationale 554
Cinéma et les Etudes Humaines 72
Cinéma et les Images Collectives 897
Cinéma et les Jeunes 177
Cinéma et les Réactions des Enfants et des Adolescents 603
Cinema Experience 523
Cinema Going in Greater London 323
Cinema, Grande École du Soir des Peuples 242

Cinema, Great Evening School of the People 242
Cinema Habits of Finnish Children 592
Cinema in American Education 132
Cinéma, le Meurtre et la Tragédie 151
Cinema Makes the World Picture 1072
Cinéma Québeçois: Une Recherche sur la Voie de l'Ecriture 1108
CinemaScore: Poll Created Out of Frustration 746
Cinema Spectator in Spain 402
Cinemas and Cinema-Going in Great Britain 134
Cinematic Neurosis Following "The Exorcist": Report of Four Cases 117
Cinematic Neurosis: A Brief Case Report 472
Cinematic Neurosis: Scary Movies Can Drive You Crazy 1044
Cinematógrafo y Criminología 500
Cinematógrafo y Delincuencia 571
Cinematograph and Hygiene 552
Cinematographic Experience and its Educational Elaboration. A Record of Activities Organized in Connection with the Film "It's Midnight, Dr. Schweitzer" 460
Cinematographic Experience and the Mental Life of the Child 1074
Cinematographic Experience and the Personal Problems of the Child 1075
Cinematographical Leisure Activities and Popular Culture 277
Cinepatriotism 444
Classification by the Motion Picture Industry 917
Clozentropy: A New Technique for Analyzing Audience Response to Film 705
Clozentropy: A Technique for Studying Audience Response to Films 704
Collecting Evidences of Children's Preferences 377
College Students' Attitudes Toward Movies 66
Comment Evaluer l'Influence du Cinéma sur les Enfants? 699
Comments on Mr. Zeisel's Note 543
Commercial Practices in Audience Analysis 859
Communications Research and the Concept of the Mass 367
Communicative Significance of Musical Affect in Eliciting Differential Perception, Cognition, and Emotion in Sound-Motion Media Messages 1148
Community and the Motion Picture 197
Comparative Effect of Color and Black and White Film Clips Upon Rated Perception of Reality 1140
Comparative Effectiveness of Pictorial Teaching Aids: An Experimental Investigation in Safety Education at the Elementary School-Level 439 & 441
Comparative Study of Presentation in the Media of Radio, Motion Pictures, and Television 306
Comparison Between Those Elementary School Children Who Attend Moving Pictures, Read Comic Books and Listen to Serial Radio Programs to Excess with Those Who Indulge in These Activities Seldom or Not at All 497
Comparison of the Movie and Non-Movie Goers of the Elementary School 496
Comparison of Color and Black and White Films in the Modification of Attitudes 990
Comparison of Interests of Delinquent and Non-Delinquent Boys 1109
Comparison of Responses of Adolescents to Narrative and Lyric Literature and Film 671
Comparison of Responses of Selected Eleventh-Graders to Written and Filmed Versions of Selected Short Stories 1206
Compensatory Function of the Movies 650
Compréhension du Langage Cinématographique par les Enfants 559
Computer-Testing to Pick Up Lost Elements of Film Audience 198
Concours International du Film Récréatif pour Enfants 1225

Condizionamenti Sociali Attraverso Tecniche Cinematografiche: Determinazione dell' Effetto "Power" di Proiezioni Filmiche 220
Consideracões sobre a Crianca e o Cinema 436
Considerations Concerning the Child and the Cinema 436
Consistenza Intraindividuale e Differenze di Gruppo nella Testimonianza sul Contenduto di Breve Sequenze Filmiche a Significato Ambiguo 65
Consumption of Communication in the Danish Population 81
Consumption of Mass Media by Polish-American Children 369
Content of Films 614
Contributions of Psychiatry to Filmology 510
Contributions to the Psychology of the Cinema Spectator 98
Contributions to the Study of the Relations Between the Cinema and Young People 206
Contributo allo Studio dei Rapporti tra Cinema e Gioventù 206
Control Investigation of the Success of Film Education 1231
Coping Style as a Factor in Psychophysiological Response to a Tension-Arousing Film 433
Correction of "Motion Picture Attendance and Social Isolation" 850
Correlation Between Media Variables and Birth Rate 1088
Correlation Between the Cinema and Juvenile Delinquency 1032
Correlations Entre le Cinema et la Délinquance Juvenile 1032
Crime and the Cinema in the United States 219
Criteria for the Selection of Pictures for the Investigation of Adolescent Fantasies 1083
Critical Evaluation of Films by Repertory Grid: Value Patterns of Working and Middle Class Youths Compared with Those of Professional Critics, 167
Critical Research on Movie Effects: On the Conduct of Inquiry in Communication 33
Critical Summary of Studies of the Effect of Motion Pictures Upon the Habits, Ideals, and Attitudes of Children 881
Criticism of the Choices of Films for Children 783
Cross-Cultural Study of Film Preferences on an Indian Student Population 860.
Cultural Influence of the Talkies 502
Cumulative Effect of Selected Educational Motion Pictures on the Attitudes of High School Boys and the Relationship of Attitude Changes to Selected Personality and Intelligence Factors 1056
Curve of Retention in Moving Pictures for Young Children 898

Dailies Fuel Exhib Fear of Fans Lost to Stay-at-Homes; Menace of Cheap Cassettes 227
Dangers and Disadvantages of Motion Pictures for Children 168
Dangers of "La Symphonie Pastorale" 926
Dangers of Sensational Films 136
De ce Merg Tinerii la Cinema? 732
Definition of Motion-Picture Research 7
Degeneration of Emotional Response Upon Reshowing of Motion Picture Situations 919
Demographics Favoring Films Future 813
Description of Fear Induced in Children Attending a Film as Indexed by the Number of Trips to the Restroom 720
Despite Video, X-hibition is Stronger than Ever 791
Deti i Kino 636
Deuxième Concours International du Film Récréatif pour Enfants. Compte-Rendu et Premières Déductions 635
Developing Scientific Attitudes by Responding Actively to Motion Pictures: A Study to Determine if Responding Actively to Selected Motion Pictures

By Identifying the Problem-Solving Skills They Portray Reinforces or Develops a Scientific Attitude in College Freshman 256
Development and Use of Educational Motion Pictures in New York City 739
Developmental Studies of Children's Fright from Mass Media 157
Di Alcune Osservazioni Psicologiche fatte Durante Rappresentazioni Cinematografiche 891
Diagnosis in Leisure-Time Activities 230
Die 13-14-Jährigen und das Theater 326
Differential Movie Appeals as Correlates of Attendance 23
Differential Movie-Viewing Behavior of Male and Female Viewers 726
Differential Prediction of Learning from a Motion Picture by Means of Indices of Identification Potential Derived from Attitudes Toward the Main Character 620
Differential Psychology and Filmology 900
Differential Psychology and the Cinema 156
Differentiation of Popular Culture Audiences 670
Dinamica Psichica e Dinamismo Cinematografico 24 & 25
Discussions on Juvenile Film Psychology 192
Does the Film Bring About Superficial Observation? Theoretical Contribution for Practical Application 986
Does the Film Play a Part in the Genesis or Progress of Psychic Disturbances of Children? 405
Does the Public Know What it Wants? 640
Dogmatism and the Movie "Dr. Strangelove" 957
Dream Factors and Juvenile Dreams. A Psychological Study of the Film 494
Drive-Ins have Arrived 271

Edinburgh Cinema Enquiry: Being an Investigation Conducted into the Influence of Films on School Children and Adolescents in the City 728
Effect of Advertising and Other Factors on a Consumer's Decision to Attend a Movie 1200
Effect of Black Films on the Self-Esteem of Black Adolescents 451
Effect of Cognitive Complexity, Interaction Style and Liking on Adolescents' Impression Complexity of Characters in a Film 1154
Effect of Criticism on Urban Film Taste 314
Effect of Educational Motion Pictures Upon the Retention of Informational Learning 480
Effect of Emotional Arousal on the Retention of Aggressive and Nonaggressive Movie Content 723
Effect of Emotional Arousal on the Retention of Film Content: A Failure to Replicate 724
Effect of Film on Young People 1111
Effect of Film Treatments on Attitudes that Correlate with Drug-Behavior 1176
Effect of Filmed Modeling on the Self-Reported Frequency of Masturbation 492
Effect of Film-Mediated Fantasy Aggression on Strength of Aggressive Drive in Young Children 1015
Effect of Films on the Importance of Behavioral Freedom 1204
Effect of Image Iconicity on Film Interpretation 60
Effect of Laughter on Evaluation of a Slapstick Movie 662
Effect of Motion Pictures Portraying Black Models on the Self-Concept of Black Elementary School Children 267
Effect of Motion Pictures in the Social Attitudes of High-School Children 1009
Effect of Motion Pictures on Body Temperature 130, 623
Effect of Motion Pictures on the Intellectual Content of Children 525

Effect of Motion and Cutting Rate in Motion Pictures 870
Effect of Motivational Film on the Attitudes and Understanding of High School Students Concerning Science and Scientists 1184
Effect of Movies on Children 1022
Effect of Murder on Movie Preference 115
Effect of Personality on the Perception of a Motion Picture 1055
Effect of Positive and Negative Prior Information on Motion Picture Appreciation 148
Effect of Preliminary Information on Choice of Movie 239
Effect of Science Motivational Films on the Attitudes of Secondary School Pupils Toward the Field of Science 1177
Effect of Selected Film Sequences on Individuals Toward Nature and Art Forms 315
Effect of Self-Selected Movies, Popular Songs, and Books on Selected High School Students 1144
Effect of Self-Selected Movies, Popular Songs, and Books on Selected High School Students 745
Effect of Sound Motion Pictures as Measured by Differential Achievement of the Motivation of College Freshman Chemistry Students 719
Effect of Television on Cinema Going 80
Effect of Two Sound Slide-Films on the Development of Desirable Social Attitudes 479
Effect of a Liberal Persuasive Film in Shifting Attitudes of a Group of Journalism Students 834
Effect of a Motion Picture Film on Children's Attitudes Toward Germans 880
Effect of an Erotic Movie on the Sleep and Dreams of Young Men 166
Effect of the Cinema on Young People 83
Effect of the Cinema on the Sight 551
Effect of the Motion Picture "Gentleman's Agreement" on Attitudes Towards Jews 956
Effect on Education and Morals of the Moving-Picture Shows 388
Effectiveness of Selected Motion Pictures in Changing the Beliefs of Nebraska Secondary School Students Relative to the United Nations and its Activities 879
Effectiveness of a Motion Picture Trailer as Election Propaganda 872
Effects of Censorship and Uniqueness Motivation on the Valuation of Sexually Explicit Messages 538
Effects of Cinema Attendance on the Behavior of Adolescents as Seen by Their Contemporaries 1159
Effects of Different Litter Control Procedures on Movie Audiences 1218
Effects of Erotic Films on the Sexual Behaviors of Married Couples 736
Effects of Film Material Upon Children's Behavior 143
Effects of Film Repetition, Programmed Discussion and Audience-Set on the Changing of Verbally Professed Attitudes Towards Due Process of Law 873
Effects of Film and Discussion on Facilitating Shift in Kohlberg's Stages of Moral Development Among Adolescents 452
Effects of Films and Reading and Test Materials on Attitudes Toward Due Process of Law 464
Effects of Mass Media on the Sexual Behavior of Adolescent Females 981
Effects of Mental Hygiene Motion Pictures on the Self-Regarding Attitudes and Self Perceptions of College Girls 764
Effects of Motion Pictures on the Response to Narrative: A Study of the Effects of Film Versions of Certain Short Stories on the Responses of Junior High School Students 663
Effects of Prestige and Identification Factors on Attitude Restructuring and Learning from Sound Films 621
Effects of Prior Information Desensitization, and Denial on Physiological Reactivity to a Stressful Motion Picture 618

Esplosione Delinquenziale in un Ragazzo per un Moto d'Animo Indotto del
    Cinema   977
Esquema General de los Efectos Sociologicos del Cine   225
Essai de Mise en Relation de Certain Types de Contenus Filmiques et des
    Réactions des Spectateurs Enfants   874
Estimating the Net Effect of a Commercial Motion Picture Upon the Trend of
    Local Public Opinion   542
Estudio sobre Cine   1058
Etat Actuel de la Recherche Filmologique en Neuropsychiatrie Infantile   924
Ethnic Prejudice and Susceptibility to Persuasion   772
Etude Objective du Comportement des Spectateurs   100
Etude du Comportement Emotionnel Enfantin au Cours de la Projection d'un
    Film Comique   659
Evaluating Motion Pictures   380
Evaluating Social Consequences of Erotic Films: An Experimental Approach
    738
Evaluation in Context: A Comparative Study in Film Evaluation   971
Evaluation of American Feature Film Age Suitability, Quality and Popularity:
    1965-1967   423
Evolution of an Image: Marketing Techniques of the American Motion Picture Industry 1946-1969   675
Exception to the Law of "Adult Discount": The Need to Take Film Content
    into Account   131
Experience sur la Compréhension du Film   1224
Experiences sur la Compréhension du Langage Cinématographique par l'Enfant
    769
Experiencing the Popular Film: An Audience Gratifications Study   843
Experiment at Biarritz   742
Experiment in Film Understanding   1224
Experiment in Propaganda   104
Experiment in Pupil Appraisal   866
Experiment to Determine the Most Effective Method of Teaching Current History   286 & 287
Experiment with Entertainment Films   680
Experiment with Films: Parts I and II   279
Experiment--The Child's Matinee   638
Experimental Appraisal of Films and Verbal Incited Discussion in Church
    Youth Groups   1135
Experimental Determination of the Effects of a Film About Moral Behavior
    and of Peer Group Discussion Regarding Moral Dilemmas Upon the
    Moral Development of College Students   842
Experimental Evaluation of Certain Motion Picture Films in Selected Educational Psychology Classes in Kansas College   169
Experimental Inquiry into the Effects of Pictorial Fidelity on Audiovisual Communication   1116
Experimental Methods of Investigating Taste in Films   634
Experimental Research in Audio-Visual Education   440
Experimental Studies of Motion Pictures: Comprehension and Reaction of
    Feebleminded and Character Disturbed Children   518
Experimental Study of Learning and Attitude Change Through Film and of Effects of Music-Montage Interludes in a Film   522
Experimental Study of the Comparative Effects of Aggressive Film and Television Content on Physiological Arousal and Psychological Mood   838
Experimental Study of the Effect on an Audience of Two Showings of a Sound
    Film Utilizing Two Narrations from Opposite Points of View   918
Experimental Study of the Influence of Motion Picture Films on Behavior   364
Experimental Study of the Meaning of Cutting-Rate Variables in Motion Pictures   869

Effects of Radio and Motion Pictures on Children's Behavior 318
Effects of Size and Movement of Shots on the Reactions of Juvenile Spectators 1222
Effects of Sound Films on Opinions About Mental Illness in Community Discussion Groups 712
Effects of Television on the Interests and Initiatives of Adult Viewers 79
Effects of Television on the Motion Picture Theater 982
Effects of Television on the Motion Picture and Radio Industries 1069
Effects of Two Types of Sound Motion Pictures on Attitudes of Adults Toward Minority Groups 428
Effects of Two Types of Sound Motion Pictures on the Attitudes of Adults Toward Minorities 429
Effects of Vicariously Experiencing Supernatural-Violent Events: A Case Study of "The Exorcist's" Impact 498
Effects of Viewer Distance on Film Induced Anxiety 936
Effects of the Motion Picture on the Mind and Morals of the Young 408
Effects on Aggression of Viewing Sadomasochism and Beastiality After Longitudinal Exposure to Standard Erotica 144
Effets de la Grosseur et de la Mobilité des Plans sur les Réactions des Spectateurs-Enfants 1222
Ego-Involvement and the Mass Media 1005
Egyptian Picture-Goers 103
Einfluss des Kinos auf die Kinder (Zusammenfassung) 254
El Proceso del Cine en el Mundo y en la Cultura y la Deformacion de los Temas Culturales al Traves del Cine 311
Electric Movie "Reviewers" Reaction to Film 291
Emotional Reactions to Abstract Motion on Films 545 & 546
Emotional Reactions to Film 649
Emotional Responses of Adolescent Groups to Certain Films, Part I 1160
Emotional Responses of Children to the Motion Picture Situation 281
Emotional Sensitivity of Neglected Female Adolescents: A Study Based on Talks About Movies in a Girls' Home 509
Emotionality, Understanding and Identification in Pre-School Children's Reactions to Western Films 415
Empathetic Perception of Emotional Displays in Films as a Function of Hedonic Excitatory State to Prior Exposure 1230
Empirical Analysis of Theatrical Movie Popularity 677
Enfant Devant le Cinéma 793
Enfant au Cinéma 241
Enfant au Cinéma; Spectateur et Sujet d'Etude 485
Enfant et le Cinéma d'Aujourd'hui 661
Enfant et le Film 446, 1164
Enfants au Cinéma 792
Enfants et Adolescents Devant les Films 450
English children and the "Movies" 300 & 301
Enquête Filmologique chez les Enfants et Adolescents Inadaptés 516
Enquête sur le Cinéma et la Lecture chez les Adolescents 1223
Enquête sur les Effets du Cinéma sur la Vue 302
Enquête sur les Raisons d'Interêt pour les Genres des Films en Relation avec l'Âge, le Sexe, le Type de Comportement et le Milieu Social et Familier 1094
Enquiry Respecting the Cinematograph Made in the Schools of Geneva, Lausanne and Neuchâtel 251
Erzieht der Film zu Oberflächlichen Sehen? Ein Theoretischer Beitrag für die Praxis 986
Espace et le Temps Filmiques 1165
Españoles y el Cine 852
Espectador Cinematográfico en España 402

Experimental Study of the Relationship Between a Conscious and an Unconscious Measure of Audience Response to a Motion Picture Film 507
Experimental Study of the Relationship of Film Movement and Emotional Involvement Response and its Effect on Learning and Attitude Formation 776
Experimental vs. Survey Techniques for Determing the Effects of Motion Pictures 697
Experiments on the Understanding of Film Language by the Child 769
Exploding a Myth: Motion Pictures are not Responsible for Juvenile Delinquency 207
Exploitation of Pleasure: A Study of Commercial Recreations in New York City 237
Exploration of Elite Audience Attitudes Toward Television and Theater Movies 945
Exploration of the Concepts of Secondary School Boys and Girls Concerning the Roles of Parents in Family Living as Indicated by Their Responses to Certain Family Situations in Selected Motion Pictures 487
Exploration on the Utility of Motion Picture Media in Personality Assessment 59
Exposure of Adults to Erotic Materials 292
Exposure to Pornography and Sexual Behavior in Deviant and Normal Groups 434
Eye Strain in Motion Picture Theaters 310

Factor Analytic Study of Attitudes Toward Motion Pictures 52
Factor Cinematográfico en la Delincuencia Infantil 12
Factor Criminogeno Secundario (Cinematografo y Criminalidad) 18
Factors Affecting the Decline of the Motion Picture Audience in the United States Since World War II 940
Factors Influencing Attitudes and Attitude Change 915
Factors Influencing Verbal Learning From Films Under Varying Conditions of Audience Participation 770
Factors Which Appear to Influence the Subjective Evaluation of a Motion Picture 1061
Facts and Fiction about the Educational Values of the Cinema 763
Feature Films Preferred by Danish Youth 826
Feature Films as Historical Data 1153
Female Responsiveness to Erotic Films and its Relation to Attitudes, Sexual Knowledge and Selected Demographic Variables 1059
Field Experiment on Immediate and Delayed Effects of Aggressive-Erotic, Mild- and Hard-Core Erotic Films on Attitudes Toward Sexual Violence 289
Fifty-one Percent of French Never Attend 339
Film Analyticity: Variations in Viewer Orientation 946
Film Attendance: Why College Students Chose to See Their Most Recent Film, 44 & 45
Film Audience's Awareness of the Production Process 765
Film Choices of Adolescents 1157
Film Comme Méthode Projective 412
Film Fabularny Jako Zrolo Historyczne 1153
Film Movement and Affective Response and the Effect on Learning and Attitude Formation 777
Film Music and Attitude Change: A Study to Determine the Effect of Manipulating a Musical Soundtrack Upon Changes in Attitude Toward Militarism --Pacifism Held by Tenth Grade Social Studies Students 989
Film Persuasion in Education and Social Controversies: A Theoretical Analysis of the Components Manifest in Viewer-Film Involvement as They Affect the Viewer's Urge to Further Inquiry into Social Controversies 375

Film Audience 152
Film Preference Patterns of Fourth and Fifth Grade Children 209
Film Preferences Following a Murder 116
Film Preferences Under Conditions of Threat: Whetting the Appetite for Violence, Information, or Excitement? 114
Film Scholarship: Dead or Alive? 722
Film Shots and Expressed Interest Levels 1189
Film Study, Literary Criticism, and Science: A Polemical Response to Richard Dyer MacCann 362
Film Subject Matter Looms Large in Stay-Away; Ticket Prices are Related to Age; Income Strata 342
Film Supply in Polish Cinemas 1216
Film Talk: Viewers Responses to a Film as a Socially Situated Event 224
Film Tastes of Urban Population 313
Film als Erziehungsmacht 1073
Film als Psycho-Traumatisches Kindheitserlebnis Psychotherapie 137
Film and Child Delinquency 893
Film and Education at School 1043
Film and Everyday Life 261
Film and Juvenile Criminality 1105
Film and Juvenile Delinquency 419
Film and Public: Chance of a Lifetime 340
Film and Society in Tamil Nadu 484
Film and Youth 782
Film and its Audience 341
Film and its Public 84
Film and Mass Culture 1233
Film and the Communication of Values 566
Film and the Family 109
Film and the Measurement of its Effects 1131
Film and the Projective Methods 385
Film as a Projective Device 412 & 413
Film as a Research Tool 212
Film as an Aid to Education: A Pedagogic Study Carried Out with the Aid of the Film "The Great Adventure" 951
Film as an Educational Force 1073
Film as Mental Reaction 1087
Film as Psychotraumatic Experience in Childhood 138
Film di Gangster e Riflessi Psicologica sui Fanciulli 20
Film e la Delinquenza Giovanile 419
Film es Kozonsege 84, 341
Film es a Mindennapi Elet 261
Film for Children in Italy 161
Film for Young People 984
Film i Kultura Masowa 1233
Film im Weltbild unserer Jugend 593
Film per Ragazzi e Pericoli del Semplicismo 1095
Film pour Enfants en Italie 161
Film som Psyko-Traumatisk Barndomsoplevelse 138
Film und Familie 109
Film und Jugend 782
Film und Jugendkriminalität 244
Film und Jugendkriminalität 1105
Film, Danger for Youth 89
Film, Politics and the Press: The Influence of "All the President's Men" 296
Film, Procédé d'Analyse Projective 413
Film-Facilitated Arousal and Prosocial Behavior 810

Film-Induced Arousal, Information Search, and the Attribution Process 426
Film-Mediated Fantasy Aggression and Strength of Aggressive Drive 1016
Filmdiscussiegroep in een Inrichting 273
Filmeinflüsse bei Kinder und Jugendlichen und die Problematik ihrer Feststellung 604
Filmens Rollei den Sociale Oplysning 297
Filmerlebnis 523
Filmerlebnis der Jugend 602
Filmerlebnis und seine Pädogogische Vertiefung. Erfahrungsberichte zum Film "Es est Mitternacht, Dr. Schweitzer" 460
Filmi Dete: Clanci, Dokumenti i Informacije 324
Filmivaatage Tupoloogiast 1141
Filmmaking and Politics: The Cuban Experience 505
Filmnezes Szabad Szombatokon 381
Filmologia e Psicologia Infantile 386
Filmologia e Psicologia Infantile 384
Filmologie et Sociologie 28
Filmology and Child Psychology 386
Filmology and Infantile Psychology 382, 384
Filmology and Sociology 28
Films and Attitudes 99
Films and Australian--Asian Relations 958
Films and Fans 343
Films and the British Public 458
Films for Adolescents and Dangers of Over-Simplicity 1095
Films for Children and Dramas for Children 821
Films in Changing Ethnic Attitudes and Behavior in the Elementary Grades 837
Filmseende och Mognad 555
Finland Still Goes to Movies 709
First Contribution to the Psycho-Analysis and Aesthetics of Motion Pictures 784
First Motion Picture Audiences 587
Five Hundred New Screens Due 349
Flicker of Hope? Things May be Looking Up for the Movie Theatres 1110
Fonctions Psychologiques du Cinéma 260
For a Sociology of the Cinema 141
Formation and Recall of Structurally Equivalent Stories in Movie and Text 61
Fortune Survey: Movies and Movie Stars 356
Fortune Survey: Moving Pictures 355
Fortune Survey: The Movies 357
Fortune Survey: The People's Taste in Movies, Books, and Radio 358
Frekwencja w Kinematografach natle Roezwoju Konjunktury 370
French Public and the Japanese Film 120
Frequency of Attendance at Motion Pictures by School Children in Nebraska, the Nature of Shows Attended 181
Frequency of Attendance of High-School Students at the Movies 875
Functions of Mass Media in the Political Socialization of Adolescents 10
Fundamentals of the Reaction of Children and Adolescents to Films 605
Further Findings from Audienscope Pre-Release Survey 389

G-GP-R-X: A Q-Study of the Movie Industry's Latest Attempt at Self-Regulation 1211
G-PG-R-X: The Purpose, Promise, and Performance of the Movie Rating System 54
Gallup Check Re Likes: Theatre, and/or Homes 999

Film Audience 154

Gallup Gadget Charts Movie Appeal 395
Gallup Gadget 394
Gallup Looks at the Movies 396
Gallup Survey Reports Movie Popularity Up Since '66 Poll 397
Galvanic Changes in Clinical Patients Resulting from the Motion Picture Situation 454
Galvanic Skin Responses to Motion Pictures 590
Gangster Films and Their Psychological Effects on Children 20
Gefährdung der Jugend durch den Film 89
Gefühlsansprechbarkeit von Verwahrlosten Weiblichen Jugendlichen: Ein Studie auf Grund von Filmgesprächen in einem Mädchenheim 509
Gegenwärtige Stand der Filmsoziologie 226
General Occurrence of Stressful Reactions to Commercial Motion Pictures and Elements in Films Subjectively Identified as Stressors 573
General Outline of the Sociological Effect of the Motion Picture 225
German Drive-Ins Boom 416
Getting Them Back to the Movies 418
Go to the Cinema. Buy a Life Style 119
Golemijat i Malkijat Ekran v Predpocitanijata na Zritelite 695
Gratifications Found in Media by British Teenage Boys 252
Grundzüge des Filmerlebens der Kinder und Jugendlichen in der Ausgehenden Kindheit und Beginnenden Pubertät 605

Hard Night Out 153
Health and Psychic Equilbrium of Children at the Cinema 653 & 654
Heroic Personification of Juvenile Delinquency: Eddie Constantine 863
Hierarchy of Empathy Applied to Child and Adolescent Response to Filmed Literature 1202
High Versus Low Camera Angle in Film Production as a Factor Influencing Viewers' Predictions of Performance 526
Hollywood Films on the British Screen: An Analysis of the Function of American Popular Culture Abroad 400
Hollywood Letter 942
Hollywood Market Research 478
Hollywood and Pedagogy 570
Hollywood is Sick 435
Hollywood's Foreign Correspondents 1057
Hollywood's Movie Star System and the Film Industry in the 1940's 616
Home from Home 921
Homicida Menor de Edad. Influencia del Cinematografo y del Ambiente Hogareno y Social 679
How Children See Films 1070
How Children are Entertained 531
How Do Motion Pictures Affect the Attitudes and Emotions of Children? 966
How do Motion Pictures Affect the Conduct of Children 489
How do Students form an Opinion About the Cinema? 1151
How People Spend Their Time 533
How School Achievement Relates to Mass Media Use 307
How the New TV Forms Affect Movie-going 532
How the United Parents Associations Regards Radio and Motion Pictures as These Affect Children 979
How to Evaluate the Influence of the Cinema on Children? 699
How TV and Film Portrayals Affect Sexual Satisfaction in College Students 67
Hudozestvennoe Kino vospitalel 'noj Rabote Skoly 1043
Husbands and Wives in Bergman Films: A Close Analysis Based on Empirical Data 698

I Ragazzi votano per "Domani e Troppo Tarde" 884
Identification Héroique de l'Adolescent Délinquent: Eddie Constantine 863
Identification and Observational Learning from Films 725
Identified Auteurs Among Top-Grossing American Film Directors, 1945-1969 1027
Il Fanciullo Davanti al Cinema Spettacolare 751
Immediately Detectable Influence of Film from Age 10 Years On 515
Immediately Discernable Influence of the Cinema From the Age of 10 Upwards. International Meeting of Experts to Consider the Psychological, Technical and Social Aspects of Problems Concerning the Cinema and Young People, Luxembourg 512
Immoral Education 1033
Impact of Film Violence on Viewer Mood and Masculine-Feminine Self-Concept 288
Impact of In-Flight Entertainment Upon Passengers on Selected Flights of a Recognized Commercial Airline 854
Impliciations Behind the Social Survey 693
Importation of Films for Cinema and Television in Egypt 911
In Canada's Centennial Year, U. S. Mass Media Influence Probed 73
In Defense of Popular Taste: Film Ratings Among Professional and Lay Audiences 1167
In the Pursuit of Happiness? Consumers of Erotica in San Francisco 824
Inchiesta sul Cinematografo 108
Inchiesta sulla Cinematografia per Ragazzi 170
Incidental Learning of Film Content: A Developmental Study 468
Incidenza del Cinema sul Costume e sulle Norme di Comportamento 330
Individual Differences in the Affective, Evaluative, and Behavioral Responses to an Erotic Film 345
Industry 1024
Influence du Cinéma sur l'Enfance et l'Adolescence, l'Enquête Nationale Française 882
Influence du Cinéma sur l'Enfant et l'Adolescent 243
Influence du Cinéma sur la Jeunesse: Etudes Experimentales 840
Influence Immédiatement Décelable du Film à Partir de 10 Ans. Rencontre Internationale d'Experts sur les Aspects Psychologiques, Techniques et Sociaux des Problèmes du Cinéma et de la Jeunesse, Luxembourg 512
Influence Immédiatement Décelable du Film à Partir de l'Age de 10 Ans 515
Influence of Age Upon Movie Scores in a Rural Community 528
Influence of Cinematographic Experience on the Mental Life of Children 1091
Influence of Color on Acquisition and Retention as Evidenced by the Use of Sound Films 683
Influence of Color on Audiences' Rated Perception of Reality in Film 710
Influence of Motion Pictures Upon Sunday School Children (Ages 11-17) of Christian Churches in Los Angeles, California 549
Influence of Motion Pictures on Children's Attitudes 1115
Influence of Motion Pictures on Moral Attitudes of Children and the Permanence of the Influence 585
Influence of Movies on Adolescents 589
Influence of Movies on Children: Summary 254
Influence of Moving Pictures on Students in India 213
Influence of Subliminal Suggestion on the Response to Two Films 1146
Influence of the Cinema on Childhood and Adolescence, French National Investigation 882
Influence of the Cinema on Children and Adolescents 243
Influence of the Cinema on Children and Adolescents, and How to Assess It 604
Influence of the Cinema on Delinquent Girls 656

Influence of the Cinema on Habits and Norms of Behavior 330
Influence of the Cinema on Juvenile Delinquency. A Few Ideas About an Inquiry 1031
Influence of the Cinema on Young People: Experimental Studies 840
Influence of the Cinema on Youth 403
Influence of the Cinematograph on Childhood Affectivity 754
Influence of the Denver Film Critics Upon the Movie Selection Habits of the General Audience 1021
Influence of the Entertainment Film on Youth 1071
Influence of the Film 943
Influence of the Kinematograph Upon National Life 1175
Influence of the MPAA's Film Rating System on Motion Picture Attendance: A Pilot Study 42 & 43
Influence of the Movies on Attitude and Behavior 320
Influence of the Social-Cultural Standing of the Spectators on Acceptance and Interpretation of an African Film 1118
Influencia del Cine en la Juventud 403
Influencing Ethnocentrism in Small Discussion Groups Through a Film Communication 780
Influenza dell'Appartenenza Socio-Culturale Degli Spettatori sull'Accettazione e Interpretazione di un Film Africano 1118
Infrared Motion-Picture Technique in Observing Audience Reactions 591
Inleidend Onderzoek tot het Problemn Film en Jeugd 486
Inquiry Into the Influence of Motion Pictures on Children 864
Inquiry into Cinema for Children 170
Inquiry on Movies and Reading Among Adolescents 1223
Inquiry on the Cinema 108
Intensive Politicization Episodes: Movies, Melas, and Political Attitudes in a North Indian District 760
Interests of High-School Students in Motion Pictures and the Radio 1198
Internalization of Filmic Schematic Operations in Interaction with Learners' Aptitudes 973
International Competition for a Recreational Film for Children 1225
International Survey, Conference of Filmology 553
Intrusive and Repetitive Thought After a Depressing Film: A Pilot Study 1191
Investigation of the Amusements of School Girls. II. The Cinema as an Amusement of School Girls 1086
Investigation of the Dimensions of an Instrument for Measuring Audience Reaction to Motion Pictures 160
Investigation of the Influence of Motion-Pictures on a Group of High School Boys and Girls 221
Investigation of Two Different Film Presentations as the Psychological Cause of Emotional Stress 490
Investigation on the Effects of the Cinema on Vision 302
Investigations on the Influence of the Movie Upon Youth Turned Criminal 350
Is Media Exposure Unidimensional? A Socioeconomic Approach 748
It's Film Plot, Not Star, That Attracts Moviegoers 557
Izucenie Detskogo Kinozriteljz 409

"Jaws" Neurosis 948
Jeune Spectateur et Son Entourage 660
Jeunes Spectateurs 445
Jeunesse Devant les Images 883
Jeunesse et le Cinéma: Etude Experimentale du Centre Internationale de l'Enfance Effectuée au Laboratoire de Psychobiologie de l'Enfant 1226
Jido Eiga to Jido Geki 821
Jogakusei no Goraku Chosa. II. Jogakusei no Goraku Toshiteno Eiga 1086

Jugend Kriminalität Durch Film--und Umwelteinflüsse 633
Jugend und Film 912 & 998
Jugendfilm 984
Jugendliche vor der Leinwand 1185
Jugendlichen und das Filmtheater 811
Juvenile Criminality as Influenced by Films and Environment 633
Juvenile Delinquency and Dramatized Entertainment 798

K Aktualnym Problemom Vyuzitia Kratkeho Filmu 733
K Voprosu o Vosprijatii Ocenke Kinoiskusstva Zritelem 1050
Kartlegging av Kinobesokende i Oslo 594
Kila pa Bio. Kop en Livsstil 119
Kind und Film 767
Kind und Film. Der Einfluss des Filmes auf das Seelenleben des Kindes. Eine Experimentelle Studie unter Verwendung des Pigem- und des Tuanima-Tests 1013
Kind und Kino. Neue Betrachtungsmethoden 437
Kinden Bioscoop. De Juiste Verhouding 499
Kinder und das Filmverbrechen 265
Kinematograf kak Predmet Massovogo Potreblenija, Kino i Massovye Zurnaly 1132
Kino Fabriziert das Weltbild 1072
Kino i Gorodskoj Zritel 303
Kino i Teatr a Uczestnictwo w Kulturze 1207
Kino i Zritel': Opyt Sociologicekogo Issledovanija Pod Obscej Redakciej 629
Kino Studyjne w Zielonej Gorze 1047
Kontrolluntersuchungen über den Erfolg Filmischer Erziehung 1231

Laboratory Study of Psychological Stress Produced by a Motion Picture Film 645
Land-Jugend und Kino 820
Lasten Elokuvissa Kayminen 592
Latin American Audience Viewpoint on American Films 836
Latino Audience: This Market Translates into Dollars 673
Learning of Peripheral Content in Films: A Developmental Study 491
Leisure 534
Leisure Activities of Secondary Children 276
Leisure Revolution: Recreation in the American City, 1820-1920 1048
Limited Social Effect of Radio Broadcasting 90
Literary Trash, Movies, and Juvenile Delinquency 1124
Loisir Cinématographique et Culture Populaire 277
London Children and the Cinema 540
London Filmgoer 682
Look at Southern California Movie-Going 687
Lost Audience 1152
Lure of the Films 278

M. P. A. A. Film Rating Influence on Stated Likelihood of High School Student Film Attendance: A Test of Reactance Theory 48
M. P. A. A. Ratings and the Box Office: Some Tantalizing Statistics 57
MPAA Film Ratings and Film Attendance: A Test of Reactance Theory 51
MPAA Interprets ORC Survey 674
MPAA Survey Seeks Answer to Biz Decline; TV Still Chief Villain 807
Main Influences of the Cinema on the Public 312
Majority of Students Approve Film Ratings 1

Film Audience 158

Market Analysis of Sex-Oriented Materials in Denver, Colorado, August, 1969 --A Pilot Study 753
Market Research for Film Sell; Parables for Believers, Skeptics 744
Market Research: Beyond the Fanny of the Cohn 1026
Marketing Aspects of Drive-In Theatres 701
Marketing and Attitude Research Applied to Motion Pictures 876
Marketing of Motion Pictures 819
Mass Communication and Para-Social Interaction 529
Mass Communication Behavior of Young People in Grades 5, 7, 9, and 11, in Des Moines Public Schools in 1958 as Compared with the Mass Communication Behavior of an Equivalent Group in Des Moines Before the Advent of Television 70
Mass Communication Media and Public Opinion 833
Mass Communication no Baitai to Shite no Eliga-sono Tokushitsu Nitsuite 548
Mass Communications: The Cinema in India 107
Mass Media Preference Patterns: A Cross Media Study 1187
Mass Media Use by Sub-Elites in 11 Latin American Countries 264
Mass Media and Children: A Study of Exposure Habits and Cognitive Effects 63 & 64
Mass Media and Young People 71
Mass Media in Los Angeles Since the Rise of Television 994
Mass Media in an Underdeveloped Village 263
Mass Propaganda in the War Against Bigotry 351
Measurement and Analysis of Physiological Response to Film 664
Measurement of Change in Social Attitude 1114
Measuring the Influence of Motion Picture Attendance on Conduct and Attitude 1012
Measuring "Intangible" Effects of Motion Pictures 916
Measuring Motion-Picture Preferences 376
Measuring the Effect of Motion Pictures on the Intellectual Content of Children 1067
Media Use and Political Interest at the University of Costa Rica 718
Medias Audiovisuels Face à Leur Public 250
Méfaits de la "Symphonie Pastorale" 926
Mémoire des Films 786
Memoria del Film 1093
Memory for Trade Names Presented in Screen, Radio and Television Advertisements 295
Memory of Films 786
Menace of the Movies 284
Mental Hygiene and Film Control 93
Mental Level and Understanding of the Cinema 1227
Methoden der Jugendfilmforschung: Ein Überblick 1128
Methodes voor het Onderzoek van s de Invloed van de Film op de Jeugd 935
Methods for Analyzing the Content of Motion Pictures 229
"Middletown" Study of Hollywood 961
Mild and Hard-Core Erotic Films on Attitudes Toward Sexual Violence 280
Minds Made by the Movies 612
Minds and Movies 672
Mise en-Scène Versus Montage: Viewer Response to Two Styles of Visual Communication 145
Miterzieher Film: Eine Pädogogische Studie im Anschluss an den Film "Das Grosse Abenteuer" 951
Modern Youth and the Movies 1079
Molodez i Kino. Opyt Analiza Cennostnyh Orientacij Molodez na Kinematograf 459
Monde Scolaire et le Film d'Enseignement 245

Montclair Children and the Movies. A Survey in 1933 785
Mood Change as a Function of Stress of Protagonist and Degree of Identification in a Film-Viewing Situation 1089
Mood and Sleep: II. Effects of Aversive Pre-Sleep Stimulation 193
Moral Effect of the Cinema on Individuals 266
Moral Evaluation of Films by 10-14 Year Olds: A Psychological-Pedagogic Study Concerning the Film "Teufelskerle" 949
Moral Evaluation of Films. A Test with 10-14 Year Old Girls Concerning the Film Teufelskerle (Boys' Town) 13
Moral Influence of the Movies on Children and Adolescents 1017
Morals and Movies 789
Motion Picture and the American School 632
Motion Picture as Communication 483
Motion Picture as Informal Education 216
Motion Picture as a Medium of Mass Communication 548
Motion Picture Attendance and Factors Influencing Movie Selection Among High School Students 40
Motion Picture Attendance and Social Isolation 849
Motion Picture Economics 240
Motion Picture Experience as Modified by Social Background and Personality 217
Motion Picture Habits of Pupils in the Four Upper Elementary Grades in the Mesa Schools 762
Motion Picture in the Soviet Union, 1918-1952: A Sociological Analysis 939
Motion Picture Industry and Public Relations 234
Motion Picture Preferences of Passaic High School 283
Motion-Picture Preferences of Adults and Children 3
Motion Picture Psychotherapy of Psychotic Depressions in an Army General Hospital 964
Motion Picture Research and the Art of the Film Maker 952
Motion Picture Research: Content and Audience Analysis 346
Motion Picture Research: Response Analysis 347
Motion Picture Versus the Church 1178
Motion Pictures a Stimulant to Reading Interest 757
Motion Pictures and Crime 886
Motion Pictures and Juvenile Delinquency 244
Motion Pictures and Our Youth 164
Motion Pictures and Radio as Factors in Child Behavior 582
Motion Pictures and Social Research 406
Motion Pictures and the Public 327
Motion Pictures and Youth: A Review 689
Motion Pictures as a Medium of Instruction and Communication 321
Motion Pictures for Children 1201
Motion Pictures in the Classroom 453
Motion Pictures, Radio Programs, and Youth 643
Motion Pictures, the Theater, and Race Relations 717
Motion Pictures. Social Implications 855
Motiv Navstevnosti Filmu a Socialne Psychologicke Funkce Filmoveho Umen 11
Motivational Research in Promotion: Why Folks Go To, Stay From Pics 799
Moulding of Mass Behavior Through the Motion Picture 102
Movie Attendance Levelling Out in Finland 800
Movie Attendance in Los Angeles 688
Movie Code: A View from Parents and Teenagers 944
Movie Content and Behavioral Disturbance in Psychiatric and Neurological Patients 700
Movie Going in the Metropolis 830
Movie-Going in the United States and Canada 831

Film Audience

Movie Habits and Attitudes of the Underpriviledged Boys of the All Nations Area in Los Angeles 211
Movie Ratings and Revenues: Eleven Years of Success Ratios 56
Movie Ratings and Their Effect on Movie Attendance 49
Moviegoers Favor at Home Viewing, Claims Gallup Study 801
Moviegoers Tell What Pleases them ... What Turns Them Off 802
Moviegoing and American Culture 740
Movies Children Like 779
Movies Defy Polls and Projections 421
Movies and Audiences 937
Movies and Children: A Challenge to Parents 1053
Movies and Delinquency 462
Movies and Propaganda 962
Movies and Propagandizing 774
Movies and Sociology, Marginal Notes on a Congress 1117
Movies and the Students 755
Movies and the Teenager 162
Movies for Children 328
Movies in Russia 519
Movies' Effect Depends on Mood of Audience 803
Movies: Stereotypes or Realities? 463
Moving Attitudes with Moving Pictures 521
Moving Picture: A Primary School for Criminals 715
Moving Picture and the National Character 806
Moving Picture as a Psychopathogenic Factor: A Paper on Primary Psychotraumatic Neurosis 139
Moving Picture Drama for the Multitude 1166
Moving Picture Habits of High-School Students 805
Moving Picture Patronage and General Business Conditions 370
Moving Picture Preferences 38
Moving Picture Show 173
Moving Pictures Attended and Preferred by Children 85
Moving Pictures and Criminology 500
Moving Pictures as a Factor in Municipal Life 804
Moving Pictures as an Aid in Community Development 652
Münchner Vorstadtkinder und Film 569
Music of Colors and the Cinema 316
Musique des Couleurs et le Cinéma 316
Musische Erziehung nach Filmeindrücken. Schülerzeichnungen Bezeugen Bildungsmöglichkeiten der Filmerziehung 190

"Nanook of the North": Evaluation of a Film by Secondary School Pupils 191
"Nanuk der Eskimo": Oberstufenkinder Urteilen über Einen Film 191
National Types as Hollywood Presents Them 631
Need for Statistical Research 171
Need for Study of the Newsreel 232
Needs of Motion Picture Audiences 404
Neuen Götter. Zur Problematik des Starkultes 1232
Neuere Psychologische und Pädagogische Forschungsergebnisse auf dem Gebiet "Jugendschutz und Film" 607
New Approaches Developed by Relating Film Production Techniques to Theater Exhibition 983
New Gods. Problems of Film-Star Worship 1232
New Motion Picture Rating Code and its Effect on Teenage Audiences 934
New Survey: Metropolitan New Yorkers Better Film-goers than Surburbanites 829
New Techniques for Studying the Effectiveness of Films 348

Nickel Madness 223
1981 Set New Boxoffice Records, MPAA Reports 832
Niveau Mental et Compréhension du Cinema 1227
Note on the Effect of a Motion Picture on Public Opinion 1228
Notes on Commercial Movie Technique 902
Notes on the Sociology of the Film 488
Notities uit de Provincie 561
Notiunea de "Public" nu Spune Nimic, Daca nu Stim din Cine e Format Acest Public 885
Nova Filme Dintr-un An 976
Nursery School Teacher and Parent Group Perceptions in Film Choices 118

O Ekspererymentalnych Metodach Badania Upodoban Filmowych 634
O Konkretno-Sociologiceskih Issledovanijah Kinematografo 647
O Nekotorych Rezul'tatach Sociologiceskogo Issledovanija Vosprijatija i Ocenke Kinoiskusstva Zritelem 1051
ORC Poll: Non-Urban Attendance Up, Teenage Market Share Down 853
Objective Study of Spectators' Behavior 100
Observation of Maladjusted Children 511
Observation sur les Enfants Inadaptés 511
Observations on the Preferences of the Italian Public for Films of Various Kinds 325
Older Audience Needs a Fresh Sell on Film 1133
On Cinematographic Concrete Sociological Researches 647
On Some Results of Sociological Research on Acceptance and Judgment of Film Art by Audiences 1051
On the Application of Psychotechnical Valuation to a Publicity Film 467
On the Frequency of Cinema Attendance. Role of Some Soci-Demographic Factors as Well as Relations Connected with Other Cultural Activities Among Adult Inhabitants 1084
On the Psychological Significance of Cinematic Images 383
On the Question of Judging Film Art by Audiences 1050
On the Use of the Mass Media for Important Things 596
Opinions Concerning Motion Pictures and Their Influence in a Large Mexican City 508
Opinions of the Columbian Movie Artist 30
Optiunea Pentru a Adolescentilor Scolari 980
Orientations and Preferences Towards Motion Pictures 253
Osservazioni sulle Preferenze del Pubblico Italiano per Films di Diverso Gènere 325
Our Youth and the World of the Cinema 601
Outbreak of Delinquency in a Child due to Emotions Aroused at the Cinema 977

Package Deal in Film Opinions 1003
Part of Motion Pictures in Juvenile Delinquency 12
Patterns in Mass Media Use and Other Activities 37
Patterns in the Mass Communications Tastes of the Young Audience 706 & 707
Peligros e Inconvenientes de Cinematógrafo para los Ninos 168
People and Appeals of Newspaper Movie Ads: A Content Analysis 657
Perceived Similarities Between the Personalities of Viewers and Characters of Television and Film Drama 503
Perception Research and Audio-Visual Education 835
Perception Visuelle des Images du Cinéma de la Television et du Radar 848
Perception and Interpretation of Cinematographic Pictures by Children 16 & 17

Film Audience 162

Percezione e Interpretazione di Immagini Cinematografiche nei Ragazzi 16 & 17
Performers' Marquee Values in Relation to Top-Grossing Films 1025
Personaggio ed Attore nei Film per Ragazzi 1092
Personal Factors in Motion Picture Writing: I. Interests and Attitudes 766
Personality and Movie Preference 993
Personality Correlates of Physiological Responses to Motion Pictures 950
Personality Determinants of Mass Media Preferences 22
Photoplay and Character Development 1006
Place of the Mass Media in the Lives of Boys and Girls 708
Place of the Motion-Picture in Modern Life 825
Pluralistic Perspectives on the Black-Directed, Black-Oriented Feature Film: A Study of Content, Intent and Audience Response 95
Points of Departure 97
Policeman Goes to the Pictures 390
Polska Mladez a Film 809
Popular Favorites and Critics' Darlings Among Film Directors in American Release, 1930-1971 1028
Portrait of a Cult Film Audience: The Rocky Horror Picture Show 46 & 47
Portrait of a First-Run Audience 1042
Portrait of an Art-Theater Audience 1041
Portrait Robot du Spectateur de Cinéma 262
Posestaemost v Kinata 29
Possibilités Actuelles de la Recherche en Belgique sur le Cinéma et son Publique 105
Pour une Sociologie du Cinéma 141
Pourquoi les Jeunes Vont-ils au Cinéma? 259
Pre-Testing Movies 1199
Pre-testing a Motion Picture: A Case History 184
Predicting Film Potentials 422
Predicting Success of Theatrical Movies: New Empirical Evidence 678
Predicting the Box Office Returns of Motion Pictures 965
Predicting TV Ratings for Theatrical Movies 676
Prediction of Differential Learning from a Motion Picture by Means of "Indices of Identification Potential" Derived from Attitudes Toward the Main Character 622
Preferences of a Small Town Motion Picture Audience 913
Préliminaires à une Sociologie du Cinéma 795
Preliminaries to a Sociology of Cinema 795
Preliminary Investigation of the Problem of Film and Youth 486
Preliminary Survey of Interest and Preferences of Primary Children in Motion Pictures, Comic Strips, and Radio Programs as Related to Grade, Sex, and Intelligence Differences 1212 & 1213
Present Condition of the Sociology of the Cinema 226
Present Possibilities for Belgian Research Concerning the Cinema and Its Public 105
Present State of Filmological Research in Infantile Neuro-psychiatry 924
Presleep Determinants of Dream Content: Effects of Two Films 359
Principales Influencias del Cine Sobre el Público 312
Problem der Reizüberflutung. Bericht über die Ergebnisse einer Testvorführung des Films "Die Feuerspringer von Montana" 524
Problem of Excessively Sensational Films. Results of an Experimental Screening of the Film "Die Feuerspringer von Montana" 524
Problem of the Dangerous Effects of the Cinema 794
Problème des Effets Dangereux du Cinéma 794
Problèmes Sociaux du Cinéma: Cinéma et Criminalité Précoce 905

Problèmes de Méthode Posés par le Cinéma Considéré comme Experimentation Psychologique Nouvelle 1049
Problems in the Sociology of Cinema 431
Problems of Method in the Cinema Considered as New Psychological Experimentation 1049
Proceso del Cine en el Mundo y en la Cultura y la Deformación de los Temas Culturales at Través del Cine 311
Process of Identification and the Importance of Suggestibility in the Cinema 111
Process of the Cinema in the World and in the Culture and the Development of Methods for Culture and the Parts for the Cinema 311
Processus de l'Identification et l'Importance de le Suggestibilité dans la Situation Cinematographique 111
Profile of Typical German Filmgoer 906
Progrès des Films pour Enfants en Angleterre 333
Progress in Films for Children in England 333
Przyczynki do Psychologji widza Kinowego 98
Psicologia Diffenerziale ed il Cinema 156
Psicología del Cinema 1125
Psychanalyse et Cinéma 648
Psychiatric Patient Audience Reactions to Types of Motion Pictures 1183
Psychic Dynamics and Cinematographic Dynamism 24 & 25
Psychic Trauma Through the Cinema--An Illustrative Case 140
Psycho-Physiological Problems of the Cinema 1163
Psychoanalysis and Cinema 648
Psychodrama and Therapeutic Motion Pictures 790
Psychological Effects of the "Western" Film: A Study in Television Viewing 298, 299
Psychological Functions of the Cinema 260
Psychological Reactance as a Causative Factor in Film Attendance 39
Psychological Reactions to Pornographic Films 796
Psychological Studies of Motion Pictures II. Observation and Recall as a Function of Age 584; III. Fidelity of Report as a Measure of Adult Intelligence 199; IV. The Technique of Mental-Test Surveys Among Adults 200
Psychological Study of Film Production for Child Audiences 1098
Psychological Study of Motion Picture Audience Behavior 954
Psychologie Différentielle et Filmologie 900
Psychologie des Filmerlebens 332
Psychologie du Cinéma 637
Psychologocial Causes of Interest in Cinema Projection 410
Psychology and the Film 608
Psychology and the Films 317
Psychology of Film Experience 756
Psychology of Films 466
Psychology of Movie Attendance 332
Psychology of Natural Color Motion Pictures 1129
Psychology of the Cinema 637 & 1125
Psychophysiological Reactions of Male and Female Subjects with Varying Film Viewing Experience While Viewing Selected Cinemagraphic Elements 1038
Psykisk Hygien och Filmkontroll 93
Public Attendance at the Cinema 247
Public Français et le Film Japonais 120
Public Opinion and Crossfire 920
Public Opinion and the Motion Picture 909
Public Reaction: The Lion has Wings 907
Public Tastes and the Entertainment Film 78
Público Cinematográfico 1137

Publiek van de Nederlandse Speelfilm: Gelegenheidspubliek 759
Punitiveness in Responses to Films Varying in Content: A Cross-National
  Field Study of Aggression 432
Puppet and the Moppet 443

Quand et Comment les Jeunes Fréquentent le Cinéma 246
Quantitative Analysis of Motion Picture Content 579
Quantitative Nonreactive Study of Mass Behavior with Emphasis on the Cinema
  as Behavioral Catalyst 1020
Quarter's Poll: Moving Pictures 908
Quebec Cinema: An Investigation on the Medium of Writing 1108
Quelques Aspects du Rapport Entre le Cinéma et un Type d'Adolescents:
  l'Elève du Centre d'Apprentissage 425
Quelques Problèmes Psycho-Physiologiques que Pose le Cinéma 1163
Quelques Problèmes de Sociologie du Cinéma 431
Quelques Réactions d'Enfants Inadaptés 517

Radio and Motion Pictures 568
Radio, Motion Picture, and Reading Interests: A Study of High School Pupils
  1064 & 1065
Radio, Movies, Publications Increase Each Other's Audience 475
Ragazzi al Cinema 182, 205
Rapport am Forsoket med Filmundervisn pa Ruselokke Skole 741
Rassegna Cinematografica 155
Rating Films on TV 504
Rating The Movies 41, 1142
Ratings and Revenues 55
Réactions Affectives au Film 649
Réactions des Petits Enfants au Cinéma: Résumé d'une Série d'Observations
  Faites au Danemark 1018
Reactions of Sixth Grade Children to Commercial Motion Pictures as a Medium for Character Education 202, 203
Reactions of Small Children in the Cinema: Summary of a Series of Observations Made in Denmark 1018
Reactions of Three Different Social Groups to a Film Inquiry on Youth 1119
Réactions Respiratoires au Cours de Projections Cinématographiques 1122
Réactions Sociales du Cinéma en Angleterre 730
Reactions to Films and Maturity 555
Reactions to Viewing Films of Erotically Realistic Heterosexual Behavior 236
Reazioni di Tre Gruppi Sociali Diversi a un Film-Inquiesta sulla Gioventù
  1119
Recall of Filmic Material: An Experimental Study 135
Recherches Experimentales Filmologiques; Compréhension et Réactions des
  Enfants Débiles et Caractérials 518
Recherches sur les Problèmes du Cinéma 752
Recollection of Films 360
Recollections of a Film 1093
Recreational Cinema and the Adolescent 613
Recreational Cinema and the Young 646
Regression Analysis of Prior Experiences of Key Production Personnel as
  Predictors of Revenues from High-Grossing Motion Pictures in American Release 1023
Relation of Motion Pictures to Standards of Morality 877 & 878
Relation of the Motion Picture to Changing Moral Standards 1062
Relation of the Social Situation of Contact to the Media in Mass Communication 368

Relationship Between Images Actualized by Verbal Description and Motion Pictures   841
Relationship Between Mental Age and the Types of Motion Pictures Liked by Children in Grades 4 to 9, Inclusive   816
Relationship Between Motion Picture Attendance and Scholastic Achievement in the Seventh Grade   96
Relationship Between Religious Beliefs and Attending the Fear-Provoking Religiously Oriented Movie: "The Exorcist"   1147
Relationship of Acquired Information or Knowledge Obtained from Certain Educational Motion-Picture Films to the Intelligence, Grade, Age, Sex, and Type of Educational Training of Pupils   929 & 930
Relationship of Marketing Strategies Used by Walt Disney Productions to The Evolving Family Audience   175
Relative Effectiveness of Motion and Still Pictures as Stimuli for Eliciting Fantasy Stories About Adolescent-Parent Relationships   290
Relative Effectiveness of the Motion Picture and the Single Still Picture Presentation Modes in Facilitating the Perception of Dynamic Action Concepts   1130
Relative Values of the Use of Motion Pictures with Bright and Dull Children   781
Remémoration du Material Filmique: Etude Experimentale   135
Repeat Audience for Movies on TV   1099
Replicating Photographic Lighting Effects to Elicit Certain Conditioned Responses in Motion Picture Audiences   527
Replies to a Questionnaire   932
Report of BFI Summer School 1978: "Film Audience"   716
Report on an Experiment with Film Teaching in Ruselokke School, 1956   741
Report on Cinema and the Public: A Pilot Survey of Audience Reaction in Greater Bombay   556
Report on Pre-Release Preferences of Moviegoers for December 1976   933
Research and Considerations on the Influence of Eutaneous Spatial Representations   892
Research in Radio, Television, and Film by Graduate Students in Speech   827
Research into the U. K. Cinema Advertising Audience   185
Research Methods used in Examining the Influence of Films on Young People   935
Research on Cinema Problems   752
Resistance of the Closed Mind to a Novel and Complex Audio-Visual Experience   1217
Respiratory Reactions During Cinema Projections   1122
Response of the Deaf or Blind Child to Talking Motion Pictures   544
Responses of Adolescent Groups to Certain Films, Part II   1161
Responses of College Students to Film   1174
Responses of Pakistani College Students to a Selected American Film   941
Responses of Theatre Audiences, Experimental Studies   721
Responsiveness of Rhesus Monkeys to Motion Pictures   149
Rest--and Unrest   1039
Results of Recent Psychological and Pedagogical Research on the Protection of Youth and the Cinema   607
Results of a Motion-Picture Survey   541
Results of the Experiment with Eastman Classroom Films   344
Retention Related to Arousal in Film and Television   238
Retention of Film Content Under Conditions of Self-Selection and Individual Viewing   208
Retention of Sequential Events in Dramatic Narrative Film   927
Review of Research Bearing on the Impact of Television and Motion Pictures on Children and Adults   694
Review of the Payne Fund Studies   1214

Ricerche e Considerazioni Intorno all'Influenza dell'Escercizio sulle Rappresentazioni Spaziali Eutenee 892
Rise of the Problem-Film: An Analysis of Changes in Hollywood Films and the American Audience 401
Rola Kina W Zainteresowaniach Dzieciecych 1104
Role of "Cutting" in the Perception of the Motion Picture 430
Role of Films in Creating Social Public Opinion 297
Role of Mass Media and the Effect of Aggressive Film Content upon Children's Aggressive Responses and Identification Choices 14
Role of Movies in Morale 1168
Role of the Cinema in Children's Interests 1104
Role of the Critic in Mass Communications: II. The Critic Speaks 15
Role of the Film in our Youth's Conception of the World 593
Rorschach Test, Children's Drawings and the Cinema 778
Rural Communication Patterns: A Study in the Availability and Use of Print, Radio and Film in Shelby County, Missouri 684
Rural Preferences in Motion Pictures 583

Salience of Selected Variables on Choice for Movie Attendance Among High School Students 50
Sampling of High-School Likes and Dislikes in Motion Pictures 4
San Francisco Erotic Marketplace 823
Santé des Enfants et Leur Equilibre Psychique en Face du Cinéma 653 & 654
Satiation of the Transient Stimulating Effect of Erotic Films 737
Saturday Night Fever and its Audience 31
Scale for Measuring Attitude Toward the Movies 1113
School Children and Moving Pictures in England 987
School Children and the Cinema 681
School World and the Educational Film 245
Schund, Film und Jugendkriminalität 1124
Scot Filmgoing Up, Statistics Reveal 992
Screen Answers Back: A "Films and Filming" Survey 995
Screening of America: The Use and Influences of American Films and Television Programs by Adolescents in a Romanian Community 586
Second International Competition of Children's Entertainment Films. Report and Preliminary Findings 635
Secondary Community Influences and Juvenile Delinquency 188
Secondary Factor in the Genesis of Crime. Motion Pictures and Criminality 18
Seelenlage und Filmerleben beim Kind 1074
Seishonen no Eiga-Kogyo Kanran-jokyo Chosa Gaiyo, Chu 563
Seishonen no Eiga-Kogyo Kanran-jokyo Chosa Gaiyo, Ge 564
Seishonen no Eiga-Kosyo Kanran-jokyo Chosa Gaiyo 565
Seishonen no Eiga-Kogyo Kanran-jokyo Chosa Gaiyo, Jo 562
Selected Characteristics of the X-Rated Movie Audience: Toward a National Profile of the Recidivist 624
Selective Exposure to the Film "Close Encounters" 857
Selective Exposure: The Potential Boomerang Effect 858
Selective Retention by Attitude in Film 122
Self-Consistency and Group Differences in Reports on the Content of Short Ambiguous Film Sequences 65
Sensationskulturfilm-Eine Warnung? 136
Sex and Age Determinants of Theatre and Movie Interests 641
Sex, Age and Iconicity as Factors Influencing Projection Onto Motion Picture Protagonists 714

Title Index

Sex Differences in Response to Psychosexual Stimulation by Films and Slides 985
Sex Differences, Sex Experience, Sex Guilt, and Explicitly Sexual Films 797
Sex, Individual Differences, and Film Effects on Responses to Sexual Films 609
Sexually Dimorphic Image: An Empirical Analysis of the Influences of Gender Differences on Photographic Content 189
Significance of Audience Measurement in Motion Pictures 270
Significance of the Cinema to Children 558
Sittliche Filmbeurteilung Zehn- bis Vierzehnjähriger: Eine Psychologische-Pädogogische Studie zu dem Film "Teufelskerle" 949
Sittlichen Beurteilung von Filmen. Test mit 10-14 Jährigen Mädchen über Teufelskerle 13
Sixty Percent of People Polled by Hong Kong Survey Attend Pix Year Round 1035
Sleep Mobility as an Index of Motion-Picture Influence 931
Sobre el Valor Psicológico de la Imagen Cinematográfica 383
Social and Emotional Effects of the Cinema 1029
Social and Political Aspects of Films 963
Social Aspects of the Cinema 550
Social Aspects of the Cinema in England 730
Social Conditioning Through Movies: The Determination of the "Power" Effect in Movie Projection 220
Social Context and Mass Media Reception 577
Social Effects of the Film 448 & 449
Social Function of the Cinema 201
Social Obligation of Motion Pictures 476
Social Problems of the Cinema: Cinema and Early Criminality 905
Social Psychological Study of Motion Picture Audience Behavior: A Case Study of the Negro Image in Mass Communication 101
Social Psychology of Film 110
Social Role of Motion Pictures in an Interstitial Area 214
Social Role of the Motion Picture in an Interstitial Area 215, 218
Social Study of the Motion Picture 1008
Social Uses of the Motion Picture 761
Social Value of the Film 1149
Socialization Patterns and Preschool Children's Television and Film-Related Play Behavior 975
Sociological Approach to Communications Research 938
Sociological Approach to Esthetics: An Analysis of Attitudes Toward the Motion Picture 222
Sociological Approach to Motion Pictures in Relation to Education 1112
Sociological Aspects of Film 1030
Sociological Aspects of the Cinema 77
Sociological Research on Films 572
Sociologiceska Harakteristika na Kinopublikata 1060
Sociologie du Cinéma 374
Sociologie et Filmologie 373
Sociology and Filmology 373
Sociology and the Cinema 691
Sociology of the Cinema 374
Sociopsychological Aspects of the Influence of the Cinema 427
Sohn-Problem als Schlüssel zum Filmerleben 1075
Some Aspects of the Relationship Between the Cinema and a Certain Type of Adolescent: The Trade School Pupil 425
Some Comments on Motion Picture Research 955
Some Considerations on the Rise of the Art-Film Theater 1134

Some Effects of Film-Mediated Professional Models on the Self-Perceptions of Black School Children   904
Some Effects of Films of Successful Blacks on Racial Self-Concept   1102
Some Effects of Guilt-Arousing and Fear-Arousing Persuasive Communications on Opinion Change   465
Some Effects of Motion Pictures Upon Junior High School Children   150
Some Effects of the Cinema Situation on Character   735
Some Galvanic Responses of Psychopathic Individuals   455
Some Observations of Patrons of Adult Theaters and Bookstores   1193
Some Patterns of Mass Media Use in Santiago de Chile   165
Some Psychological Aspects of Motion Picture Montage   457
Some Psychological Bases for Split-Screen Utilization   274
Some Psychological Problems in the Film Industry   1036
Some Reactions of Maladjusted Children   517
Some Sociological Notes on the Boom in Film Interest   372
Some Sources of Confusion   319
Some Studies of the Influence of Films on Mood and Attitude   839
Sootnoshenie Obrazov, Akutualizairuemykh Slovesnym Opisaniem i Kinofilmom   841
Sound Motion-Picture Technique for Teaching Beginning Reading   27
Soviet Film Audience: A Confidential View   391
Sozialpsychologische Aspekte der Filmwirkung   427
Space and Time in the Film   1165
Spaniards and the Cinema   852
Spectrum Report on Australian Film Audiences   1052
Speelt de Film bij het Onstaan of in het Verloop van Psychische Stoornissen van het Kind een Rol?   405
Star Wars and its Audience   32
Statements by Young People About a Film   889 & 890
Statistical Analysis of Non-Theatrical Feature Film Exhibition: A Predictive Model for University Film Attendance   615
Strategy of Terror: Audience Response to Blitzkrieg im Westen   142
Structurally Equivalent Stories in Movie and Text and the Effect of the Medium on Recall   62
Structure of the Motion Picture Industry   576
Student Attitudes Toward the Foreign Film   275
Students and the Didactic Film   248
Studies in Radio and Film Propaganda   644
Studies of the Motion Picture Audience   473
Study Blames TV for Theatre Drop   1076
Study Group on the Cinema in an Institution   273
Study in Suitability of Motion-Picture-Theater Programs to the Needs of the Child   1011
Study in the Sociology of Communications: Determinants and Consequences of Exposure to American Motion Picture Films in the Near and Middle East   773
Study of Attitudes Concerning the Entertainment Film of Pupils of Both Sexes Ages 13-15, Using the Questionnaire Method   1120
Study of Audience Reactions to Two Educational Films   1078
Study of Children's Attitudes and the Influence of a Commercial Motion Picture   1186
Study of Cinema Attendance by 15-18 Year Olds and the Methods Used   599
Study of Consumers of Explicitly Sexual Materials: Some Functions Served by Adult Movies   1194
Study of Indian Students' Attitude Towards the Motion Picture   861
Study of Man--Can We Fight Prejudice Scientifically   352
Study of Parents' Attitudes Towards the Motion Picture Association of America Rating System   844
Study of Reactions to the Film "Confrontations of Death"   304

Study of Some Communicator Variables Related to Attitude Restructuring Through Motion Picture Films 991
Study of Television Interests and Viewing Habits, and a Comparison of These with the Interests and Habits in Radio, Motion Pictures, and Reading, as Shown by Students in Selected Senior High Schools in Metropolitan New York 1034
Study of the Attitudes of Selected Officers of the California Congress of Parents and Teachers Toward the Relationship of Motion Picture and Television to Children 414
Study of the Comparative Effectiveness of Three Methods of Using Motion Pictures in Teaching (I) 481
Study of the Comparative Effectiveness of Three Methods of Using Motion Pictures in Teaching (II) 482
Study of the Effect of Film Upon the Religious Attitudes of High School Students 828
Study of the Effect of a Subliminal Stimulus Upon Attitudes Developed Toward a Character Portrayed in a Motion Picture 899
Study of the Effects of Motion Pictures on the Attitudes of Seventh Graders 1066
Study of the Emotional Behavior of Children During the Projection of a Comic Film 659
Study of the Influence of Conventional Film Lighting on Audience Response 1107
Study of the Influence of Documentary Films 914
Study of the Influence of the Film, "The Birth of a Nation," on the Attitudes of Selected High School White Students Towards Negroes 787
Study of the Learning and Retention of Materials Presented by Lecture and by Silent Film 567
Study of the Motion Picture Preferences of the Horace Mann High Schools 2
Study of the Motion Picture as a Factor in the Life of 242 Girls from Subadequate Families 658
Study of the Reasons for Interest in Different Kinds of Films as Related to Age, Sex, Behavior, Social and Family Milieu 1094
Study of the Relationship Between Certain Kinds of Film Sequences and the Reactions of Juvenile Spectators 874
Study of the Rendition and Suggestion of Motion in the Animated Film 575
Study of Verbal Accompaniments to Educational Motion Pictures 1180
Study on the Cultural Effect of Moving Pictures 1085
Study to Determine the Drawing Power of Male and Female Stars Upon Movie-Goers of Their Own Sex 477
Study to Develop a Cognitive Preference Test Based on Motion Picture Stimuli 862
Suburban Children of Munich and the Cinema 569
Suitability of the Commercial Entertainment Motion Picture to the Age of the Child 1010
Summary of Methods Suitable for Young Persons 1128
Summary of Surveys on Film-viewing by Children and Adolescents, Vol. 3 564
Summary of Surveys on Film-viewing by Children and Adolescents, Vol. 2 563
Summary of Surveys on Film-viewing by Children and Adolescents, Vol. 1 562
Summary of Surveys on Film-viewing by Children and Adolescents 565
Sur la Mémoire des Films 360
Survey of Children's Cinema Matinees in Sheffield 1004
Survey of Children's Cinema 94
Survey of Los Angeles Theater Attendance of Two Motion Pictures Which Were Advertised on Television 547

Survey of Maladjusted Children and Adolescents 516
Survey of the Cinema 1058
Survey of the Cinema Audience in Oslo 594
Survey of the Leisure Time of West Lothian School Children 187
Survey of the Reading, Radio and Motion Picture Habits of Royal Oak Public
 School Students and Their Parents 420
Survey of the Relative Influence of Color and Black and White on Audience Recall and Emotional Response to a Documentary Motion Picture 146
Survey on Film-viewing by Secondary School Pupils 856
Szkic do Badan Potocznego Odbioru Filmu 398

Talking Movie and Students' Interest 186
"Talking" Picture and the Drama 447
Talking Picture in Psychiatric Teaching and Research 651
Taste in Art: Experience of a Concrete Sociological Study on Taste of Theater and Moviegoers in the Cities in the Ural 628
Technique for Evaluating Family Life and Mental Health Films 887 & 888
Technique for Studying a Social Problem 176
Technique Used in the Study of the Effect of Motion Pictures on the Care of
 the Teeth 363
Téléspectateurs et le Cinéma 407
Televiewers and the Movies 407
Televised Movies: Directors Win Audience 1101
Television and its Effects on Other Related Interests of High School Pupils
 88
Television and the Future of Motion Picture Exhibition 702
Television and the Motion Picture Industry 1171
Television and the Rest of Leisure 768
Television Movie Audiences and Movie Awards: A Statistical Study 1100
Television Owning and Its Correlates 1081
Television Viewing Habits of College Students 747
Television/Film Attitudes of Upper-Middle Class Professionals 947
Television's Effect on Leisure-Time Activities 194
Témoignages d'Adolescents sur un Episode Filmé 890
Temps au Cinéma 578
Ten Years of Attendance Fall in U. K. 1103
Tendency Systems and the Effects of a Movie Dealing with a Social Problem
 1192
Test de Rorschach, les Dessins d'Enfants et le Cinéma 778
Testimonianze di Adolescenti su un Episodio Filmico 889
Testing Some Objectives of Motion-Picture Appreciation 379
Theatergoer's Reaction to the Audible Picture as It Was and and Now 471
Thematic Expectations in Movies Viewed by Young Workers Interested in
 Formal Groups 438
Thirteen- and Fourteen-Year-Olds and the Theater 326
This Thing Called Audience Research 474
Three Studies Examining the Effect of Film Exposure on Dreams 627
Time in Films 578
Traumatic Commercial Film Experience: An Extension of Laboratory Findings
 on Stress in a Naturalistic Setting 399
Traumfabrik und Jugendträume. Eine Filmpsychologische Studie 494
Trends in Mass Communications Research 560
Trib-Star Checks Out Film Fans, and Where They Get Info (Not TV) 1126
Troubles du Caractère et Cinéma 514
Two Main Reasons for Cinema Attendance of Adolescents Between the Ages
 of Fifteen and Eighteen 600
Typology Study of Movie Critics 174
Typology of the Recipients of Artistic Films 1141

U. S. Film Journalism--A Survey 152
Über den Versuch einer Feststellung des Einflusses von Theater und Kino auf die Schuljugend im Alter von 11-14 Jahren (Zusammenfassung) 268
Unfinished Project 334
Ungdom og Kino-En Undersoking over Kinovaner of Filminteresser hos Oslo Ungdem i Alderen 12 til 18 Ar 1121
Unsere Jugend und die Welt des Films 601
Untersuchung Zweier Verschiedener Filmdarbietungen als Psychologische Ursache für Emotionalen Stress 490
Untersuchung über die Einstellung 13-15 Jahriger Schüler und Schülerinnen zum Spielfilm unter Anwendung der Fragebogenmethode 1120
Untersuchungen über den Einfluss des Films auf Kriminalgewordene Jugendliche 350
Upodobania Filmowe Ludnosci Miejskie 313
Urban Working-Class Adolescents and Sexually Explicit Media 82
Urges Close Study of MPAA Report 1138
Use of Film in Opinion Measurement 665
Use of Film in the Diagnosis of Neuroses 988
Use of Films in Psychotherapy 901
Use of the Mass Media in France and Egypt 686
Using the Mass Media: Need Gratification and Perceived Utility 619

Value Implications of Popular Films 293
Value of Movies and Film Strips as Devices to Motivate Ninth Grade Home Economics Students to Improve Their Food Habits 1210
Value of the Motion Picture in Education with Special Reference to the Exceptional Child 121
Variacie Filmoveho Zazitku u Mladeze 589
Veda-Film-Divak 1080
Versuche mit Spielfilmen 680
Visual Perception of Cinema, Television and Radar Images 848
Visual Physiology of the Cinema 76
Vliyanii Predvaritel' noy Informatsii na Vybor Fil'ma 239
Vycteno z Anket 808

WBBM in Live-Lens Survey 1173
War Films and Child Opinion 309
War and Child Opinion 308
Warum Gehen sie ins Kino? Eine Untersuchung uber die Würzeln Kindlicher Filmbegeisterung 1106
Was Bleibt? Kinder Besinnen sich auf einen Film 867
Welche Rolle spielt der Film Tatsächlich im Leben unseres Jugend? 16,000 Wiener Jugendliche geben Antwort 75
What Children Like 775
What Do They Like? 280
What Does the Child Think of the Film? 1179
What is the Nature of the Drive-In Theater Audience 129
What is the Role of the Cinema in the Life of Our Young People? 16,000 Viennese Young People Give Their Answers 75
What Motion Pictures Mean to the Child 1068
What One Public Says it Likes: Comments on the Bernstein Questionnaire 354
What Remains? Children Recall a Film 867
What Says Poll About Film Fans 1181
What Shall We Read About the Movies, Radio, and Audio-Visual Methods? 669

Film Audience 172

What Students Think of Movies 1182
What to do with the Motion-Picture Show: Shall it be Censored? 535
What Women Think of the Movies 506
When and How Children Go to the Cinema 246
Who Goes to the Cinema 470
Who Goes to the Cinema and Why? 180
Who Goes to the Movies 910
Who's Watching? 172
Why do Adolescents go to the Cinema 259
Why do People Go to the Movies?--A Study of Motion Picture Attendance as a Socially Comfortable Activity 597
Why Do They Go to the Cinema? A Study of the Reasons for Juvenile Enthusiasm for the Cinema 1106
Why You Go to the Cinema 1019
Wie Denkt das Kind über den Film? 1179
Wie Kinder Filme Sehen 1070
Wie Urteilen die Schüler über den Film? 1151
"Wiggle Test" als Anhaltspunkt für die Jugendeignung eines Films 1172
"Wiggle Test" as an Indication of the Suitability of a Film for Young Audiences 1172
Wirklichkeitscharakter des Filmerlebens bei Kindern und Jugendlichen 606
Wirkung des Films auf Jugendliche 83, 1111
Wirkung des Spielfilms auf die Jugend 1071
Word of Caution for the Intelligent Consumer of Motion Pictures 322
Worldwide Cinemagoing 1205
Wykorzystanie Podazy Seansow Filmowych w Kinach Polskich 1216

Young Audiences 445
Young Children at the Cinema 1150
Young People and Cinema 811
Young Peoples' Impressions of War Films 249
Young Spectator and His Entourage 660
Young Spectator's Reactions Studied 409
Young Tanzanians and the Cinema: A Study of the Effects of Selected Basic Motion Picture Elements and Population Characteristics on Filmic Comprehension of Tanzanian Adolescent Primary School Children 424
Youngsters and Film Patronage 1215
Your Child and the Movies 282
Your Child and Radio, TV, Comics and Movies 1196
Youth and Film 912, 998
Youth and Pictures 883
Youth and Pictures. An Analytical Essay of Youth Valuable Orientation with Cinema 459
Youth and the Cinema--An Investigation into the Cinema Habits and Film Preferences of Young People in Oslo Between 12 and 18 Years 1121
Youth and the Cinema: An Experimental Study Carried out by the Centre Internationale de l'Enfance at the Laboratory for Child Psycho-Biology 1226
Youth Expresses its Viewpoint on Whether the Exclusion of Young People from Films is Justifiable and Effective 598
Youth's Cinema Experience 602

Zanrove a Tematicke Preferencie Slovenskeho Folmoveho Obecenstva 734
Znachenie Kino Dlia Detei 558

Zum Filmbesuch der 15-18j. Jugendlichen und Seiner Methodischen Erfassung 599
Zur Verwendung von Filmreproduktionen für die Neurosendiagnostik 988
Zwei Hauptmotive des Filmbesuch der Fünfzehn- bis Achtzehnjährigen 600

INDEX OF NON-PRIMARY AUTHORS

Alexander, Franz C. 433
Amado, G. 516

Barnett, A. 948
Bauer, Alice H. 69
Bayer, Dewey J. 148
Becker, James D. 492
Berkowitz, Leonard 737
Bernick, Niles 166
Bertagna L. 517, 518
Borowitz, Gene 166
Braucht, George N. 236
Bricker, Harry 1196
Brini, A. 926
Brink, William 1198
Burton, Roger V. 726
Byrne, Donn 345

Canestrari, Renzo 752
Cantor, Joanne R. 1229
Capriolo, E. 884
Caruso, Maria Pia 16, 17
Clemens, Theodore L. 433
Cohen, Michael F. 68
Cole, Stewart G. 1186
Collins, Forrest 950
Colvin, Oliver P. 1042
Conrad, Herbert S. 583, 584
Coomer, Anne 1197
Corbal, F. 863
Cowden, James E. 68
Crane, Jeffrey L. 624
Crawford, Winifred 785
Croce, Maria A. 24, 25
Cumberbatch, Guy 536
Curtis, Alberta 1078

Dale, Edgar 379, 380
Das, J. K. 860

Davison, Leslie A. 645
Dearborn, Walter F. 27
DeLalande, Helene 656
DeMontmollin, G. 360
Dinerman, Helen 204
Dolan, Kent 175
Donnerstein, Edward 810
Dunn, S. W. 686

Elhardt, Dale G. 371
Ellingsworth, Huber 264

Faugere, M. M. 655
Fenley, William F. 667
Flagg, Glenn W. 433
Fonseca, Eugenio 718
Fontanesi, M. 26
Fowler, George 142

Gaer, Eleanor P. 1089
Garfield, Sol 1198
Gaskell, George D. 432
Germeten, Elsa 741
Golden, N. D. 836
Gregory, John R. 1042
Guitton, R. 863
Gurevitch, Michael 596

Hass, Hadassah 596
Hagens, Richard B. 858
Handel, Leo 346, 347, 348
Hansen, H. Lund 1018
Harwood, Kenneth 1027, 1028
Hassett, Christopher A. 922
Hendrich, Clyde 1147
Hennebelle, G. 501
Heuyer, Georges 111
Hoefer, Carolyn 364

Hoffberg, William A. 982, 983
Horn, Aaron 584
Horowitz, Mardi J. 1191

Izcaray, Fausto 748

Jahoda, Marie 352
Johnston, Ray 700
Jones, Harold Ellis 199, 200
Jones, Robert B. 433
Jones, Robert L. 1081

Kant, H. 434
Kanungo, R. N. 860, 861
Katz, Elias 964
Kejlina, I. 636
Kelly, Marynell 1217
Kenyon, Judy 1019
Kern, Joseph C. 652
Koon, Judith 858
Kowalewicz, K. 398
Krishnamurthy, Nagid 307
Kronenberger, Louis 717

Lana, Robert 712
Lebovici, Serge 111, 514, 515, 516, 517, 518
Leighton, Frederick A. 652
Levin, Harry 723, 724
Lewis, Charles A. 1041
Lewis, Jerry M. 66
Leyens, Jacques-Philippe 504
Lidz, T. 651
Livsic, G. M. 303
Lusk, Parker B. 1041

Maccoby, Nathan 770
Mace, William 662
McGinnies, Elliott 780
McNelly, John T. 264, 748
Marston, Dorothea 785
Martin, David 299
Mason, Edward A. 652
Meaden, Flora 730, 731
Melies, M. G. 769
Merton, Robert K. 644
Miller, Leon K. 468
Minsky, L. 774
Mordkoff, Arnold M. 645
Morin, Edgar 374
Moroney, William 1042
Mourgue, R. 1122
Mulac, Anthony 698

Murray, Edward J. 1047
Murray, John P. 619

Nahabedian, Vaskey 420
Ness, Einar 741
Newston, Darren 115, 116
Nicolich, Mark J. 56, 57

Oglesbee, Frank W. 747
Ostrin, Alvin 1042

Paderni, Sandro 1094, 1095, 1096
Pasadeos, Yorgo 1088
Peterman, Jack N. 184
Piernot, Craig A. 371
Pietranera, Giulio 784
Podany, Edward C. 1102
Poorkaj, Houshang 625
Preuss, K. 192

Raday, Tamas 432
Ramos, Antonio 438
Rechtschaffen, Allan 359
Reilly, Sandra 158
Riesman, Evelyn 937
Riley, John W., Jr. 938
Roessler, Robert 590
Roessler, W. 949
Rosnow, Ralph L. 432
Ruckmick, Christian A. 281

Sabat, Khalil 911
Salomone, Kandice 289
Samuels, Lennox 32
Sargent, S. Stansfeld 1005
Schenck-Hamlin, William J. 296
Schneider, Fred 289
Schulze, Robert 560
Schwartz, Tanis 143
Segal, J. 392
Selya, Bruce M. 723, 724
Sepulveda, Orlando 165
Sidman, Jack 736, 737, 738
Sigusch, V. 985
Silverman, Irwin 432
Simon, Rita James 944
Simonet, Thomas 56, 57
Simson, W. A. 1159, 1160, 1161
Smith, Clagett 712
Smith, E. M. 1157, 1158
Sorrell, A. A. 134
Speisman, Joseph C. 645
Spinat, P. 863

Stark, Harold 544
Starr, Sheldon 736, 737, 738
Stevenson, Harold W. 468
Sullivan, Kevin 175

Taviani, V. 1097
Teddlie, Charles 617
Thompson, Neil 175
Thurstone, L. L. 880
Tilton, J. Warren 626
Trager, Frank N. 920

Visser, Piet 193

Voitkus, Audrey 329

Walster, Elaine 115, 116
West, Stephen 737
Whitehead, Elizabeth 858
Whitelam, Peter 15
Wikander, Eva 119
Wilson, William Cody 725, 726
Witty, Paul A. 650
Wohl, R. Richard 529
Wroblowa-Koblewska, Janina 635

Zazzo, Rene 1224, 1225, 1226
Zillmann, Dolf 144

ABOUT THE EDITOR

Bruce A. Austin is presently an Assistant Professor of Communications at Rochester Institute of Technology, Rochester, New York. He earned the Ph. D. degree from Temple University's School of Communications and Theater, Department of Radio-Television-Film. His M. S. degree is from the Department of Communication, Illinois State University and his B. A. degree from the Communications Department, Rider College. Austin has been Book Review Editor for Exchange: A Journal of Opinion for the Performing Arts since 1978. He has published articles in Communication Quarterly, Film Quarterly, Journalism Quarterly, Journal of Communication, Journal of Popular Film and Television, Journal of Psychology, Journal of Social Psychology, and Literature/Film Quarterly.